Rainmaker

Rainmaker

Superagent Hughes Norton and
the Money-Grab Explosion of Golf from
Tiger Woods to LIV and Beyond

HUGHES NORTON
AND GEORGE PEPER

ATRIA BOOKS

New York London Toronto Sydney New Delhi

An Imprint of Simon & Schuster, LLC
1230 Avenue of the Americas
New York, NY 10020

First Atria Books hardcover edition March 2024

ATRIA BOOKS and colophon are trademarks of Simon & Schuster, LLC

Simon & Schuster: Celebrating 100 Years of Publishing in 2024

For information about special discounts for bulk purchases, please contact Simon
& Schuster Special Sales at 1-866-506-1949 or business@simonandschuster.com.

The Simon & Schuster Speakers Bureau can bring authors to your live event.
For more information or to book an event, contact the Simon & Schuster Speakers
Bureau at 1-866-248-3049 or visit our website at www.simonspeakers.com.

Interior design by Silverglass

Manufactured in the United States of America

1 3 5 7 9 10 8 6 4 2

Library of Congress Control Number: 2023950288

ISBN 978-1-6680-4526-8
ISBN 978-1-6680-4528-2 (ebook)

Contents

Author's Note VII

Prologue 1

CHAPTER 1

Two Roads Diverged 3

CHAPTER 2

Active Agent 13

CHAPTER 3

A Rising Tide 43

CHAPTER 4

Growing Pains 73

CHAPTER 5

Landing a Shark 103

CHAPTER 6

Blond Ambition 123

CHAPTER 7

Finding (and Funding) Tiger 157

CHAPTER 8

Managing the Maelstrom 183

CHAPTER 9

Fired 207

Epilogue 223
Acknowledgments 233
A Note on Sources 234
Index 235

Author's Note

....

I'm thinking you may have a couple of questions for me: (1) Why write this book? and (2) Why now?

The answer to the second question is easy. I've always been a bit obsessed with numbers, and as *Rainmaker* makes its appearance, a few of my life numbers have clicked into perfect alignment: I'm seventy-five years old, it's the fiftieth anniversary of my joining IMG, and the twenty-fifth anniversary of getting fired by both Tiger Woods and IMG. If ever there was a moment for me to reflect on and record a few things, this is it.

As to the bigger "why," well there's never been a book about what it's like being a sports agent. The movies *Jerry Maguire* and *Air* have painted Hollywood versions—caricatures—but no book has captured the blocking and tackling behind the glitz and glamour of managing superstar athletes. More specifically, there has never been a history of the world's largest and most famous (some would say infamous) management firm, Mark McCormack's International Management Group.

In telling the story of my rise and fall, I've tried to do the same for IMG. I've also tried to chronicle the astonishing growth of professional golf, from the mom-and-pop operation it was when I began my career to the multibillion-dollar juggernaut it is now, an enterprise that has suddenly become imperiled.

This is not a vanity book—at least I hope you won't find it that way. Nor is it an exercise in "woe is me" self-pity. I've tried to keep the narrative both real and balanced, have included things I'm proud to have accomplished but also things I'm not proud of—the good and the bad—with a perspective only possible after a quarter century of being away from it all.

Finally and fundamentally, however, I've written this for my daughters and grandchildren, a way of letting them know what Dad/Papia did way back when. They are my target audience—but I'm very glad to have you as a reader as well.

Hughes Norton
March 2024

Rainmaker

Prologue

On August 28, 1996, two words changed golf forever.

That day, twenty-year-old Tiger Woods stepped to the podium at the Greater Milwaukee Open. As dozens of flashbulbs popped, he smiled widely, if sheepishly, and uttered his first words to the public since turning professional two days earlier: "Uh . . . I guess . . . Hello, world, huh?" Those assembled laughed, clearly charmed by what appeared to be a spontaneous statement.

It was anything but.

Two days later Nike launched an ad campaign with a three-page spread in the *Wall Street Journal* and a series of thirty- and sixty-second spots on CBS and ESPN, all carrying the same message:

I shot in the 70s when I was 8.
I shot in the 60s when I was 12.
I played in the Nissan Open when I was 16.
Hello world.
I won the U.S. Amateur when I was 18.
I played in the Masters when I was 19.
I am the only man to win three consecutive U.S. Amateur titles.
Hello world.
There are still courses in the U.S. I am not allowed to play.
Because of the color of my skin.

Hello world.

I've heard I'm not ready for you.

Are you ready for me?

It was a message that sparked controversy and even boycotts. But it also reached a generation of younger consumers as no golf ad ever had. At that moment, the game of golf became cool, and very big business.

The evening before, I'd knocked on the door of a hotel suite where Tiger and his father, Earl, were waiting for me. Moments later the three of us signed three groundbreaking contracts: (1) a five-year, $40 million agreement with Nike for Tiger to wear their shoes and apparel; (2) a $20 million agreement with Titleist to play their golf balls and clubs, also for five years; and (3) an agreement to be represented by my firm, International Management Group, for an unprecedented ten-year term.

It was a huge moment for Tiger Woods—but just one of many more to come. For me, on the other hand, it was a crowning achievement. No agent in the history of sports—or anything else—had ever delivered so mightily for a client on the first day of his professional career. I'd hit the pinnacle, climbed to the mountaintop, and I was loving the view.

Two years later, I'd be out of a job.

1
....

Two Roads Diverged

On the final hole of the 99th Open Championship, thirty-six-year-old Doug Sanders faced a putt to beat Jack Nicklaus, to become the Champion Golfer of the Year. The biggest putt of his life, it was less than three feet.

The thousands of spectators ringing the green, along with the millions watching on television, held their breath as the flamboyant Californian, clad in purple from head to toe, surveyed his task from both sides and then hunched over the ball.

The stroke he made was painful to witness—a convulsive stab that pushed the ball so far right it never touched the cup. The following day, in an eighteen-hole playoff with Nicklaus, Sanders lost by a stroke as Jack notched the eighth of his record eighteen major titles.

On that same weekend, precisely three thousand miles to the west, another competition took place—the men's championship of the Portland Country Club—and, as at St. Andrews, it came down to a short putt and the jittery fellow standing over it: me.

My opponent was Ray Lebel, a forty-seven-year-old oral surgeon, World War II navy fighter pilot, and father of seven. To call him the "Jack Nicklaus of Maine Golf" would be demeaning Ray. A member of the Maine Sports Hall of Fame, he'd won the state amateur seven times. Inside the Portland clubhouse, on a plaque honoring past champions,

"Dr. R. Lebel" had made twenty-five appearances, including twelve of the previous thirteen years. (I'm not sure what happened in 1961—maybe he had jury duty.) Ray would ultimately win thirty-two Portland Country Club titles, along with fifteen more at a handful of other clubs, for a total of forty-seven club championships. According to *Golf Digest*, that's the all-time record.

I was half his age, a wiry five ten and 160 pounds with a 5 handicap and a self-taught swing. I lacked Lebel's stature in every sense. On a really good day I could bump it around Portland's 6,200 yards in something close to par, but I was no match for Ray. Two years earlier, I'd made it to the final against him and he'd beaten me 7 and 6. Suffice it to say, I wasn't brimming with confidence as we shook hands on the first tee that Saturday in 1970.

But somehow, after seventeen holes we were all square. I don't recall much about our match except that I double-bogeyed the par-4 fifteenth and got away with it, as Ray, in a rare lapse, also made a 6. The eighteenth was a reachable par-5, and a solidly struck 3-wood got me home in two, pin high and about thirty feet from the hole. Ray, after outdriving me, came up short on his second shot and then played a mediocre pitch (by his standards) that settled on the front of the green, a bit farther from the hole than I was. He was now putting for birdie, while I had a look at eagle.

A handful of club members were watching all this, including my mother, along with my aunt and uncle, who were visiting us. My regular golf buddies were absent; knowing I'd had my ass kicked by Ray the last time, they'd opted out rather than bear witness to a second brutal slaying.

Ray's putt burned the edge before stopping a foot away. So my situation was clear: two putts for victory. Of course, the only thought in my mind was *For God's sake, don't three-jack—if you have to go extra holes with this guy, you're toast.* Despite that less than buoyant inner monologue, I was able to hit a solid putt, but a bit too solid, as it stopped just beyond the hole.

I had about three feet, slightly downhill, with a bit of slide to the right—the same putt Doug Sanders had faced.

I took a deep breath and managed to shake it into the hole. (Do you really think I'd be telling this story if I'd missed it?)

I remember thinking, *Has this really happened?* Indeed, more than half a century later I still look back at that day as my most surreally blissful moment on a golf course. On that blessed afternoon, the game I so loved had decided to love me back.

Word got around the club. It wasn't long before my pals came out of the woodwork to offer incredulous congratulations. We were having a beer in the locker room when one of them said, "Hey, we need to go out and celebrate!"

"I'd love to," I said, "but I'm on the air in forty-five minutes."

During my formative years I'd developed two strong and abiding passions—one for sports, the other for the communications media. Always in the back of my mind was the notion, or at least the hope, I would someday find a job related to one or the other of them.

Of course, a lot of red-blooded American boys had similar ambitions, still do. Sports and media: If those two industries don't spur you to embellish your résumé and knock on a few doors, what does? But I did have a couple of advantages, and the first of them was my dad.

John Hughes Norton Jr. (and yes, I'm John Hughes Norton III) was an executive in the broadcast business and held a variety of positions at networks and stations in several different cities—New York, Chicago, Portland, and Buffalo—which made for a peripatetic childhood for me and my older sister, Gini, but also gave me an early and inside look at the magic of television and radio.

The Portland station he managed had a Saturday morning kids' show, a poor man's *Captain Kangaroo*. Back when I was in the third or fourth grade, the highlight of my week was to go to the office with Dad on those Saturdays and watch the show unfold live from the studio. It wasn't the actors or the show itself that captured me; rather, it was the process, the mesmeric coming together of all that lights-camera-action.

That said, my father and I weren't particularly close. Like many fathers of that era, I guess, he was absent a lot, either at work or traveling for his job, and the child-nurturing was left to my mother, Virginia. Dad and I didn't go on fishing trips or wrestle around on the floor together, and he wasn't one for heartfelt guy chats or chats of any kind. (Even the whole sex-talk thing was left, weirdly, to my mother.)

I've often regretted never sitting down and asking him about his past, asking about his hopes and dreams, his worries and concerns, asking how and why *he* got into broadcasting, a reticent man in the communications business. Although he worked hard, I don't think he ever felt appreciated. I know he had trouble holding on to jobs. He and Mom also had their difficulties, though they remained married for thirty-nine years until Dad's death in 1977 at the age of sixty-nine.

One of the few tidbits of worldly wisdom my father shared with me came out of nowhere one day when he said wistfully, "Hughes, never feel bad when you are alone, because you're in good company." So many times in my life, I've had reason to recall those words.

All this to say those Saturday mornings in the Portland studios of WMTW were about as close to bonding as Dad and I ever got. The connection my father did provide, however, to the world of broadcasting would only deepen and endure.

A few years later at WKBW in Buffalo, the Saturdays with Dad continued, but this time it was not television that fascinated me but radio. WKBW was a Top 40 station where the smooth-talking disc jockeys leaned into a vintage RCA microphone and spun vinyl on a sixteen-inch turntable. In the era of "cool" they were the coolest.

So was the music they played. This was the late fifties, the heyday of Elvis, Buddy Holly, Chuck Berry, Connie Francis, Ricky Nelson, among many others. The uncomplicated melodies and pounding beats of that era somehow spoke to me. Even now, my satellite radio is locked on '50s Gold.

By 1962, my sister and I had attended schools in three different states, and my mother had become unhappy with the choppy education we'd gotten. A graduate of Agnes Scott, a private women's liberal arts college in Decatur, Georgia, she was focused on getting Gini and me the best possible schooling. She'd also pushed us to work hard in school.

Her family had been in America for several generations, and her grandfather, a soldier in the Confederate army, was wounded at Pickett's Charge, the Gettysburg conflict cited as the turning point in favor of the Union forces. I've often thought about that and marveled at the power of fate, the almost mystical way its unexpected consequences can change lives. After all, during that fierce 1863 battle, had Great-grandpa been killed rather than wounded, I wouldn't be here!

Mom had decided I needed to complete grades ten through twelve at a boarding school. I wasn't crazy about moving away from my family and friends for three years, nor was my father. Gini was on her way to Vassar and now he'd be looking at two hefty tuitions that would consume a major chunk of his salary. But Mom was on a mission: I would serve a three-year sentence at an institution that would propel me into an Ivy League school.

I didn't want to let down my mother or myself, so I became a grinder; a highly organized, goal-oriented overachiever. When I joined the Boy Scouts, for instance, it wasn't for the joy of fireside camping, it was to make Eagle Scout, and I systematically knocked off merit badge after merit badge until I had the requisite twenty-one of them at age fourteen, two or three years sooner than most.

And so, I left Buffalo and traveled five hundred miles east to Phillips Exeter Academy, a leafy bastion of the proud and privileged in Exeter, New Hampshire.

My first few weeks there were more intimidating than anything I'd ever experienced, both socially and academically. Being away from home for the first time was bad enough, but as the new kid, and entering as a sophomore, I felt estranged and out of step with my classmates, who had already gone through an initiation.

In public school, I'd grown used to big classes, heterogeneous groups of thirty or so kids sitting at assigned desks, with little oversight or pressure to excel. Suddenly I found myself in cozy seminars of ten or twelve, with some of the smartest kids I'd ever met and instructors whose mission was to challenge us. There was nowhere to hide. Over time, however, I came to see my mother's point. I was getting a very good education and learning to understand the significance of it all.

Serendipitously, at the beginning of my senior year a few enterprising students started to set up a student radio station. It was a modest operation, housed in the basement of one of the dorms with a mighty signal strength of ten watts, barely reaching the perimeter of campus. The format was all music—a mix of rock, Motown, and blues. When I heard they were looking for deejays, I couldn't resist. I'd absorbed enough from watching the guys in Buffalo that I figured I could at least fake it. Besides, how many superstar disc jockeys could there be within the Exeter student body?

When in the spring semester WPEA launched, I volunteered for the 7 to 8 a.m. slot. It was perfect, save for the fact that each day at Exeter began with Assembly, when everyone was required to gather in the imaginatively named Assembly Hall at 8 a.m. sharp. One lateness was permitted; after that, with each violation you were grounded for a weekend. So, I made sure to sign off my show by 7:55 and then sprinted a quarter mile across campus, sweating through my mandatory blazer and tie.

Meanwhile, I was able to find an outlet for my other childhood passion, sports. During three long, cold winters in Buffalo, I'd learned how to play ice hockey on the backyard rink my father had put together. Now at Exeter, I played sparingly on the hockey team. In the spring, I was a utility infielder on the jayvee baseball team (good field, no hit).

I wasn't a sufficiently skilled golfer to make the Exeter team, but in the eight years since my family had left Portland, we'd kept a nonresident membership at the Portland Country Club, renting the same place we'd rented when we lived there. That's where I'd spent my childhood summers, getting a little better at golf each year. When I returned to Exeter for my senior year, I saw a notice for the Exeter Academy fall golf championship, a match-play event held on the town's nine-hole course. On a whim, I entered and won. The 1964 "Laurence M. Crosbie Fall Golf Championship" plaque still hangs on a wall in my home, but the cool part was that my win was announced during Assembly the next morning.

The following spring my mother's grand plan came to fruition when, along with a number of my Exeter classmates, I got accepted to Yale.

My last Portland summer before heading to New Haven saw some excitement when the country club staged a high-profile charity golf event. A few thousand folks bought tickets to the clinic, and my best buddy, Chris Pierce, and I were among the first to sign up as marshals, thus guaranteeing ourselves ringside seats.

This was 1965, and the lineup that day included the reigning Masters champion Jack Nicklaus, the reigning U.S. Open champion Gary Player, and the soon-to-be-crowned PGA champion Dave Marr, along with England's top player, Tony Jacklin.

I'd never been so close to pro athletes, especially guys I'd been watching and worshipping throughout my childhood, and it was cool to see them interact with each other, tease each other during the clinic, see them as real people rather than distant icons. The day began with a luncheon and questions from the audience. Then it was off to the range for the clinic. In between, Nicklaus had slipped out to the men's room. As he emerged, I overheard one of the other marshals say to him, "Jack, how you feeling?" to which he replied, "About ten pounds lighter." It was a revelation—these guys talked just like we did!

They had all been brought to us that day through the auspices of a fledgling sports management firm out of Cleveland. Little could I have imagined in the moment, that company was where I'd be spending my entire business career.

But first: I had some schooling ahead of me. Thanks to the rigorous

academics at Exeter, Yale turned out to be less demanding than I'd antici-
pated. There was plenty of time for fun and games, the latter including four
years as a marginal contributor to the hockey team and three years on the
golf team.

As for the fun part, it began the moment I joined WYBC, the Yale radio
station, where I worked as a deejay and did play-by-play of home football
games and the occasional hockey game when I didn't suit up.

Doing sports radio was exhilarating and at times I could really get
into the flow of the action. Etched in my memory is a football game
against the University of Connecticut. It was a warm September afternoon and the window in our radio booth was propped open. On a particularly exciting play I stood up to better describe the action, bumping
into the support rod that held the window open. Down crashed the
window, the frame hitting me smack in the head.

"Holy shit, what was that?" I blurted, adding a couple more expletives
likely never heard in Connecticut broadcasting history. I'd completely forgotten I was live on the air. Blessedly there was no reaction from the FCC.
I kept the recording of that game for years.

Despite that gaffe and others, I was able to splice together enough of my
Yale airtime for a demo tape, which I sent to WGAN, a top radio station in
Portland. To my surprise, the station program director said he'd like to hire
me to do the all-night show, midnight to 6 a.m., the week between Christ-
mas and New Year's. I couldn't say yes fast enough. That led to a summer
job as the station's "swingman." When the regular deejay from 10 a.m. to
2 p.m. took his vacation, I filled in. Then the 6-to-midnight guy would
leave for two weeks, and I'd move into that slot, then the morning-drive
guy, etc.

It was an absolute dream job. I was learning a lot while doing something
I loved, I had plenty of time for golf, and I was making more money than
my friends, who were lifeguarding or doing construction. I hung on to that
WGAN gig for six glorious Maine summers. Life was good.

Then Vietnam happened.

Just before graduation in 1969, I got a letter from my draft board in Connecticut informing me that I would be drafted by the end of the year. I'd done two years of ROTC at Yale before dropping out, thank goodness, or I would have been on my way to the Mekong Delta as a second lieutenant with a life expectancy of about twenty minutes.

Desperate to avoid combat, I determined that my best chance was to enlist in some division of the Reserves, which would guarantee to keep me stateside. On August 15, I signed up for a six-year hitch in the Maine Army National Guard: six months of active-duty training, then one weekend per month and two weeks of summer camp each year through 1975.

The drive from the Portland Country Club to the WGAN studio was less than fifteen minutes, and when I slipped on my headphones for the 6 p.m. show, I was still on adrenaline from my match against Ray Lebel. For the next six hours I did my best to focus, but I'm sure I sounded goofy that night, floating on a self-congratulatory cloud nine.

The euphoria was short-lived, however, as I realized my summer was about to end with a couple of serious challenges. First was summer camp for the Reserves, two weeks in the company of kindred draft dodgers, playing soldier sixteen hours a day at a training center in the Maine woods. Then came a different sort of test: business school.

My commitment to the Reserves had forced me to put all future plans on a one-year hold, but I'd sent applications to a few business schools and was fortunate to get an acceptance from Harvard. I say fortunate because, although my college grades were good enough, my score on the business school exam was less than stellar, and I lacked what Harvard valued most—real work experience. The majority of those accepted by HBS had logged two or three years of meaningful employment, and others were accepted on the condition that they would put in those two years before enrolling. I guess a former part-time deejay was just what they were looking for.

It was a two-year program, and by the start of my second year I'd begun to think about how to put my MBA to use. When I asked myself in what field I wanted to forge a career, the answer came immediately: the one I'd grown to know and love, the broadcast business.

After a bit of research I targeted one company—a fast-growing conglomerate of radio and TV stations called Capital Cities. They owned WKBW in Buffalo, where my father had worked, and had recently acquired the New Haven station, WNHC, so I figured I had some karma going. On top of that, their two top guys, CEO Tom Murphy and President Daniel Burke, were both HBS alumni.

I wrote a letter to Murphy and it was Burke who replied. Over the next several weeks we corresponded, each of us getting a sense of what the other was after, and by the middle of my final semester at Harvard I had an offer to become Tom Murphy's executive assistant, helping with a variety of Cap Cities projects.

I couldn't believe my good fortune. Thanks to my hardworking father and iron-willed mother, so many good things had come my way. And now I had the opportunity to work beside a brilliant executive at the helm of his thriving company in the industry that had enthralled me for a decade. There was no way I could turn it down.

And then I met Mark McCormack.

2

Active Agent

The hallmark of the Harvard Business School curriculum is the "case method," an innovative teaching system based on discussion rather than lectures. Students are provided detailed studies of complex business situations—challenges faced by actual companies, both domestic and international—and are then asked to evaluate those cases, think nimbly and critically, and recommend a course of action. The cases are read the night before class, and the classroom becomes both a competition and a forum for the exchange of ideas. It's a powerful way to learn.

During my time there, one of the most popular courses was a second-year elective I took called "Starting New Ventures," where the cases involved entrepreneurs wrestling with their nascent businesses. One of the attractions was that several of the actual protagonists from these cases came to Boston and made presentations to the class. For many of them it was smart business, a low-cost way to hear some fresh ideas and do some head-hunting.

I had zero interest in most of these cases beyond the fleeting moments of attention I was required to give them. Then one night we were presented one on a company called International Management. Its founder, a fellow named Mark McCormack, had had some early success and the class assignment was to identify his best strategy for the future.

"Oh my god, what the hell is this?" I said to myself as I began to read it. McCormack was a sports agent. I didn't know there even was such a thing. And this guy was the agent for Arnold Palmer, Gary Player, and Jack Nicklaus, the top three golfers on the planet!

The next day, at the podium of the amphitheater classroom, there he stood: forty years old, six foot five, with a Robert Redford–worthy mop of blond hair and a smile to match. The presentation he made was captivating in both content and delivery. Much of what he said was simple good-business advice, but he said it with a passion and conviction that was mesmerizing: "Believe in what you're selling . . . Personal relationships are the key . . . Do what you say you're going to do for clients, colleagues, and bosses . . . Hire people smarter than you, and give them the freedom to do their jobs."

During the Q and A that followed I raised my hand and asked, "What do you look for in a client?" and he pointed to three things: (1) Someone young with the potential to become a superstar; (2) Someone who may never become a superstar but for whom we can earn a lot of money and who will be happy with our services at the end of the day; (3) Someone who, having signed with us, will be unable to develop a relationship with any of our competitors (playing defense as well as offense).

Typically, when the entrepreneurs spoke, one or two students would stay after class to learn a bit more. This time at least ten of us bounded down the steps to the front of the classroom, all, I suspect, with the same question I posed when my moment with McCormack arrived:

"Do you ever hire people from here?"

"Yes, I do," he said. "Here's my business card. Write me a letter."

I wrote to him the next day and a couple of weeks later heard back: "We don't have any openings at the moment, but I'll be back to Harvard to give the same presentation to the spring semester class. Let's plan to get together then."

I was excited by those words, but I also had a dilemma. Just two days earlier I'd gotten the letter from Cap Cities offering me a job. It was as if I'd spent months courting the woman of my dreams, had become engaged, and now suddenly someone even more intoxicating had come along. With a very carefully worded letter to Dan Burke at Cap Cities, I all but accepted, stopping short of a formal commitment. I wasn't proud of that, but I simply had to see where this thing with McCormack might lead.

A couple of weeks before he was scheduled to return to campus, I contacted his secretary to see where things stood.

"Oh yes," she said, "you're all set. Your interview with Mark will be on his way back to the airport."

That, I would soon learn, was the way Mark McCormack operated. He was constantly in motion, every moment of every day meticulously scheduled. I'd been slotted in for the twenty-minute drive from Harvard to Logan Airport, and I'd also be providing the transportation. My first thought was, *I wonder which one of my classmates is picking him up?*

On the appointed day I sat in on McCormack's re-presentation, surprised to hear how many new things he had to say. Once again, he was surrounded after class by job seekers. Finally, my time came.

"I have a tight schedule," was the first thing he said as we power walked to the parking lot. He also had a tight squeeze, shoehorning his six-foot-five frame into the passenger seat of my rust bucket Chevy.

Once we were on the road and chatting, he pulled a stack of 3x5 cards from the breast pocket of his jacket and disconcertingly began making notes. I don't recall much of our conversation, but it must have been engaging, since I managed to miss the ramp for the American Airlines terminal—which meant we had to circle back around, a delay of ten minutes that had McCormack repeatedly checking his watch, apparently in danger of missing his flight.

Just before we reached the terminal he asked me, "What sort of a starting salary are Harvard Business School graduates getting these days?" For a split second I considered bumping it up a couple thousand, then thought better of it, figuring he probably knew the answer.

"It's fourteen thousand dollars, sir," I said.

This prompted an entry on one of his cards, after which he said, "We'll be heading south from there." And with that he was out of the car.

A month later I received a letter offering me a job as Mark McCormack's executive assistant at International Management Group in Cleveland, starting salary $13,500, starting date August 15.

Suddenly I faced the biggest decision of my life. I'd been presented with two spectacular opportunities, reporting directly to a pair of titans in the two arenas that had been my passions, broadcasting and sports. Which door to open?

I'm not sure what it was—maybe Mark McCormack's charisma, maybe my father's less-than-stable career in broadcasting—but something deep inside told me to go with IMG.

It was a decision I've never regretted, but at the same time I've never stopped wondering what might have been, especially after 1985 when Tom Murphy's company acquired ABC and then was bought by the Walt Disney Company for $19 billion—at that time, the second largest acquisition in U.S. history.

There was also the personal side: I'd forgone the opportunity to work with a man who became one of America's most admired chief executives. When Murphy died in 2022, Disney CEO Robert Iger said, "Tom Murphy was unrivaled in our industry, not just for his business achievements, but for his impeccable ethics, his unwavering kindness, and his boundless generosity."

Mark McCormack would never be described quite that way.

In the city of Chicago in 1936, the mysterious forces of fate had again conspired to my advantage, this time smiling on the world of professional golf as well—when six-year-old Mark Hume McCormack, the only child of Ned and Grace McCormack, was struck by a car and suffered a fractured skull. His recuperation was lengthy, but his parents drew comfort from friends, among them Mark's godfather, who dedicated a poem to him, "Young Mark Expects," a not insignificant gesture since his godfather was poet Carl Sandburg.

Restricted from playing contact sports, young Mark turned to golf and became a fine player, winning a Chicago schoolboy championship, playing number one on the team at William & Mary, and qualifying for two U.S. Amateurs plus the 1958 U.S. Open at Southern Hills. It was while at

William & Mary, during a 1951 match against Wake Forest, that he met the ace of the Demon Deacons team, Arnold Palmer.

Seven years would pass before they reconnected. In the meantime McCormack earned a law degree from Yale, served a hitch in the army teaching military justice in Augusta, Georgia (where he managed to get in a few rounds at Augusta National), met and married his first wife, Nancy, and landed a job with the Cleveland law firm of Arter, Hadden, Wykoff & Van Duzer at an annual salary of $5,400.

"I didn't really find law all that thrilling," he told *Sports Illustrated* years later. "There were all these 80-year-old guys shuffling around the halls, and when someone died everyone moved offices. It was like my whole life was programmed. All I was really interested in was golf."

In an effort to merge his passion with his career, McCormack and a friend in 1958 formed National Sports Management, a company that lined up exhibition matches for some of the touring golf pros. (In those days of very modest tournament purses, such exhibitions provided the better players with a much needed second source of income.)

Within a short time, a few of those players were coming to McCormack, asking for advice with their endorsement contracts, and one of the first was Palmer, who had a deal with Wilson Sporting Goods. He'd signed a lifetime agreement to endorse their clubs and balls worldwide for an annual payment of just $5,000. The contract also was littered with restrictive clauses, as McCormack recalled in his book *Arnie: The Evolution of a Legend*. "One stipulated that all the golf equipment Palmer used belonged to Wilson and was supposed to be returned to them after the contract expired. Even golf balls? It also said that if Arnold endorsed any other product—be it soap suds, toothpaste, automobiles, hair tonic or breakfast cereal—Wilson Sporting Goods had to be mentioned. ('I start off every morning with a hearty bowl of Crunchy Corn Crackles and my trusty Wilson wedge.')"

Arnie had been perfectly happy with all that, but Mark was not. He negotiated a new deal, got rid of the lifetime shackle and limit on endorsing other products, and changed Wilson's rights from worldwide to only areas where the company had outlets, thus freeing Palmer to do business all over the world. The result was the now famous Golden Handshake in 1960 that made Mark McCormack the exclusive business representative for Arnold Palmer. And that deal *would* last a lifetime.

It was a beautiful marriage, Arnie's star power and Mark's business savvy, and their timing was perfect. Mark had created an industry just as Arnie's career and televised sports were taking off. In the first two years of their relationship Palmer's off-course earnings soared from $6,000 a year to $500,000, the equivalent of $5.2 million in today's dollars. (Arnie, in fifty-two years of playing the PGA and Champions Tours, would earn only $3.6 million in prize money, but thanks in equal parts to his own visceral appeal and McCormack's magic, he would amass a fortune of nearly $1 billion.)

McCormack's strategy was based on what he called the "brand-name principle." In *Arnie* he explained: "I once wrote to a manufacturer who wanted to put out an Arnold Palmer golf shoe. We liked the company, but the suggested royalty to Arnold was too low, and in telling the gentleman that I said, 'Regardless of what you pay for Arnold Palmer, it would be exceedingly less than what you would have to pay to build a brand name from the beginning. Arnold Palmer *is* a brand name.'"

A LESSON FROM ARNIE

Not long after Mark started to represent Palmer, the two of them were at a swanky hotel in Los Angeles. The guy working at the pool confused their drink orders and was slow bringing towels to their cabana. McCormack read him the riot act.

As the guy shuffled away humiliated, Arnold grabbed Mark by the arm and said: "If you ever treat anyone like that again, our relationship is over."

Mark, to his credit, told that story on himself. From that point forward, he never forgot Palmer's message: no matter how successful you become, treat people well. It epitomized what Arnold Palmer was all about.

When word spread of Palmer's lucrative alliance with McCormack, a budding South African star named Gary Player came looking for help. He, too, had a lopsided contract in hand, one that required him to win tournaments before he could earn any appreciable income. Mark fixed that one simply by rewriting the relevant clause to read "attempt to win" and Gary came on board as National Sports Management's second client.

Then, a bit more cautiously, came Jack Nicklaus. In his book *The Greatest Game of All*, Nicklaus recalled the start of his relationship with McCormack:

I wasn't seriously thinking of turning professional at the time. I was thinking more along the lines of what I would have to do to double or triple the $6,000 I was making by selling insurance. However, I wanted to find out the facts about professional golf. When Mark, at my request, came to Columbus to see me after the Amateur, he went over, item by item, a breakdown he had prepared on the various contracts he believed would be available to me if I decided to turn pro. They came to about $100,000, exclusive of the tournament prize money I might win. I told Mark that my plans were to remain an amateur but that I would think the matter over more fully at my leisure, and we left it at that.

When Jack decided to make the leap, Mark was quick to deliver:

At a press conference in Columbus I announced that I was turning pro, that Mark McCormack would be managing my business affairs. That same night I received a call from a Mr. Joel Gordon of the Revere Knitting Mills, in Boston. He had heard the news on the radio, he explained, and wondered if I would be interested in endorsing a line of sport shirts and sweaters. I told him to get in touch with Mark and later that month we all met in New York and worked out a contract. I mention this affiliation with Revere, my first commercial plum, not only because it proved to be a long and happy one, but also because of its importance to me at the time. Now that I had taken the plunge, in order to compete on the Tour I would need to get an Approved Tournament Player card from the PGA, and one of the requirements was that the applicant be able to show that he had $12,000 in the bank or was backed by a sponsor who did. By taking to my banker the written commitments from the Revere people and from a deal that Mark had quickly arranged with a publishing house (actually for this book), I got the letter I needed.

THE JOY OF BEING THIRD

Mark told me how in the early days of representing Arnold, Jack, and Gary, a company or advertising agency would call, usually seeking Palmer's endorsement or appearance.

Mark would quote a fee, which the caller usually ridiculed.

"That's way too much. I'm going to call Nicklaus."

Mark: "You don't have to, sir. I also represent Jack."

Caller (slightly flummoxed): "And what will he cost?"

Hearing Jack's fee, the caller fumed a bit more.

"Look, you give me no choice—I'll have to call Gary Player."

Mark (pause): "I represent him, too."

Gary was unique in many ways. Superstar golfers resent any perception that they are not top priority. Their egos won't allow it. It's basically why Nicklaus left IMG in 1971, feeling he would always play second fiddle to Palmer.

Player was the ultimate pragmatist. I asked him once if it was difficult being seen (especially in America) as number three behind Arnold and Jack.

"Laddie," he said with a sly smile, "I made millions on deals those two turned down."

That was 1961. Almost overnight McCormack's three clients began to win everything in sight. During the seven-year span that began in 1960, nobody but Arnie, Jack, and Gary won the Masters. They would account for seventeen of the forty major championships played during the 1960s. Arnie in that decade alone won forty-three tournaments; Jack, thirty; and Gary, ten.

Mark's company, now renamed International Management Group, took full advantage, crafting contracts for his three titans that demanded—and got—record cuts of the action, bonuses for each victory, and right of approval over all ads in which their names or images appeared. "Athletes were being ripped off for so long that I felt like Robin Hood," McCormack said.

Wrote *Sports Illustrated*'s Ray Kennedy, "The Big Three became the biggest moneymakers this side of Kuwait. Palmer was president of more than a dozen companies grossing $25 million, and young Jack was the mogul of such grand-sounding enterprises as the Jack Nicklaus Western Hemisphere Trading Co. With seven different golf equipment contracts for as many areas of the world, Player was kept busy switching clubs and muttering things like, 'If this is Spalding, it must be New Zealand.'"

THE PIONEER

It would be easy to declare Mark McCormack golf's first impresario, but that title belongs to a rotund, affable Bostonian named Fred Corcoran.

Corcoran spent his entire life immersed in the game, starting as a caddie at the Belmont Country Club, where, in an early display of his managerial chops, he rose to caddiemaster at age twelve. Before long he was running events for the Massachusetts Golf Association, where, with a box of crayons, he created the first tournament scoreboards.

A scratch-handicap backslapper and storyteller, Corcoran wooed local sportswriters and got golf into the Boston area newspapers. He also caught the attention of Pinehurst owner Richard Tufts, who hired him to run the press room at the 1936 PGA Championship, where he so impressed PGA of America president George Jacobus that he was hired as the association's tournament director, as close as there was in those days to being commissioner of the PGA Tour.

When Corcoran took over, the circuit was a loosely stitched patchwork of twenty-two events played during the winter in Florida, Texas, and on the West Coast. With a total purse of barely

$100,000, it was little more than a traveling circus. Most of the players were nameless, faceless itinerants sleeping in their cars as they hustled from event to event hoping to break even. The real goal was to attract enough attention to land a legitimate job as head professional at a posh private club.

So desperate were those post-Depression days that the resourceful star Gene Sarazen suggested an early version of crowdfunding: charge every golf fan ten cents to be used for prize money. He reasoned that, with 4 million golfers in America, if each of them could be dunned for a dime, it would reap $400,000. The idea went nowhere.

It was Corcoran who turned things around, using his PR and marketing savvy to convince auto dealers, resort hotel owners, and city chambers of commerce that sponsoring a professional golf event was good business. When he left his job in 1947 the Tour schedule had more than doubled to forty-seven events, the total prize money was over $600,000, and salivating sponsors were being turned away. Big-time professional golf had arrived.

So packed was the calendar that, for a brief moment, consideration was given to forming a satellite tour for lesser players, until it was decided that the pool of playing talent simply wasn't deep enough to pull it off. The idea would simmer for half a century before resurfacing as the Ben Hogan (now Korn Ferry) Tour.

Corcoran did not share materially in the success he brought the Tour pros. (His salary as tournament director was $5,000 a year plus $5-a-day expense money.) However, the PGA allowed him to supplement his income by handling the business affairs of one of the young players, Sam Snead, who became his lifelong client and friend.

Snead was a country boy from the backwoods of Hot Springs, Virginia, with enormous natural talent—he'd actually played much of his formative golf barefoot—and Corcoran did his Barnumesque best to milk that image. A story he loved to tell related to the time Sam learned that his picture had appeared in the *New York Times* and wondered how that could be, as he'd never been to New York. With Corcoran working on his behalf, Snead would become the first professional golfer to bank a million dollars.

Another Corcoran client was America's first great woman athlete, Babe Didrikson Zaharias, who excelled not just at golf but baseball, basketball, and track and field as well, winning two gold medals in the 1932 Olympics before turning to golf and winning ten major titles. In 1945, Corcoran brought Babe worldwide attention when he landed her a spot in the Los Angeles Open, the first woman to compete in a PGA Tour event.

Among Corcoran's closest friends was fellow Bostonian Ted Williams, who became his client and brought him valuable contacts in baseball, where he produced a series of three golf challenge matches between archrivals Babe Ruth and Ty Cobb (Cobb won, 2–1). He also staged exhibitions for Bing Crosby and Bob Hope, bringing sports-themed shows to U.S. troops abroad.

Corcoran was a cofounder of both the Ladies Professional Golf Association and the Golf Writers Association of America. He was the manager of three U.S. Ryder Cup teams and official scorer for thirty-four USGA Championships. When the World Golf Hall of Fame opened in 1975, he was among the charter inductees. The title of his biography says it all: *Fred Corcoran: The Man Who Sold Golf to the World.*

In the midst of all that 1960s success, however, came a major crisis when a civil war erupted within the PGA of America.

Since its founding in 1916 the PGA had focused on club professionals— the guys who ran pro shops and gave lessons. With the clubs in the northern tier closing for the winter, many pros would head south to pick up extra work and compete in tournaments. As the tournament circuit expanded and the prize money swelled, so did the flock of snowbird pros, and by the 1960s, several of them had decided to play for pay full-time. Suddenly the PGA comprised two factions—six thousand golf pros and two hundred pro golfers—with decidedly divergent agendas.

Television had played a major role. Thanks in large part to the appeal of Palmer, Nicklaus, and Player, the major TV networks were paying substantial fees for the right to broadcast events. The PGA was using that income to strengthen the greater organization and its programs, but the Tour players felt it was they who should be getting the lion's share of the largesse. They also wanted more authority over tournament scheduling and operations, and the hiring of Tour-related personnel, all of which was then under the firm control of the PGA home office.

The conflict inflamed in 1966 when a proposal came in for a $200,000 tournament to be sponsored by Frank Sinatra and held at the Canyon Country Club in Palm Springs. The PGA's tournament committee, consisting of four players and three PGA officials, voted 4–3 to hold the event. But the event would be played within a few weeks of the established Bob Hope Desert Classic in Palm Springs, and the PGA's executive committee, feeling the area couldn't properly embrace two events so close in time, met in special session and used its veto power (for the first and only time in fifty years) to kill the tournament. That set in motion a battle that lasted nearly three years.

Leading the PGA forces was the association's president, Max Elbin, with the backing of the broader membership as well as three of the game's most revered figures—Bobby Jones, Walter Hagen, and Sam Snead. The chief spokesman for the Tour players was Jack Nicklaus, and behind him stood virtually every significant player. At the 1967 U.S. Open at Baltusrol, 135 of them signed a petition listing seven demands (one of which was that the PGA relinquish its veto power) and insisted that if those demands were not met, all 135 of them would boycott that year's PGA Championship.

Nicklaus, despite all the distraction, won that U.S. Open at Baltusrol with a record seventy-two-hole total. The runner-up, and the man caught smack in the middle of the schism, was Arnold Palmer.

More of a traditionalist than his younger colleagues, Arnie had always been a staunch supporter of the PGA, which had been a big part of his life since childhood, his father, Deacon, being the green superintendent and then head professional at Latrobe Country Club in Pennsylvania. There was also the fact that his Arnold Palmer line of golf clubs was then being sold exclusively through PGA pro shops rather than more widely through sporting goods and department stores (a decision Arnie had made out of loyalty to his club pro brethren). Alienating those club pros now by siding with the Tour players would be unwise for business. Foremost in Palmer's mind, however, was a concern for the future health of both sides of professional golf.

LV YEARS BEFORE LIV

What was Mark McCormack's view of all this wrangling between the PGA of America and the Tour players? In his biography of Arnold Palmer, written in 1967 during the height of the conflict, he left no doubt—while also offering an eerie foreshadowing of today's situation with LIV Golf:

"I often wondered if the best thing that might happen for professional golf would be for Arnold Palmer to lead a group of players to a new pro tour. This almost occurred in 1964.

"A corporation, a very big corporation, guaranteed $4,000,000 to sponsor a golf tour of the top thirty players. The basic stipulation was that three of the players would be Arnold Palmer, Jack Nicklaus, and Gary Player. Twenty-seven others would be selected, but after Palmer, Nicklaus, and Player, we could pick any 27 we wanted.

"We would have had a tie-in with a television network and every tournament would have been on national television. The tour would have consisted of about 20 tournaments a year, which would have been spaced around the major championships—the Masters, U.S. Open and British Open. Presumably our players would no longer have been eligible for the PGA Championship.

"The prize money would have been better than then existed on the tour. In addition, each player would have received a salary of between $20,000 and $40,000 a year, depending on his

stature. The players also would have received profit sharing,
pension plans, and insurance benefits, none of which they get
now. The financial backing for this plan was no dream. The
money was on the table.

"The reason that new tour was not established is Arnold
Palmer. He feared for the future of the PGA."

Two weeks after the U.S. Open, the PGA of America agreed to six of
the Tour players' seven demands, enough of a concession that the players
all showed up at the PGA Championship. But the one item on which the
PGA did not budge was the veto that assured PGA executives final control
over the Tour, and that was a sore that would fester.

A year later, after no progress had been made, the Tour pros pulled the
trigger and formed their own association, American Professional Golfers,
Inc. Cynics called it Arnold Palmer's Golfers, and Arnie was not amused.
Although he gave verbal support to the breakaway group, he did not join it.
Instead, he met clandestinely with Max Elbin both in Latrobe and at the
PGA headquarters in Dunedin, Florida, and the two of them came up with
a compromise proposal, a one-year trial during which the Tour would be
run by a fourteen-person board consisting of seven players, four unaffiliated
businessmen, and three PGA officers.

The Palmer-Elbin proposal failed to gain favor on either side, but it did
spur broader talks, and in December of 1968, just weeks before the start of
the Tour's first season, a solution finally was reached. The short-lived APG
became the Tournament Players Division (TPD) of the PGA (later renamed
the PGA Tour), to be run by a twelve-member board comprised of PGA
executives, Tour players, and businessmen, and overseen by a commissioner.
The PGA of America thus withdrew itself from the business of tournament
golf, retaining oversight of only the PGA Championship and the Ryder Cup.

Joseph C. Dey, the highly respected executive director of the USGA,
became the first commissioner, and under his steady hand the rift

healed. Within a short time both the PGA of America and the PGA Tour were on paths to great prosperity.

No one would navigate this new world more deftly than Mark McCormack. Quite literally, he became the agent of change in modern golf.

I have no recollection what sage advice my business school class offered Mark on the conduct of his empire, but of one thing I'm certain: he didn't need our help. He was always way ahead of us. That became clear the moment I went to work for him.

I was twenty-five, and had been enjoying one final carefree summer in Portland—playing some golf, doing the fill-in deejay gig, slogging through another fortnight with the Maine Army Reserves—when I got a surprise phone call from Mark. He was going to be in New York the following week and wondered if I could join him there for a day, to get a bit better acquainted and learn about a number of the projects he had going.

I met him at the General Motors Building, where IMG had a suite of offices overlooking Central Park. I'd had no idea the company had a physical presence beyond Cleveland. That was just the first of several eye-openers that day.

Mark began by introducing me to one of his lieutenants, Rick Isaacson, an MBA out of Dartmouth who'd joined the company four years earlier and was now managing Gary Player and Ray Floyd. Short, bespectacled, prematurely balding, and chain-smoking, he looked more like a press agent than a sports agent, but he would become a close friend and mentor during my first years at IMG. Rick had me copy him on most of my memos and letters and invariably returned them with corrections, comments, and clarifications, always full of exclamation points in his trademark red ink. He had strong opinions—often less than complimentary—on everything and everyone in the company, and wasn't shy about expressing them, but I think I was spared the worst of his vitriol. Early on he started calling me

"Hugs," and I loved the guy despite moments when I (and others within IMG) wanted to kill him.

Rick was in New York that day to launch a new division of IMG called Merchandising Consultants International. Mark had correctly intuited that most major companies were ill-equipped to evaluate the myriad proposals they received from people like himself. That responsibility typically fell to in-house executives or lawyers with zero expertise in sports or talent management. Invariably mistakes were made—bad choices and bad deals. So Mark had created MCI on the hunch that such corporations would pay significant monthly retainers to subcontract that job to a knowledgeable specialist.

He was right. Within a year or two MCI would have lucrative agreements with the likes of Colgate-Palmolive, Hertz, Miller Brewing, Princess Hotels, Rolex, Seagram's, and Wilkinson, among many others.

Most of the rest of my day in New York was spent riding around the city with Mark, listening in on an endless string of phone calls he fielded in the back of his limousine. That afternoon we stopped at a law firm for a short meeting. Going up in the elevator Mark explained that Lee Trevino's agent, Bucky Woy, was suing IMG for infringing upon Trevino's commercial rights without approval or compensation. IMG had made a documentary titled *The 30 Days of Lee Trevino*, about the magical period in 1971 when Supermex had won the U.S. Open, Canadian Open, and British Open, a golf triple crown never accomplished before or since. (I happened to know the third leg of that triple well. Best friend Chris Pierce and I had been at Royal Birkdale on that day in July when Trevino sank the winning putt, on our first-ever trip to Britain the summer between my two years at HBS. Little could I have imagined there would be 103 more major championships in my future!)

Listening to Mark and the lawyer he'd retained to defend IMG, I got a quick tutorial in sports litigation, an athlete's right to compensation versus what is already in the public domain, etc. But mostly I remember marveling at Mark's mind in action, an astute lawyer and imaginative problem solver.

Toward the end of the day he handed me a lengthy list of administrative tasks to tackle when I got to Cleveland, briefly explaining each one as I frantically took notes. "Sorry, sir—what's TWI?" (Trans World International, IMG's television division.) "David's last name again?" (Rees, our South African CFO.) "MMI?" (Motor Marketing International, our auto racing division.)

On the flight back to Maine that evening, I tried to process it all. IMG was a lot more than Arnold Palmer's agent; it was a sports-marketing powerhouse. Cleveland may have been its birthplace, but within its first decade the company had expanded to offices in New York, Los Angeles, London, Paris, Geneva, Tokyo, Cape Town, Sydney, and Christchurch. The original client base—a small stable of golfers—had exploded to include dozens of athletes, with entire divisions of the company now devoted to tennis, skiing, auto racing, and team sports. They'd started IMG Literary Management (first client *Dennis the Menace* creator Hank Ketcham), IMG Models (first client British supermodel Jean Shrimpton), and IMG Broadcasting (first client the voice of ABC Sports, Chris Schenkel). In addition to the MCI consulting arm, there was a division charged with creating and managing sporting events, another aimed at working with sports leagues and associations, and a huge and fast-growing division in L.A. producing television programming and films. And Mark McCormack was just getting started.

A month later I joined him.

As eager as I'd been to get started, I was less than excited about the prospect of moving to Cleveland, Ohio. A xenophobic northeasterner, I had no clue where Cleveland was on the map, figured it was somewhere west of Chicago. Imagine my surprise to find it just over the Pennsylvania border. I didn't even have to change time zones!

Still, it was Cleveland. There was a guy in my section at HBS who'd grown up there, and when I asked him about his hometown, he said, "The main drag is Euclid Avenue, and if you're downtown at seven p.m. and roll a bowling ball down Euclid Avenue, you won't hit anything for forty blocks." Expectations managed.

The IMG offices were in the Cuyahoga Savings Bank building, a fifteen-story steel-and-glass monument to charmlessness at 1360 East

Ninth Street, a few blocks from Lake Erie. About a hundred employees were spread over three floors. My office was on the thirteenth, which was a bit unusual—because of the superstition about the number 13, most buildings of that era had elevators with buttons marked 1 through 12, then 14 upward. The joke around the office was that when Mark set up shop he chose the thirteenth floor and then leveraged the triskaidekaphobia thing to get a sweet deal on the rent.

On the northeast corner of the headquarters Mark ran things from a large office with a sitting room, a private bathroom, and a commanding view of the lake—except that he didn't run things from there because he was constantly traveling, almost never in Cleveland. Two doors down, next to the kitchenette, was the notably less lavish workspace where yours truly would be spending sixty hours a week.

It would be more than a month before Mark made his first appearance, but that was fine, as it enabled me to get a sense—not so much an overview as an underview—of the operation. My first impression was that Mark must have lowballed a lot of guys the way he had me on the hiring salary, because a surprising number of the executives were not the best and the brightest I'd expected them all to be. Instead, a handful of extremely smart individuals stood out amid much mediocrity.

In addition to the aforementioned Rick Isaacson there was Ian Todd, an Englishman who handled the pro skiing clients. A former Olympic skier himself, he had a law degree and an exceptionally quick mind. Ian was around for only a year or so before Mark recognized just how sharp he was and sent him to Geneva and then London, where he oversaw IMG operations in Europe, Africa, and the Middle East.

IMG Tennis was a fledgling operation until Bob Kain arrived and built it into a one of the company's most profitable divisions. Bob had shrewd business sense, worked his tail off, and knew how to get things done, but I think a big part of his success came from the warmth of his personality and the ease with which he related to everyone. For years Mark had tried to sign Billie Jean King, but she never liked his manner and approach. Then Bob came on board, Billie Jean made the leap, and many of the top male and female tennis pros followed. When Bob arrived at IMG the tennis division's annual revenue was $650,000; when he left it was $110 million.

When I joined IMG in 1972, IMG's fastest-growing division was the television production company Trans World International. (I'd taken a job in the broadcasting world after all!) At the helm was one of the true geniuses in that field, Barry Frank, who had been hired away from ABC, where he'd been vice president of programming under the legendary Roone Arledge. Barry would leave IMG in 1976 to become president of CBS Sports, but then return to run TWI and IMG Broadcasting, where he attracted an all-star cast of clients, including Bob Costas, Al Michaels, Jim Nantz, and Mike Tirico.

Another Barry Frank client was football commentator John Madden, who one year reaped a $7.5 million salary bump thanks to Barry's creating a bidding war for his services among ABC, CBS, and Fox. Madden was an odd duck, however, who required more than the usual care and feeding. He insisted that all the income he'd earned through IMG agreements be paid directly to him, then he would send commission checks back to us—and he was notorious for being late with those checks. More than once at senior executive meetings Mark went ballistic over this, reaming Barry at length, but Barry knew how to handle both his client and his boss.

"I'm not happy about it, either," he said, "but eventually John always pays—wouldn't you rather have this be our problem than some other agent's?"

The best sense of humor in the office belonged to a diminutive former North Carolina newspaperman with the unfortunate name Bev Norwood. "I was named after four cities in Massachusetts," he was fond of saying, "Beverly, Norwood, Marblehead, and Athol."

Bev attended Wake Forest, where the commencement speaker his graduation year was Arnold Palmer. They became friends, and after a stint as a sportswriter on the *Winston-Salem Journal* he joined IMG as sort of the company editor in chief, producing McCormack's annual tome, *The World of Professional Golf*, and editing corporate client-sponsored books that recapped the U.S. Open, Open Championship, Ryder Cup, and Presidents

Cup. He also served as literary agent for our top golf clients, pairing them with writers who penned books by and about them. Another classic Norwood line: "Not only has Arnold Palmer not written any of the fourteen books under his byline, he hasn't *read* any of them."

And another: after Curtis Strange, hands down the thriftiest client I managed, became the first player to win $1 million in a season, Bev quipped, "By my calculation, this allows Curtis to enjoy twenty thousand nights at the Red Roof Inn."

Among Bev's closest pals in the game was Dan Jenkins, with whom he shared many cocktails on the tournament trail. In fact a Bev-like character appears in a couple of Dan's books under the name Smokey Barwood.

And then there was my Cleveland roommate for the first few months, Alastair Johnston, a Glasgow-born accountant who at age twenty had approached Mark at the 1968 Open Championship at Carnoustie and suggested rather cheekily that if Mark ever wanted to open an office in Europe, he was the man. Mark didn't take him up on that, but they kept in touch, and the summer I came to Cleveland so did Alastair.

His big break came a few years later when Mark made the difficult decision to step away as Arnold Palmer's personal handler and transferred the reins to Alastair, who went on to serve Arnie, and then Arnie's estate, for more than forty years. During that period Alastair found time to become chairman of the Glasgow Rangers soccer team, while also amassing the largest private golf library in the world, over thirty thousand volumes, which he ultimately donated to the Royal and Ancient Golf Club of St. Andrews.

My relationship with Alastair began cordially enough, but over time, and for a variety of reasons, it became strained, and when my tenure at IMG ended, there was no one at the company for whom I had less respect, a feeling that was shared by many others there.

At the start, however, the only relationship that mattered to me was the one with Mark McCormack. When he finally appeared in Cleveland in mid-September, I had several sit-downs with him and began to get a sense of the man behind the magnate—to the extent that anyone could get to know Mark McCormack.

He wasn't much for eye contact, small talk, or any real depth of connection. There was always too much work to be done, always the next fire to put out or goal to pursue. Mark wasn't distant or aloof, he was simply two steps ahead of everyone. The words used most often to describe him are "visionary" and "driven," ideal assets for an entrepreneur, but less conducive to forming meaningful relationships.

I'm not sure why, maybe it was the way he ran his business-centric life—in constant motion, on the road two hundred days a year, logging 250,000 miles around the world annually, eyes on the prize—but I had the sense that beneath the veneer of his success was a sad sort of aloneness, a guy who had never stopped to smell the roses. He was also a man of vexing contradictions—demanding yet open-minded, generous yet tightfisted, appreciative yet unpraising, trusting yet paranoid.

His work schedule would have been unbearable for most humans—awake at 4:30 a.m., dictating letters and making phone calls overseas from 5 to 7, then hammering through a gauntlet of tasks and meetings scheduled in half-hour segments, followed invariably by dinner with a client or prospective client and/or a few phone calls to Australia and Japan. Some were turned into the fifty or more letters and memos that he dashed off each day. And those who reported to him were expected to have a similar work ethic. In the words of one of his early vice presidents, Bud Stanner, "If you're not working 24 hours a day, seven days a week, Mark figures you're taking too much time for lunch."

Mark actually kept track of exactly how many hours he worked, slept, exercised, spent time with his family, and relaxed, and once told me his first marriage had failed because he'd spent only 38 percent of his time with his family.

His son Breck shared a story that reveals a bit about the way Mark's mind worked. Mark and his parents always rode the train from Chicago on vacation trips to Mississippi. Mark as a child memorized every stop along the route—seventy-eight of them—and as an adult he could still recite all seventy-eight in order to Breck and his siblings growing up.

With the same anal retentiveness, Mark constantly jotted notes on his 3x5 cards, labeling each item "future," "soon," "very soon," and "now!" then at the end of each day transferring that information to a yellow legal pad where he kept his schedule for the next several weeks. And he was quick to chastise any employee who wasn't similarly slavish. "How do you expect to remember everything if you don't write it down?" One of his mantras in managing clients was: "Do everything you said you were going to do. Then do more."

Punctuality was another of his obsessions. Anyone booked into one of Mark's half-hour slots knew to do three things: be on time, be prepared, be succinct. "He has a tendency to finish your sentences for you because he thinks it saves time," Arnold Palmer once said, while the impish Dave Marr had a slightly different view. "Let's face it," he said, "Mark is hard of listening."

McCormack's answer: "It's my job to be abrupt. I don't believe in talking around subjects. It's so easy to turn a two-minute conversation into a 10-minute ordeal. I like to cut through all the bull, so I'll have time to do some small talk in my own forum."

His attitude toward compensation and spending was baffling in a Jekyll and Hyde way. He never paid himself much from IMG, although he did take a big annual salary out of Arnold Palmer Enterprises which he and Arnold owned 50–50, and his travel and entertainment expenses were exorbitant. No doubt he reasoned: "I'm working 18 hours a day seven days a week, so everything I do is deductible." A hotel key display hanging on the wall of his office in Cleveland was legendary. Large, bizarre keys from every country in the world. When visiting clients or corporate execs stopped to look, Mark would joke: "I guess what you've heard about me is true—I *am* a thief."

He could be almost profligate in his willingness to gamble on a good idea, whether it was his own or from one of his lieutenants. Bob Kain one day pitched him on the notion of expanding a division representing professional ice-skaters by launching a national skating show featuring Olympic stars, on the surface a shaky (or at least slippery) notion, but Kain had the facts and numbers to support his hunch, and Mark didn't hesitate, investing deep into six figures of start-up money. *Stars on Ice* became a huge success.

Mark compensated his top-level executives generously, with annual performance-based bonuses occasionally rivaling those of Wall Street firms—"golden handcuffs" paid out over four years to keep everyone working hard. (There was very little turnover within the upper ranks at IMG.) When it came to the smaller things, however, he could be absurdly petty. Many of us traveled constantly, and Mark periodically required us to disclose our mileage balances with each airline as well as the extent to which we'd used those programs for personal travel. Although he never let on, I always suspected he deducted something from our compensation.

In a similar way, he made us wring every commissionable penny out of our clients. Often we'd book players to appear in two consecutive international tournaments, with each event providing round-trip airfare as part of the inducement. If, for example, a golfer competed in the Lancôme Trophy and World Match Play events back-to-back, he'd receive the cash value of two first-class tickets to and from Europe. One of my first assignments was to look into those double bookings, calculate the exact value of the airfares, and bill the clients our full 20 percent commission for the unused portion.

Lord knows why such penny-pinching gave him satisfaction, but he couldn't help himself. Another example: we got lots of letters and résumés from people wanting to work at IMG, and occasionally we hired interns. One time Mark tried to take it a step further. He sent me a résumé suggesting that, since the writer was so interested, maybe he'd pay IMG to work for us. He was similarly stingy about bestowing recognition for a job well done—at least face-to-face. More than once I heard secondhand that Mark had praised or defended me profusely about something I'd done for a client or the company, but not once in nearly thirty years did he shake my hand, look me in the eye, and say, "Job well done." I think, when he crowed about any of us in public, he was congratulating himself for having the savvy to hire us.

It was all a bit ironic, because Mark's bestselling book *What They Don't Teach You at Harvard Business School* is full of insights on human nature—the importance of empathy in making a deal, keeping the other side happy—yet he displayed little of that in his own headquarters, where a cynical nickname for him was the Jolly Blond Giant, a creature possessed of regrettably little "ho, ho, ho."

Instead, what those of us who reported to him sensed often from Mark was paranoia. Another McCormack mantra was: "In the representation business, every hour of every day someone is out there trying to steal your client." That was surely one of the reasons be began his days at 4:30 a.m.

But I think he also lived in fear of mutiny within IMG. It was well known in the head office that Mark on occasion asked secretaries to eavesdrop and report on conversations. I believe he was afraid that a handful of us driving the majority of the company's revenue might break away and form our own company, and he thus required us to sign non-compete agreements, sidelining us, in most cases, for two years. Were they enforceable? A gray area, but the cost of litigating that question would have been huge, and Mark would have drawn it out to the hilt.

Such insecurity helped explain Mark's compulsion to see copies of every scrap of correspondence that passed through his network of offices, and to check in with his direct reports at dawn each workday—whether he was phoning them from Cleveland or Katmandu. It also explained, in part, why each of us was the unceasing focus of a breast-pocket 3x5 card crammed with notations in Mark's pencil-scratch shorthand. He kept those thoughts literally close to the vest, erasable, and, if for some reason they were discovered, decipherable only by him.

So Mark McCormack was complex, enigmatic, ultimately unknowable. He was also the most intuitively brilliant businessman I've ever met, with the rare ability to see the big picture clearly from fifty thousand feet, while also staying on top of the most minute details.

Mark never stopped learning, adapting, and innovating, and two of the most important lessons he'd learned came from the man he called his mentor, Lew Wasserman, a Cleveland-born talent agent who had risen to become the chairman of MCA, one of the largest and most powerful companies in the entertainment business. Shortly after Mark had made the decision to become an agent, he paid a visit to Wasserman's world in Los Angeles and had his eyes opened.

MCA might represent an actor such as Tony Curtis to get him movie roles, but at the same time Curtis would have a business manager, a PR person, a financial advisor, an accountant, an insurance expert, and a personal assistant—each of them with his or her hand out. Even worse, they all competed for Tony's time and attention.

Mark at that time was running full speed to maximize the opportunities for Palmer, Nicklaus, and Player. In exchange, they were paying him 10 percent of their worldwide income—everything they made on and off the course—and whenever Mark took a trip, the three players split his expenses. As you might imagine, the expenses part could prompt the occasional probing question when, for instance, Jack noticed that Mark had spent a week in South Africa with Gary. By and large, however, the three players were happy with this setup.

Once having seen the disarray of Hollywood, however, Mark saw an opportunity and he instituted a sea change in his operation. Tripling his office space, he hired full-time lawyers, accountants, and financial experts, and became a one-stop shop, providing his clients a "service umbrella" that saved them the hassle and expense of dealing with multiple providers. At the same time he doubled his own commission from 10 percent to 20. It was a masterstroke that worked for both sides and would change the business of client representation forever.

At around the same time, Mark had seen an emerging strategy in Lew Wasserman's empire, one that fascinated him. In the process of building the agent business at MCA, Wasserman had expanded to include a television production company. Then he'd purchased the Universal Pictures motion picture studios. Suddenly he had a vertical operation, producing his own TV shows and movies and then casting them with his in-house talent. It was ingenious, and for a while it was hugely profitable. But it was also monopolistic, and within a short time the U.S. Justice Department shut it down.

The golf business, Mark reasoned, was not nearly as big or eye-catching as the entertainment business. He could use Wasserman's vertical strategy while staying under the radar, especially with just three clients.

But did he want just three clients? Would the vertical thing even work with just three?

"I had a decision to make," he told me. "I could semi-retire and have a comfortable life, representing my three friends and playing lots of golf. Or I could go for something bigger. Did I want to be Colonel Tom Parker to Elvis, Brian Epstein to the Beatles, or did I want something more?"

The stakes were high. Managing three players had made him a millionaire—imagine what managing thirty or three hundred might do, especially on a 20 percent commission. At the same time, Mark realized how lucky he'd been.

"Somehow, with two hundred and fifty players on the pro tour, my first three clients had turned out to be the era's preeminent superstars. I'd gone three-for-three; it was like winning the lottery. I knew lightning wouldn't strike again. I'd have to make things happen."

He decided to go for it and began by expanding his stable of players from three to dozens. At the same time, he decided to dive into television. "In the 1960s an unholy alliance was developing. Sports was helping to make television and television was helping to make sports," he wrote in *What They Don't Teach You at Harvard Business School*. Not surprisingly, Lew Wasserman had seen the same thing at the same moment, and was thinking of starting a leisure sports division at MCA. He sent one of his most talented executives, Jay Michaels, to Cleveland to find out whether Mark was interested in running the show.

Mark thought it over carefully and decided to pass. However, in his chat with Michaels he'd been very impressed. "I told Jay of our desire to become more involved in the television business. I told him what I felt the potential was, the degree of commitment I was willing to make in order to reach that potential—and I told him I wanted his help." In 1967 Jay Michaels left MCA to become head of IMG's new division, Trans World International. It would become the world's largest independent producer of sports programming.

With his vertical strategy begun, McCormack's next aim was to expand laterally, and that meant two things—taking his services beyond golf to other sports and making IMG an international business. His game plan was simple: find and sign the world's best athletes.

In the United Kingdom he solidified his golf presence by luring England's best player, Tony Jacklin, then signed race car driver Jackie Stewart and launched IMG Motor Sports. In France, he signed the skier who had just won three Olympic gold medals, Jean-Claude Killy, and built IMG Skiing around him. In Australia he landed Rod Laver and IMG Tennis was born.

Each of those coups also led to bigger prizes. The Jacklin connection brought an introduction to the Royal and Ancient that resulted in a contract that has lasted more than fifty years. Through the Jackie Stewart alliance, IMG created and sold sponsorships to auto races around the world and even brought a Grand Prix to Cleveland. With the help of Killy, IMG became the official marketing arm of the Winter Olympics, and the agreement with Laver not only gave the company a foothold in a major new sport but led to contracts with the Australian Open, Wimbledon, and the U.S. Open—three of tennis's four Grand Slam events.

Such larger affiliations not only were highly profitable, they gave the young company gravitas, they presented opportunities for film and television projects, and perhaps most important, they provided income streams far more dependable than the performance of individual athletes. One of Mark's favorite lines was: "Unlike Björn Borg, Wimbledon never sprains an ankle, fails a drug test, loses six–love, or retires."

All of these affiliations were put together in the space of a few years. By the end of the sixties, IMG also had begun to rep team sport athletes with the signing of its first baseball player (Brooks Robinson), basketball player (John Havlicek), football player (Fran Tarkenton), hockey player (Stan Mikita), and soccer star (Pelé). All of which surely brought Mark a measure of solace when, in 1970, the company suffered its first major loss as Jack Nicklaus severed his relationship with IMG and set out on his own. Nicklaus was said to be frustrated at playing second fiddle to Palmer, and McCormack didn't disagree.

"When I decided to diversify the company, I could no longer give Jack the kind of personal attention he expected," he said. "I'd have won the battle and lost the war."

Instead he'd won the war and had achieved his vision, expanding his company into an international dynamo based on the representation of athletes, but broadened into a creator and promoter of major sporting events, a global leader in sports-based television and video production, and a merchandising consultant to several of the world's largest corporations.

That was the IMG I'd walked into in August of 1972, and as McCormack's executive assistant I was quickly exposed to all of it. The list of projects he'd given me was, I realized later, purposely too long, and many of the assignments required sufficiently in-depth attention that I would never complete all of them, especially as Mark heaped on new duties daily. This was part of his modus operandi: keep everyone moving just as he was, at full throttle.

I watched him operate—the long hours, the yellow pad full of things to do and cross off—and I began to mimic him, arriving at dawn and working late, trying to check as many things off my list as possible. I became the personification of that line by poet Stephen Dobyns: "Each thing I do, I rush through so I can do something else."

Hey, it was Cleveland and I had no social life, few friends beyond my IMG colleagues. My only interaction beyond the office was playing pickup hockey in a weekly men's league and attending my weekly Army

Reserve meeting. (I'd traded the one-weekend-a-month routine in Maine for weekly meetings.) Trouble was, the only ice time the hockey league could get was very late on Tuesday night and that was the same evening as the Reserves. So my Tuesday schedule was: work from 7 a.m. to 6 p.m., quick dinner, Reserves from 7 to 11, hockey from 11:30 p.m. to 1 a.m. Oh, to be young, energetic, and driven.

After about three months I'd settled rather happily into a life that was comfortably chaotic. Then Mark dropped a bombshell.

"Our man on the golf tour is leaving the company," he said. "How would you like to replace him?"

3

....

A Rising Tide

I was incredulous. "Mark, are you saying you want me to go out onto the Tour to work with our clients?"

"That's part of it," he said, "but what I really want you to do is find us some new clients—good ones. We're getting killed out there."

Then he did something Mark McCormack rarely did—he took the blame. In the course of expanding his empire, Mark had taken his focus off the golf division that had launched his company. During the same time, a number of promising young players had appeared on the scene.

At San Francisco's Olympic Club in 1966, a nineteen-year-old local kid named Johnny Miller had captured attention by finishing tied for eighth in the U.S. Open. One year later a wisecracking Mexican-American named Lee Trevino had emerged from nowhere to finish sixth at the U.S. Open at Baltusrol. Mark had been present at both of those events—all he'd needed to do was approach Miller and Trevino, and chances are, both of them would have become clients.

Then there was Lanny Wadkins, who in 1970 had capped a glittering collegiate career with a trio of wins in the Southern, Western, and U.S. Amateurs. Wadkins, an Arnold Palmer scholar at Wake Forest, was a natural fit for IMG. But again, Mark had done nothing to court him.

"I didn't think I needed to," he told me. "I just assumed kids like that would come to me. I was the guy who'd turned the Big Three into multimillionaires. Besides I was the only game in town. Who else would Johnny Miller's father ever want to call? The only other agent I knew of was old Fred Corcoran and his only client was Sam Snead. But the truth was, I'd become complacent, fallen asleep at the switch. I lost Miller, Trevino, Wadkins, and several other potential clients to competitors I never knew existed. And now it's time to turn things around."

So there it was. The father of sports management had thrown down the gauntlet to a twenty-five-year-old, fresh out of grad school and barely able to read a contract.

"We've fallen behind, Hughes," he said. "Get out there and do something about it."

There was one hitch. This was not a promotion or change of title; I was still Mark's executive assistant, so effectively I'd be doing two jobs. Mark explained that the problem with his assistants over the years was, invariably, each of them had discovered something else of great interest within IMG that he'd then allowed them to pursue. Good for them, but he was out an assistant. So I had to promise to stay for at least a year working directly for him.

At that moment my to-do list was four pages long with three dozen projects that ranged from updating framed photos for the Cleveland reception area to exploring the possibility of IMG running the Caribbean Tour, from cultivating a golf course design partnership between Tony Jacklin and architect Arthur Hills to pitching sponsors on a motorboat race in Panama. Now I'd be doing those jobs in my spare time from the locker rooms, press centers, and hotels on the PGA Tour.

There was no how-to handbook for the man-on-Tour job, and the guy who'd preceded me had made a mess of it, so I was flying blind when in October—two months after joining IMG—I boarded a plane for the Kaiser International tournament in Napa, California. Mark had given me no real direction, and my only preparation had been to read *Arnie*, his biography of Arnold Palmer, which was full of accounts of business meetings with players, golf officials, and corporate sponsors. That was my manual.

Job one was to make contact with IMG's current roster of clients. Beyond Palmer and Player, it wasn't exactly a star-studded cast. We had Raymond

Floyd and Dave Marr, each of whom had won a PGA Championship; we had Tommy Aaron, whose claim to fame was being the perpetrator of the scorekeeping error that had led to Roberto De Vicenzo's embarrassing loss of the 1968 Masters; we had Doug Sanders, who had choked away his chance to win the 1970 Open Championship; and we had DeWitt Weaver, who a few months earlier had caused a PR nightmare when, after winning a tournament sponsored by cigarette maker Liggett & Myers, he was asked what the key to his improved play had been and replied, "I gave up smoking." Rounding out the stellar stable were the less than household names of Ron Cerrudo, Dave Eichelberger, and Barry Jaeckel. Yes, IMG Golf needed resuscitating.

FLAMBOYANT FLOYD

I'd been on the job about three months when Mark dispatched me and Rick Isaacson to Chicago to finalize the sale of Raymond Floyd's bachelor apartment. Our duties included a walk-through of the place, and when we got to the bedroom I looked upward to behold a ten-by-twenty-foot mirror on the ceiling. (Babe in the woods that I was, I had no idea why someone would want such a thing. Rick had to do a bit of educating.)

Then a few weeks later came another Floyd assignment, this one directly from Raymond. In a tournament locker room one day he approached me with a small bag and a serious look on his face. "Take this back to the office," he said, "but make sure they don't commission it. This is gambling winnings."

"How much is in here?" I stammered.

"Twenty thousand cash," Ray said. This was 1972, remember— today the equivalent would be $150,000. I never let that satchel out of my sight during a sleepless night at the hotel or on the plane back to Cleveland the next day. Welcome to the world of agenting, where you never know what a client will ask.

So job number two was to do some prospecting. Mark and I had made a list of the young players who seemed to have promise, and I was glad to see that most of them were in the field at Napa. At the top was a kid with

Hollywood good looks named Grier Jones. He'd been on the Tour a few years and in 1972 had found his game, winning twice. Grier Jones was no Bobby Jones, but he seemed to have both ability and marketability.

"Sorry," he said after I'd made my pitch. "I'm with Ed Barner."

My next stop was Jim Simons, a two-time All-American out of Wake Forest who a year earlier had almost won the U.S. Open at Merion as an amateur.

His reply was the same: "I have a contract with Ed Barner."

When I got to the third kid on my list, a burly Californian named Jerry Heard, I feared I'd get the same answer—and I did.

Ed Barner was the guy who had signed Johnny Miller and Lanny Wadkins. He and Miller had attended Brigham Young at the same time, and he'd set up shop in Los Angeles, where he'd become IMG's biggest competition, quickly assembling a group of attractive young players.

All credit to him, Barner had had the brainstorm of selling these young guns as a package, and at the Ford Motor Company he'd found the perfect fit, as Miller, Wadkins, Jones, Heard, and Simons became "The Young Thunderbirds," appearing in numerous ads and commercials. Ford gave each of them two Thunderbirds for their personal use and supplied them with Thunderbird courtesy cars at the events they played. (Ironically, the Ford executive who made that deal with Barner was Ben Bidwell, who would later become CEO of Chrysler and an IMG board member.)

The Young Thunderbirds stood in bold contrast to IMG's lackluster lineup, and I didn't see many other prospective stars on the horizon. I wasn't relishing the field report I'd have to deliver to Mark.

But first I had another duty in Napa: to get our players spots in some off-season events. Back then, the PGA Tour calendar wound down in October, and during the last two months of the year the best playing opportunities were in the southern climes, mostly on the Caribbean Tour, where the tournament organizers paid appearance money to attract upper-echelon players. Gathered together at Napa was a consortium of representatives from the Ford Maracaibo Open, Caracas GM Open, Panama Open, etc., looking to strengthen their fields. My job was to negotiate with them, to try to get as high an appearance fee as I could. It was sort of a comical scene, really. I'd make my pitch for several players, then the reps all chattered animatedly in Spanish for a few moments, then a spokesman would come back with a line right out of *Jeopardy!*: "We'll take Tony Jacklin for fifteen hundred dollars."

That year I got Ron Cerrudo a spot in the Hassan II Trophy, played on the Royal Golf Dar Es Salam course inside the walls of the king of Morocco's palace in Rabat. Cerrudo was a good young player out of San José State and had won a couple of times. So he goes over there, plays great, and ends up in a playoff with Al Geiberger.

Just before they tee off, Geiberger approaches him and says, "Do you want to split the purse?" (In those days it was common for two players in a playoff to agree to split the combined prize money for first and second.) First prize in this case was $20,000, second $11,400, and after a bit of hesitation Cerrudo agreed to the split. He then beat Geiberger and brought home a bittersweet $15,700 instead of $20,000. There was a nice trophy, though—a jewel-encrusted scabbard, value unknown but substantial—and Cerrudo has kept it in a safe-deposit box for half a century.

We've remained friends and now and then I call him, never failing to ask, "Have you sold that thing yet?" Cerrudo, now head teaching pro at the Daniel Island Club in South Carolina, always has the same reply: "Hell no, that's my retirement!"

My final task in Napa was to sign up players—both IMG clients and non-clients—for a corporate outing we were running later that fall in Colorado. If you're wondering what PGA Tour player incomes were like in those days, consider this. The deal was $500 plus expenses to play the one-day outing, and not a single player I approached turned it down.

One of the non-clients I enlisted was a young Stanford graduate out of Kansas City named Tom Watson. In his first season on Tour he'd done nothing to distinguish himself. In fact, among the group of two dozen rookies that year, Watson wasn't even in the top ten in terms of college and amateur laurels. That class of 1971, arguably the strongest crop of Tour qualifiers ever, included Lanny Wadkins, Steve Melnyk, and Bruce Fleisher (all U.S. Amateur champions), NCAA champion John Mahaffey, and Canadian Amateur champion Allen Miller. Watson, only a third-team All-American, had won nothing beyond the Missouri State Amateur.

I found him to be a thoughtful, serious guy. He had a gap-toothed farm boy appeal, and was clearly driven. Following our first contact in Napa, I kept in touch, and in early 1975 we reached an agreement for IMG to represent him worldwide—with one major caveat. It was a short-term trial deal with the stipulation that Watson's brother-in-law, a Kansas City attorney named Chuck Rubin, would be involved every step of the way.

I recognized the pitfalls of such an arrangement, but felt strongly that IMG was better served having the chance to show Tom what we could do, even if we had only one year to do it. And we delivered immediately: a lucrative golf club/bag endorsement with Ram Golf, an equally attractive touring pro arrangement with a golf resort in Steamboat Springs, Colorado, and a distinctive new clothing contract with Jantzen. Meanwhile Tom did his part in spades, winning the Open Championship in a playoff at Carnoustie that summer.

That victory—the first of the five Open titles that are the capstone of Watson's career—came in part through the auspices of IMG. Watson had never played in the UK, didn't know links golf from links sausages. Realizing he'd need a good caddie, I asked Mark if he could make a couple of calls. Within a day or two, Tom was hooked up with Alfie Fyles, the feisty Englishman who had carried Gary Player to an Open victory at Carnoustie seven years earlier. It was the beginning of a partnership that would prevail through all five of Watson's wins. It was also a perfect example of the intangible advantage, the value added, that IMG, through its size, reach, and global connections, could deliver to clients, as no other agent could.

Nonetheless, what soon became clear was that Chuck Rubin, one of the more obnoxious individuals I had ever encountered (a feeling I soon learned was shared by many in the golf business) was preordained to take over as Tom's agent. Once, that is, Chuck had learned the ropes of management courtesy of IMG. In the end, family loyalty trumped business achievement and Watson terminated our agreement.

Was this kosher? Of course. I knew the risks going in, and would agree every time to such a trial arrangement for a potential superstar—particularly at that moment in IMG Golf's history. When we'd needed some star power, he'd delivered it, however briefly.

I will say this. In the history of big-name professional golfers since 1975, few have earned less endorsement or licensing income than Tom Watson. Now, Tom may have made the choice to do little or nothing off the course, to allow himself to stay on top of his golf game—and who can argue with his success? But I'm here to tell you those two things are *not* mutually exclusive. In any case, in 1976 Tom Watson became the first client to fire me. He would be far from the biggest.

Another relatively unheralded member of that rookie class was a twenty-five-year-old Australian named David Graham. This guy had already shown his chops, winning six events in Australasia as well as the Caracas Open and French Open. He'd also teamed with countryman Bruce Devlin to win the World Cup, all before ever coming to the States.

David had wasted no time making his presence felt on the PGA Tour, winning the Cleveland Open just a month before I started, so he was top of mind for me at Napa. Mark liked both his game and his dour demeanor, calling David "the Australian Ben Hogan," an apt description for a couple of reasons. Number one, at five foot nine and 152 pounds, he was physically similar to Bantam Ben. Number two, like Hogan he'd had a difficult childhood. Hogan had witnessed his father's suicide, while David, perhaps even worse, had been disowned by his father. At age fourteen he'd sat down with his parents one day and said, "I love golf; I'm going to drop out of school and become a golf pro," to which his father had replied, "If you do that I will never speak to you again," and he did not. Not surprisingly, David Graham had a tough exterior and was one fierce competitor.

Bruce Devlin was an IMG client and introduced us. David was flattered by our interest, and we signed him to a contract a couple of months later. His professional career would produce thirty-four victories around the world, including a twenty-two-month period during which he won the '79 PGA and '81 U.S. Open (the first Aussie to win two different majors) as well as the Memorial Tournament, Phoenix Open, Lancôme Trophy, and a pair of events in Australia and New Zealand. There would be no client for whom I had greater respect.

The other big "get" in my first few months on the job was a steal from Ed Barner's stable in the form of Lanny Wadkins. Lanny had become unhappy with the treatment Barner was giving him and had begun to shop around. At the 1973 PGA Championship at Canterbury CC in Cleveland, he met for dinner one night with me and Mark. It was that evening that I got my first glimpse of Mark's brilliance as a salesman. Knowing Lanny was hypercompetitive and felt underappreciated, he said, "Lanny, how would you feel if I told you Bob Charles makes more money from his golf equipment contract than you do, Dave Marr makes more on his apparel contract, and Laura Baugh makes more money off the golf course than you do? They're our clients, and we can do for you what we've done for them." Lanny was sold.

LIGHTNING STRIKES

One of my trips to the Tour took me to Chicago for the 1975 Western Open at Butler National Golf Club. Severe thunderstorms had been forecast for the second round, and that afternoon the skies darkened and the rain began to pelt down. I was scurrying from the range back to the clubhouse when there was a deafening crash of thunder with lightning flashes everywhere—the worst I had ever seen.

Players streamed into the locker room from all corners of the course. Arnold Palmer was there, telling a reporter he'd been struck by lightning while playing the 14th. He'd been about to take the club back when it was wrenched from his hands and sent flying behind him.

My client Tony Jacklin was sitting by his locker in sort of a daze. "I was in my follow-through," he said, "and suddenly my 8-iron was 30 feet away, knocked right out of my hands, and there was this burning taste in my mouth."

"Are you okay?"

"I think so, except for this strange tingling sensation in my legs."

Bobby Nichols, paired with Jacklin that afternoon, felt worse. He'd been knocked to the ground, was in pain with a severe headache and a bad taste in his mouth, but had made it back to the clubhouse. An official who'd helped him up said he knew something was wrong—Nichols's breath smelled like burnt wire. Said Nichols, "I was never so scared in my life." At the hospital, doctors found burns on his head.

Word then spread throughout the locker room that two other players had been hit, much more seriously.

Lee Trevino and Jerry Heard were approaching the 13th green when play was suspended. They decided to wait out the storm with umbrellas open, taking shelter under a tree at the edge of a lake. Trevino was sitting on the ground, leaning against his golf bag. Heard, sitting beside him, had his putter resting on his midsection. They thought they'd be fine, having taken the precaution of removing their metal-spiked shoes.

Among the most dangerous things you can do with lightning present: stand under a tree near a body of water with a metal conduit touching your body.

A bolt of lightning hit the nearby lake, jumped the banks, and flashed straight to where they were sitting. Both players were knocked out. Trevino suffered serious burns on his back and left shoulder where the bolt exited. Heard had burns on his midsection and left leg. Trevino, shaking uncontrollably, was taken by stretcher to an ambulance. Heard got up on his own and rode in the ambulance to a hospital.

When they arrived, the emergency room doctor didn't know what to do with them. "I've never treated anyone struck by lightning," he said. "They're always taken straight to the morgue."

Trevino's heart had stopped; he remained in intensive care for

three days. Heard was released the next day. Play on Saturday
had been canceled due to continued rain, and Heard stayed
in the tournament, miraculously finishing tied for third. But
damage from the electrical shock through his body necessitated
back surgery, and by his own admission he was never the same
thereafter, winning just one event.

Bobby Nichols had been coming off the best year of his career.
He never played as well again.

Trevino needed two operations for a ruptured disc and
thereafter had to alter his swing, standing more upright and
hitting less than his usual cut. "I had to learn to play completely
over again," he said. Remarkably, he won nine more PGA Tour
events and 29 Senior Tour titles.

Trevino was asked for the rest of his career about the incident.
Ever the jokester, he said he'd found a foolproof way to escape
trouble in a thunderstorm: "Just walk down the fairway holding a
1-iron over your head—even God Almighty can't hit a 1-iron!"

The last of those three players Mark mentioned—Laura Baugh—was
the first client I worked with on a day-to-day basis. A blond phenom from
Long Beach, California, Laura had graduated from high school at age sixteen and was offered a full academic scholarship to Stanford, but turned it
down because Stanford did not then have a women's golf team. That summer, at the Atlanta Country Club, she won the 1971 U.S. Women's Amateur title, the youngest champion in the event's seventy-six-year history.
That brought a berth on the 1972 Curtis Cup and World Cup teams along
with recognition as *Golf Digest*'s "Most Beautiful Golfer."

Mark McCormack may have taken his eye off the ball, but he did not
fail to notice Laura, whom he misogynistically labeled an "eminently sal-
able commodity." In January of 1972, he reached an agreement with her to
be represented by IMG as soon as she turned pro. The only problem was,
Laura was still six months short of her eighteenth birthday, when she'd

be eligible to join the LPGA Tour. Mark, as usual, had a brilliant work-around. He packed her off to play tournaments in Japan.

When she stepped off the plane, flashbulbs popped as the Japanese populace—golfers and non-golfers alike—went Baughnanas. Mark had instructed the operatives in IMG's Tokyo office to do two things: take good care of Laura and take full advantage of her appeal.

Sports Illustrated's Ray Kennedy recalled the scene:

As McCormack hoped, the golf-mad, lens-happy Japanese could not focus often enough on the curvy blonde prototype of Western pulchritude. Almost overnight her picture was everywhere; sales of a calendar bearing her blue-eyed visage had the Japanese standing in lines for up to two hours. There followed Laura Baugh clocks, photo albums, cosmetics, school supplies, "Learn English" cassettes, sporting wear, LP records, golf accessories, and a 26-week TV series that all but toppled a competing sumo wrestling show out of the ratings. Before ever teeing up as a member of the LPGA, Laura Baugh became the highest-paid woman in golf, with earnings of $100,000 in less than six months.

While all that was happening in the Far East, back home I got Laura a deal to represent the Hamlet, a golf community in Delray Beach, Florida, in exchange for a condo—her first place of her own—plus unlimited play and practice privileges. That fall she earned her LPGA players card and the very next week placed second in her Tour debut in Atlanta. I was there.

Laura seemed destined to set ladies' professional golf on fire. But that's not what happened. During a career that stretched from 1973 to 2001, she would never win an LPGA tournament, finishing second ten times with seventy-one top tens. That was the bad news. The good news was, her appeal in America, while not as visceral as in Japan, was unprecedented for a woman golfer. Within a short time we'd secured her contracts with Rolex,

Colgate-Palmolive, *Golf Digest*, and Wilson Golf. And in a nice counter-punch to Ed Barner, I got her a Young Thunderbird deal. Laura swiftly became the face of the LPGA Tour, appearing in a raft of commercials, most memorably for Ultra-Brite toothpaste, where the catch phrase was "Hey, Laura, how's your love life?" By the end of her fourth season as a professional, at age twenty-one, she'd earned close to a million dollars in endorsement income, the equivalent of five million today.

In the 1970s that kind of figure was unheard-of in golf except for the Big Three, and it sent a couple of signals. Number one, it showed the world that a player from the LPGA Tour, which was rarely televised and often ignored, could earn big money. Number two, it reinforced, throughout the golf community, IMG's unparalleled ability to maximize opportunities for its clients. We were on our way back.

After only a few trips on Tour, interacting with IMG clients and meeting other players, it occurred to me: *Most of these guys (and girls) are clueless about business. They know less about sports management than I do and I just got here.* Practicing, playing, and traveling 24/7, relying on hearsay from fellow competitors about who was making what on endorsements—how could players possibly determine a good deal from a bad one? *Wow,* I remember thinking, *it isn't just a sales pitch: IMG can make a huge difference in pro golfers' lives.*

But Laura Baugh's phenomenal off-course success also raised an issue that would haunt me, both personally and professionally, throughout my career: What's the right balance? Shoot a commercial or spend the day practicing? Make a trip to Japan for a big guaranteed paycheck or play a couple more tournaments on the Tour without the fatigue and jet lag? My first two clients—Watson and Baugh—had personified diametrically opposed approaches.

Of course, there is no correct answer because we can never know where the road not taken might have led. Just as I to this day wonder what might have happened had I gone to work for Capital Cities instead of IMG, Laura surely must ask herself if she might have achieved that elusive LPGA victory, or multiple wins, by playing more and endorsing less, and Watson,

I suspect, wonders whether he blew the chance to capitalize fully on the magnitude of his golf achievements.

I couldn't chart the course for them. My job was simply to present my clients opportunities, discuss with them the pros and cons, and offer a professional opinion. If the client didn't take the deal I was presenting, no worries, I'd develop another one.

Looking back on the eight years I managed Laura Baugh, it was a time of ups, downs, and one notably unguarded moment when we both wish we could have had a mulligan.

She'd been a pro for a number of years and was getting frustrated at being winless. Out on the Tour she felt the jealousy and resentment of her peers, many of whom had been far more successful players than she, but did not resonate with the public or with corporate America the way Laura had. And worst of all, she'd become involved in a toxic relationship with a difficult character named Wayne Dent. They'd gotten married, but one month later—after she realized what she had gotten into—she divorced him. With all that weighing on her, it was not surprising that Laura began to drink.

Her problem was exacerbated during a tournament one day when a rain delay forced players back to the clubhouse for a lengthy period. When it began to look as if play would be suspended for the day, Laura had a glass of wine, and then another and another. She was well beyond tipsy when an air horn blared and the tournament unexpectedly resumed. What happened? She birdied her five remaining holes—and perhaps became convinced of the merits of playing while under the beta-blocking benefit of alcohol.

Alcoholism was a disease Laura would fight for more than two decades, culminating in 1996 when she was hospitalized with internal bleeding and nearly died. After that she sought treatment that included a visit to the Betty Ford Clinic, which turned her life around. Laura later described her battle in a book titled *Out of the Rough*. She has not had a drink in over twenty-five years, and although she has been married, divorced, and then remarried and divorced again (to the same man, South African golfer

Bobby Cole), she leads a happy, healthy life as a teaching professional and the mother of six adult children, including professional golfer Eric Cole, who was named Rookie of the Year on the PGA Tour in 2023 (50 years after his mother won the LPGA Rookie of the Year award).

It was during Laura's lowest period, just after the divorce from Dent, that I made one of my periodic visits to the LPGA, where my schedule included a business meeting and dinner with her. During dinner we had a few glasses of wine and then, because she was holding a couple of contracts that needed signing, we went back to her hotel room, where we had some more wine.

Every once in a while a mutual attraction surfaces between agent and client. It can be enticing, but dangerous and ultimately disastrous. A professional relationship thereafter becomes nearly impossible. That night Laura and I found ourselves on the brink.

I knew I was doing something wrong. For one thing, Mark had a strict rule—no dating clients—a rule he would have to amend years later after he dated and ultimately married one of his own tennis clients, Betsy Nagelsen.

But there was also a bigger reason—and it says something very good about Laura, and not very good about me, that it was she who was the voice of better judgment.

"We can't do this," she said. "We can't do this to Candy."

I'd met Candace Anne Bidwell on a blind date, actually a blind threesome. In my first semester of business school, one of the guys in my section, a fellow from New Jersey named Bob Ihrie, said, "These two girls I went to high school with, Candy and Ellen, are rooming together in Boston. Do you want to go out with them Friday night?" Since I had no social life to speak of, that was an easy yes.

I was then playing on the HBS hockey team against other grad schools in the Boston area, and we had a game that Friday night, so the plan was to pick up Ellen and Candy at their apartment, go watch me play, then go out for drinks and dinner. All good until we got to the apartment—no Ellen. Candy explained that her roommate had had something come up at the last minute (turns out it was a date with her steady boyfriend). So it was just Bob, Hughes, and Candy.

Candy was blond, blue-eyed, outgoing, and very attractive. She worked at a trendy architectural firm just outside of Boston. She was not a huge sports fan, and watching a stranger play hockey was not high on her list of things to do, plus her good friend was not there as planned, so it was not the greatest first date, but she was a good sport about it and I was attracted to her.

I asked her out twice and was politely rejected both times. Most guys probably wouldn't have tried again; call me stubborn. The third time she said yes, and we went from there, dating from spring 1971 through HBS graduation in 1972 and my first full year at IMG.

On my Maine Army National Guard weekends I'd stay at Candy's Boston apartment Friday night, get up at 4:30 a.m., and drive to Portland for 7 a.m. roll call Saturday. Once I got the job at IMG, it was a bit more challenging, flying from Cleveland to Boston and back on weekends. The worst part was the expense, as in those days I was watching every penny, but I found a way around it. Back then, military personnel willing to fly standby could go anywhere in the U.S. for a dollar. So on Friday afternoon, I'd suit up in my Army Reserves uniform, right down to the boots, and head to the airport. No one seemed to care whether I was active duty or not, and it worked every time—back and forth for two bucks.

Candy was in many ways my total opposite. Artsy, a bit hippieish. To her I must have seemed as establishment as they come, a sports-loving preppy from three privileged educational institutions. She'd gone to high school in Fanwood, New Jersey, then to Beaver College in Philadelphia.

Opposites attract? Or are vastly different upbringings, interests, and outlooks inevitably fatal? Young and in love, we would have dismissed the latter notion. We were married in August of 1973 at Candy's home, a small wedding attended by a few of my HBS and Yale classmates, Chris Pierce as my best man, and by Candy's college and high school friends. My apartment in suburban Cleveland became our home for a year before we bought a small starter house in Shaker Heights.

By that time, another striking young woman had come into my life—Nancy Lopez. As part of the prospecting side of my job, I'd kept one eye on the junior ranks for emerging talent, and Nancy had been lighting it up for several years. Among other laurels was a victory in the women's amateur championship of her home state of New Mexico at the eye-popping age of twelve. Five years later, after she'd she won her second U.S. Girls' Junior Championship, she earned a spot in the 1974 U.S. Women's Open at the La Grange Country Club outside Chicago, and it was there that I introduced myself to her.

Seeing her play for the first time, I was a little surprised by her golf swing. On her backswing she took the club sharply to the inside, so she had to reroute it on the downswing. The only player I'd seen who'd had success swinging that way was Ray Floyd. On the other hand, results are all that matters, and Nancy also had that rare presence, a radiant smile and charismatic "girl next door" appeal, which, when combined with natural talent, is an agent's marketing dream. When a year later she again made it to the U.S. Open, and this time—at age eighteen—finished tied for second, the handwriting was on the wall: here was the next dominant LPGA player.

I kept in touch with Nancy as she played college golf at the University of Tulsa, winning a national collegiate title and playing on the Curtis Cup and World Cup teams. When in her sophomore year she signaled an intention to turn pro, I made a trip to Roswell, New Mexico, where I met with her and her father, Domingo, the owner of an auto-body repair shop.

Roswell was not an easy place to get to—even from LAX it was three flights—but I suspect that remoteness worked in my favor, as no other agent had bothered to make the trip. Domingo struck me as the classic immigrant success story—he'd energetically come across the border to America, worked his butt off providing for his family, and saved up enough to start his own business. Big smile, proud papa, super friendly.

We sat in the living room of the Lopezes' modest ranch house and made small talk for a while. Then I took out a two-page representation agreement I'd brought with me and went over it with them in detail. Domingo thanked me for coming and said, "We'll get back to you."

"No," I said firmly (and somewhat fearfully, never having taken such an aggressive approach). "Both of you know this is the right thing for Nancy. LPGA Qualifying School is just around the corner, and if IMG is going to represent your daughter properly, we need to get going on her behalf now."

Silence. I swallowed hard.

"Give us a few minutes," said Domingo, and he and Nancy retreated briefly to the kitchen. When they returned, they were still unsure, but I didn't relent. "I had to catch three plane flights on my way here today," I said, trying to make a joke of it, "and I'm not leaving this living room until you guys do the right thing."

With that, they looked at each other, then back at me, and then both nodded their heads. We had a deal. Nancy signed the contract and we all hugged. It was the beginning of a long and very profitable relationship for both sides.

At the Qualifying School, Nancy blew away the field, and her rookie year was nothing short of historic: nine victories including five in a row, Rookie of the Year, Player of the Year, and the Vare Trophy for lowest stroke average. The cover of *Sports Illustrated* and the Associated Press Female Athlete of the Year. Nancy Lopez would win forty-eight times in her twenty-five years on the LPGA Tour. She remains the most universally beloved player the women's game has ever seen.

Ray Volpe, the LPGA commissioner at the time, marketed Nancy's accomplishments and appeal brilliantly, while on the IMG side huge credit goes to Peter Johnson, a young executive I entrusted with the management of Nancy's career almost from day one. Peter, an accomplished football player in college, would go on to run IMG's Team Sports Division for decades as well as represent top tennis clients. I'm not sure he could even spell the word g-o-l-f when he took over as Nancy's agent, but she owes virtually all her tremendous commercial success to the job Peter did representing her.

BRONZING LORD BYRON

Part of the due diligence of my early days was to stay in touch with ad agencies, checking in every so often to see if they had any accounts with products that could benefit from an endorsement by an IMG pro. Usually these calls were fruitless, but one day I hit pay dirt.

"Yeah, we have a new package goods company," said the adman, "it's a sunscreen called Aztec and they're looking for a golfer to appear in a print campaign."

"Great," I said, and rattled off the names of a few of our young players.

"Actually," said the guy, "this product skews toward an older demographic—do you have maybe a distinguished veteran?"

Immediately, I thought of Byron Nelson—Hall of Famer, author of the single most dominant season in the history of the game—an unbelievable eighteen tournament victories in 1945, including an equally unfathomable eleven in a row and a scoring average of 68.33. Lord Byron was the most roundly revered elder statesman in golf, yet still very relevant as the lead golf analyst for ABC-TV.

Now, I'd never met Byron Nelson and he wasn't an IMG client, but his ABC sidekick and one of the world's finest gentlemen, Chris Schenkel, was, and through Schenkel I got Nelson's number.

"Mr. Nelson," I said, "an opportunity has come up and we're hoping you might be interested. Even though you're not an IMG client, we occasionally work on an ad hoc basis." Then I explained the deal—a one-day photo shoot in exchange for a fee of $15,000 ($85,000 today), less a 25 percent commission to us.

A bit to my surprise, he loved the idea, and loved it even more when we were able to get the photo crew to come to him in Texas. Everything went fine, he got paid the $15,000, and a few weeks later he sent me a check—for $3,000, which was 20 percent, not 25.

Now I was in the awkward position of having to grovel before a legend. Too scared to phone him, I wrote a note saying something to the effect of "Thank you so much for the check; if you'll recall, our arrangement called for a 25 percent commission to IMG. I'm afraid the check you sent was for $3,000 and it really should have been for $3,750. Hoping this is not a problem."

Then I held my breath. A week or so later my mail included
an envelope with a check for $750, attached to which was a note
From the Desk of Byron Nelson: "Hughes—how do you think I shot
all those low scores!"

Back on the men's side, there was now one player I wanted desper-
ately to land. Curtis Strange had compiled the most impressive collegiate
record since Jack Nicklaus—nine victories including the 1974 NCAA
Championship where, as a nineteen-year-old freshman, he'd eagled the
final hole to become the event's youngest individual winner, while also
leading Wake Forest to the team title. This was the guy and, just as important, this was the moment for IMG—we needed another big win on
the men's side to go with the Tom Watson signing, to put a stake in the
ground that said IMG was back on top of its game.

In the competition for Strange, however, we were five holes down with
six to play, as a formidable challenger had arrived on the scene in the person of Marvin M. "Vinny" Giles.

Following the same path as Mark McCormack, he was a college
golfer who'd gotten a law degree and decided to become an agent. But
Vinny was not just any college golfer, he was a three-time All-American
out of Georgia. Back in the days when the U.S. Amateur was a stroke-
play event, he'd finished second for three straight years, then won it in
1972 and added the British Amateur title in 1975. He'd also played on
four Walker Cup teams and had won the amateur championship of his
native Virginia a record seven times.

Curtis Strange also was from Virginia. Curtis had played on one of
those Walker Cup teams with Vinny Giles, and Curtis had been Vinny's
friend for more than a decade. In the golf community, it was a foregone
conclusion that Curtis would sign with Vinny's firm, Pros Inc., which had
already brought on board four of Vinny's Walker Cup teammates: Tom
Kite, Jerry Pate, Gary Koch, and George Burns.

But I had to start somewhere and that was at the 1975 Masters, where Curtis, as a runner-up in the previous year's U.S. Amateur, had earned an invitation. That week I introduced myself to him—just a quick hello, this is who I am. My first impression: This kid was the real deal—handsome, confident, looked me right in the eye. Knew how good he was, but came across as humbly southern with solid values. Politely cordial at first, perked up a bit meeting someone from IMG, but noncommittal. I liked him immediately, and at that moment I was more certain than ever that we had to represent him.

With Curtis that day was his uncle, C. Jordan Ball Jr. Curtis's father, Tom, was a club professional who had passed away when Curtis and his twin brother, Allan, were fourteen, and Ball, their mother's brother and a prominent business executive from Richmond, had become sort of their surrogate father. It was clear that he would play an advisory role in Curtis's future, so I made a point to follow up with him, doing my best to educate him on the big differences between IMG and Vinny Giles's nascent firm. My sense was that Jordan was on our side.

At the same time I encouraged Curtis to speak to his fellow Wake Forest Deacon Arnold Palmer about IMG. I also enlisted Mark to meet Curtis with me a couple of times. Involving Mark personally was always a powerful ploy. For one thing, it helped dispel the criticism hurled by competitors that IMG was so big and diverse, a player who signed with us would never get any attention from the big boss. But more important, when Mark came face-to-face with a prospective client, he always knew exactly what to say, when to say it, and how to say it.

Curtis qualified for the 1976 Masters as well, this time as a member of the '75 Walker Cup team, and that gave Mark and me another chance to make our case, which I felt we did, all the while being careful not to do anything that might put Curtis in violation of the NCAA regulation that stipulated: "You are not eligible in a sport if you ever have accepted money, transportation, or other benefits from an agent or agreed to have an agent market your athletic ability or reputation in that sport. [Bylaw 23.3.1]." Mark, being as recognizable as he was within the sports industry, could

occasionally become vigilant to the point of paranoia, as he did on the evening we gave Curtis a lift from the Augusta course to the IMG house for
dinner. I drove, Curtis sat in the front passenger seat, and Mark lay down
flat in the back seat, out of sight, for the 20-minute ride.

Curtis would finish as the low amateur in that Masters, impressively
tying for fifteenth (while at the other end of the stick was Vinny Giles, who
missed the cut and was dead last after rounds of 83–81). It was tempting to
enjoy that as a positive omen, but I knew we still had work to do, and over
the next couple of months, as Curtis pondered whether to return to Wake
Forest for his senior year, I kept in touch, calling him now and then, while
trying not to overdo the pitch. At one point I got in touch with another
one of Curtis's father figures, his college coach, Jesse Haddock, just to get
the temperature of things from his standpoint. In the course of a lengthy
phone call (there was no other kind with Coach Haddock), I got the feeling
we were making progress.

In the end I think it was probably Jordan Ball who made the difference,
and I suspect what he told Curtis is something similar to the advice given to
my Yale classmate Brian Dowling, a three-sport phenom who had starred at
Saint Ignatius in Cleveland and was regarded as one of the best high school
quarterbacks ever in Ohio. Aggressively recruited by Woody Hayes to play
at Ohio State, and heavily pressured locally to stay home in Ohio, Brian also
looked at Ivy League schools, something rare for an athlete of his caliber. It
was Brian's father, a successful Cleveland businessman, who swayed his son
with a simple metaphor: "Why fly coach when you can go first class?"

Late that summer, when I got the good news from Curtis, I was eu-
phoric, and yes, proud of what I'd been able to do. Through a combination
of hard work, patience, and some recruiting savvy, IMG had signed the
game's number one prospect, even as the odds had been stacked against us.

Vinny Giles was understandably angry to have had Curtis stolen out
from under him, and I know he saw me as the lead pirate; he would bad-
mouth me for the rest of my career. If there was a moment in the aftershock
that gave him any solace, it came that December when Curtis went to

the PGA Tour Qualifying School in Brownsville, Texas, and astonishingly failed to make the top twenty-five and earn playing privileges, finishing with three straight bogeys to miss by a single stroke.

"I choked and I couldn't handle it," he told the *New York Times* several years later. "You know you're choking when you're helpless, and I felt helpless. I had no control over my swing, and most of all, I had no control over my thoughts . . . I didn't know what I was going to do for a living. I felt I was a failure, and I wasn't going to be able to play golf for a living."

Yes, he was ineligible to play the U.S. Tour, at least for another six months, when the next qualifier would be held. In the meantime, however, his choice of IMG brought immediate benefits. Through our overseas offices we were able to get Curtis into tournaments in Europe and South America, which not only kept him competitive but helped keep his mind off the embarrassment of his Q-School performance. Six months later, at the spring qualifier in Pinehurst, Curtis sailed through to the PGA Tour, where, in a twenty-five-year career, he would win nineteen times including back-to-back victories in the U.S. Open in 1988 and '89, plus another ten tournaments around the world. In 1988, he became the first player to win a million dollars in a single season.

IMG would bring him many millions more in off-course income. Of all the clients I worked with, I think Curtis did the best job of balancing—balancing his family life with his work life and balancing his extracurricular work with us with his day job as a playing professional. He had a terrific and supportive wife in Sarah, and although they had moments of strife like any couple, they were always a good team and remain so after forty-seven years of marriage. I recall Curtis once saying, "When I'm home I wish I were out on the Tour, and when I'm out on the Tour I wish I were home." He got it.

Curtis also got it with his perspective about money and financial security. I think the experience of missing out in his first try at Qualifying School gave him a sense of his vulnerability, telling him how tenuous a pro golfer's status can be. Also, with his father passing away at a young age, life for him had been a bit of a struggle.

No top player I worked with ever was more willing to make appearances or enter into endorsement contracts, while at the same time he never lost his competitive fire and drive to win. And guess what? With a smart portfolio of municipal bonds, Curtis ended his playing career a wealthy man with no financial worries for the rest of his life. Half a century later, he remains my friend, one of the truly good guys in professional golf or anywhere else.

The trio of Watson-Lopez-Strange may not have been equal to Mark McCormack's Palmer-Player-Nicklaus, but they represented three major wins when IMG had needed them badly. We were well and truly back in gear and going full throttle.

Mark, in a memo to the IMG board of directors, hailed the moment as "the renaissance age of International Management and its golf activities." In the four years since my first trip to Napa, our clients also had delivered: Tommy Aaron (1973) and Ray Floyd (1976) each had won a Masters; Gary Player had won both the 1974 Masters and Open Championship; Tom Watson had followed him with his Carnoustie win in 1975; and another promising young star, Hale Irwin, had broken through impressively with a U.S. Open victory at Winged Foot in 1974 and then come on board with IMG.

Our London office was having similar success as a pair of clients, Tony Jacklin and Peter Oosterhuis, were battling it out for supremacy on the European Tour. On the LPGA side, Nancy Lopez was the undisputed queen and Laura Baugh was princess charming. Their success would bring increased involvement by IMG in women's golf, both on the player-client side and in the creation, management, and marketing of events.

Meanwhile our two main competitors—Ed Barner and Vinny Giles— had become stuck in neutral, and while other small shops had begun to pop up on both sides of the Atlantic, none had made a significant impact. "We have no competitors within light-years of where we are," McCormack told *Sports Illustrated*, "and I can't think of two companies out there who could merge and cause a ripple in our business."

At about that time, I answered the phone one winter morning at our starter house in Shaker Heights and was surprised to hear the voice of Ed Barner. "Hi, Hughes. What's the weather like there? It's seventy-two and sunny here in L.A." The start of a pitch for me to come work for him.

It didn't go anywhere—I told Mark the day it happened—but I also made sure Mark knew Ed had offered me $50,000, twice what I was making at IMG. I never was sure if Mark believed it or thought it just a ploy to increase my compensation. (I knew by then how his mind worked.) But in the absence of much direct feedback from my boss, a competitor's recruiting pitch made me feel really good about the kind of job I was doing out there.

With the dominance of IMG's core division thus reestablished, Mark had returned his attention to expanding the company's reach both within golf and beyond. One of his most ingenious ideas—a way of leveraging the company's clout—was the creation of VIP Days for our corporate clients. These were one-day golf events where company executives invited their best customers and potential customers to play eighteen holes side by side with Tour pros. IMG booked the courses and staged the events, for a fee of course, and also supplied the pros—starting with our own clients—who paid us a commission on the appearance fees they earned. It was a win for the corporations, a win for the players, and a double win for IMG.

At the same time, IMG had become a consultant to an increasing number of tournaments in the UK and Europe—the Spanish Open, French Open, Lancôme Trophy, Piccadilly World Match Play, and John Player Classic, among many others—again filling the fields with players from the IMG client roster.

The most intriguing development, however, came in 1976 when Mark called a Saturday morning meeting—something he rarely did. Even more mysterious was that he gave no agenda for the meeting. The small group in attendance included myself; Alastair Johnston, who at the time was managing Gary Player; and Hans Kramer, whose bailiwick was event management; along with Jay Lafave, a corporate VP and Mark's right-hand man; and general counsel Bill Carpenter.

When we sat down Mark said, "I have a secret new project to share with you: the Second Tour." Then he explained that it actually wasn't new at all, that he'd had the idea since 1964. As he began to describe it, my mind went immediately to his *Arnie* biography—this was the concept he'd proposed more than a decade ago, but he'd now developed it in much greater detail.

I remember thinking, *Wow, this guy is scary smart*—he'd thought of everything: an elite field of the world's best players, more prize money, fewer tournaments per year, events in every major international market, a season-ending championship. Even health benefits and a pension plan for the players, things the PGA Tour didn't offer. It really could work. The best part, Mark believed, was those who chose to defect to this Second Tour could have their cake and eat it, too. They'd still be able to play in the four major championships, as those events, in order to maintain the strength of their fields, would want and need the Second Tour players. It was the very blueprint that would come to fruition fifty years later as LIV Golf.

Mark told us his idea had germinated well past the theoretical stage. Funding was there from a major corporation, the networks were ready to bid on television rights, a commercial airline was prepared to charter the players, and a major hotel chain was on board to offer accommodations. He had quietly made all these preliminary inquiries—now he wanted to know, did those of us in the room think IMG's player clients would buy in?

We discussed the idea very positively for a couple of hours, then dispersed, returning to our normal frenetic responsibilities. The concept was brilliant and I never forgot about it. After that, strangely, nothing happened. I suspect Mark made another run at Arnold as he had in 1964 to gauge his interest and, once again, A.P. said no. In any event, that core group never reconvened on the subject, and Mark never brought it up again.

But there was perhaps a bigger reason the time was not right for a second tour. At that moment, the PGA Tour was doing a pretty good job of reinventing itself. The architect was the man who would have more influence on the development of professional golf than anyone in history: Deane Beman.

He'd become the Tour's second commissioner after a six-year competitive career that had brought him four Tour victories. Prior to that Beman had been one of the nation's top amateurs, the winner of two U.S. Amateur Championships and one British Amateur, and a member of four Walker Cup teams. Although a notably short hitter—he was five foot seven and 150 pounds—he was a superb chipper and putter and a tenacious, driven competitor. (He'd played his first round of golf at age thirteen, shooting 113 at Congressional Country Club near his home in Maryland, had that day set his mind on becoming a top player, and within two years his handicap was scratch.)

I'd actually brought Deane Beman's name up at a meeting with Mark back in 1972, just before my trip to Napa. We were identifying potential clients for me to approach, as well as players not to waste my time on. I'd studied the PGA Tour media guide the night before and made a list of names, purely as a fan who followed golf on television.

As I went through my list, Mark would say stuff like "His best years are behind him" or "Arnold really likes that guy's game." When I brought up Beman, noting from my homework that he'd just won his third tournament a couple of weeks before, Mark immediately dismissed him without further comment. Deane was never shy about expressing his opinions, and he disliked agents even back then, so I suspect Mark had seen enough to know he would not be a good fit at IMG. Or maybe he just saw Deane as an overachiever not destined for sustained success.

Beman had worked as an insurance broker before turning pro at age twenty-nine, and then he'd done a stint on the Tour Policy Board, where his sharp mind had won fans among both his fellow players and the Tour administrators. When in late 1972 Joe Dey announced his intention to retire, Beman was surprised to learn he topped the list of candidates to succeed Dey. After some soul-searching he decided that,

at age thirty-five, he likely had more to contribute to the game as a commissioner than as a player. He accepted the job, took office on March 3,
1974, and the Deane Beman era began.

It would be quite a ride. Through a combination of entrepreneurial
vision, hard-nosed negotiating, and just plain smarts, Beman revolu-
tionized modern professional golf, wrenching it from its mom-and-pop
roots into a dazzlingly profitable business. During his twenty-year tenure as commissioner, the PGA Tour's assets would grow from $400,000
to $260 million.

Many of the changes and innovations Beman wrought were dramatic,
but he began of necessity with more mundane maneuvers—blocking-
and-tackling that set the stage. Adam Schupak, in his superb book,
Deane Beman: Golf's Driving Force, described the challenges facing the
new commissioner:

> Shortly after he started, Beman was surprised to learn that the Tour-
> nament Players Division of the PGA was organized as a for-profit
> corporation. On his desk sat a series of checks for New York City
> taxes, New York State taxes, and federal taxes that awaited his signa-
> ture. They totaled $96,000. He read the documents, shook his head,
> and wondered, "What are we doing paying taxes?"
>
> He was also asked to sign a check for nearly $90,000 to the PGA
> of America for something notated as "royalties." Though the Tour
> had barely $400,000 in total assets, Beman felt he was spending
> nearly half of that sum for unnecessary reasons.

From his insurance days Beman had an understanding of the nonprofit
world, and within six months he secured approval from the IRS for the
Tour to become a 501(c)(6) association, a "business league" that was exempt
from federal taxation. That single move has meant a difference—in the
years since—of nearly $1 billion in the Tour's net income. At the same time

Beman required that all tournaments become nonprofits, partly as a way of repairing golf's image as a game for the elite, and partly because he thought a charitable component would help the events retain the support of the legions of volunteers whose work was essential.

"I believed that golf would become as big as other sports and that prize money would double and double and double again," he told Schupak. "Once the money got big, I didn't think volunteers would continue, in some cases, to take their week's vacation to help the players come in to their city and get rich." Under the new setup, 100 percent of the tournaments' profits went back into the local communities. To date, the total contribution to charities is just short of $4 billion, far more than in any other sport.

Beman also took swift action on his other big bill, the $90,000 of royalties paid to the PGA of America. The legacy of an agreement made five years earlier when the Tour players split from the PGA, it stipulated that the Tournament Players Division would pay the PGA an annual license fee equal to 7.5 percent of the Tour's annual revenue. Beman saw the Tour growing quickly and exponentially, and he didn't want that fee to do the same.

He devised an ingenious plan that involved the World Series of Golf, a four-player, thirty-six-hole exhibition showcasing the season's four major championship winners. The ten-year-old event had begun to lose its luster, and Beman revamped it to become a full-field tournament that climaxed the season, a precursor to the current Tour Championship. He then sold the broadcast rights to CBS, and approached the PGA of America, offering them the first $125,000 of profit from the event, with a fifty-fifty split thereafter, significantly more than the $90,000 they were getting—in exchange for which the PGA would agree to end the royalty fee.

The PGA took the deal, surely one of their worst-ever business moves and one of Beman's best. The estimate is, if that 7.5 percent royalty payment had continued, by this time well over a billion dollars would have transferred from the Tour's coffers to those of the PGA of America.

Beman's final fix came with the Tour's main revenue source, television rights. Part of the amateurish operation he'd inherited was a sweetheart deal with ABC-TV to broadcast the bulk of the Tour's events, a one-year agreement renewed routinely by previous commissioner Dey with only token increases paid each year by the network. There was also a clause that said, if the Tour were to receive a better offer from another network, ABC would have a chance to top it. As a result, CBS and NBC had taken little interest in golf. Another reason for CBS's reticence was the fact that they already had a very profitable show of their own in the CBS Golf Classic, a pretaped match-play series staged over thirteen weeks at Firestone Country Club in Akron, Ohio. The top stars got paid to play in it, but the Tour received only a $15,000 rights fee.

Beman did three things. First, he changed the contract with ABC to a three-year deal, thus giving himself time to regroup and better prepare for renewal negotiations. Second, he ended ABC's entitlement to, in his words, "a second bite of the apple." And third, he ended the Tour's involvement with the CBS Golf Classic, a move that was initially unpopular with both the players and television viewers, but in a very short time redounded to the benefit of both. By the end of 1975, the Tour had broadcast agreements through 1978 with CBS for twelve events and NBC and ABC for seven each.

With his financial footing thus stabilized, Beman put in motion several strategic initiatives, beginning with a major office relocation. When he'd taken the job, the Tour's home base, an office accommodating its fifteen employees, was in Midtown Manhattan, a high-rent district that was neither necessary nor sensible. Almost immediately Beman moved everyone to his hometown of Bethesda, Maryland, briefly operating out of a one-bedroom apartment until a proper office became available, and by 1979 the permanent Tour headquarters was Ponte Vedra Beach, Florida, where today more than eight hundred people are employed.

Next, he convinced the Tour to invest in marketing itself, and that began with a change in the association's name from the cumbersome Tournament Players Division of the PGA of America to simply the PGA Tour, and an iconic new logo to go with it.

Beman's timing was perfect. Golf, thanks in part to the telegenic stars in IMG's stable, was on the upswing, and with the increased television exposure it had become the game everyone wanted to try. From 1970 to 1980, the number of golfers in America would increase at four times the rate of the U.S. population—from 10 million to 25 million—and right behind them came the people trying to sell things to them. Corporate America suddenly swooned for golf, and when they realized tournament sponsorship was in part tax deductible, the attraction became even more passionate. With more and bigger sponsors came more and bigger tournaments, Arnold Palmer and Jack Nicklaus both creating events based around themselves (Palmer's, of course, managed by IMG). Professional golf was soaring.

As all this was unfolding, I was more or less oblivious. It was a time of high inflation generally, and although I could see the jumps in Tour purses, player earnings, TV coverage, etc., I just sort of kept my head down and stayed in my lane. I wish I'd stopped once in a while and smelled the roses, and I often think of the advice I got—from the first client I met on my first day at Napa in 1972.

It was the suave veteran Dave Marr, who told me, "Kid, do yourself a favor and keep a journal. There's a lot of crazy stuff that goes on in our little traveling carnival, and you'll want to remember it all." He was so right, and the craziest stuff was yet to come.

4

Growing Pains

The good times continued to roll for golf, the PGA Tour, IMG, and me—throughout the remainder of the seventies and early eighties. Our roster of clients grew to more than fifty, the company was grossing over $25 million a year, $92 million in today's dollars, and Mark had put me in full charge of the golf division. During the same time, Candy and I did a bit of expanding of our own with the blessed arrivals of daughters Stephanie (1978) and Samantha (1981). Life was good.

Not long after we signed Curtis Strange, he and I were having dinner when he said, "There's a guy you need to meet, a player IMG needs to sign."

It was very unusual for a client to tout another player like that—most of our clients preferred to keep the IMG stable as small as possible to protect their own interests—but Curtis was a special individual, and so was the guy he recommended: Peter Jacobsen.

I recognized the name from my homework on prospects. Jacobsen was a third-team All-American out of Oregon and had won a Pac-8 event as well as the Oregon Open—good, but hardly scintillating credentials.

"Believe me, this guy can play," said Curtis. He'd met Peter a year earlier when they were both on a college all-star boondoggle in Japan. "More important, he's the funniest guy you'll ever meet."

I got my chance a few weeks later, at the fateful PGA Tour qualifier in Texas, where Curtis fell short of earning his card. Ironically, the last of the twenty-five players who did make it to the Tour, finishing one stroke ahead of Curtis, was Peter Jacobsen.

He was everything Curtis said—instantly engaging, quick-witted, and full of hilarious stories—a younger Dave Marr. I liked him instantly. Peter signed with IMG a few weeks later and went on to a thirty-year career that produced seven PGA Tour victories. He added two more on the Senior Tour including the 2004 U.S. Senior Open, and three international wins. At the same time he became one of the most popular players in the game. No one was better at corporate outings than Peter, famed for his hysterical swing impersonations of Arnold Palmer, Lee Trevino, Seve Ballesteros, Craig Stadler, and many others. A self-taught guitarist, he was the lead singer for Jake Trout and the Flounders, a band that he formed with fellow Tour players Mark Lye and Payne Stewart. He also appeared as himself in the 1996 movie *Tin Cup*, where he was the winner of the fictional U.S. Open. After his playing career Peter went on to success as a TV broadcaster and also founded his own sports and entertainment marketing company, which has produced and managed over three hundred events worldwide.

Typically when talking to a potential client for the first time, I'd ask a few questions about how they got into the game. Jacobsen's answer was a bit different than most, and also revealing.

"My brother, David, and I played a lot with our dad, especially late afternoons after he got out of work. We'd tee off just after five o'clock and play until the sun went down. You'd be surprised at how many holes we were able to squeeze in. We'd hit our drives, hit shots to the green, and then, rather than waste time putting, we'd pick up the balls and head straight to the next tee."

Given that background, it's not surprising that putting was the weak link in Peter's game. He was recognized by his peers as one of the best ball-strikers on Tour, and had he been a better putter there's no telling how big a career he might have had.

By contrast, there's the other young player we signed a couple of years later in 1979. When he began playing at age six, he had just a 7-iron, a putter, and one ball, given to him by the old pro at his parents' club. The pro had him chip the ball to a hole on the practice green, then lay down the 7-iron, pick up the putter, and putt the ball until it was in the hole. The pro then tossed the ball to another spot beside the green and had the boy chip and putt again. That was all they did, not just that day but many more, before the boy ever took a full swing. The teacher's name was Harvey Penick and the boy grew up to become one of the best putters the game has ever seen, Ben Crenshaw.

A three-time NCAA Champion out of the University of Texas with blond-surfer good looks, Ben had joined the Tour in 1973 amid tremendous ballyhoo and had not disappointed, winning the first tournament he played. Much to my disappointment, he'd resisted all my approaches to be his agent, leaving his business management to a family friend in Austin.

I felt Ben had never taken advantage of his strong marketability, and I kept in touch with him over the years. In 1979 I had the inspiration to get him a birthday card, which I left in his locker at a PGA Tour event. In the inscription I wrote something like "Can't believe it's been almost seven years since you burst on the Tour, amazing how time passes. If you're ready to do a bit more to maximize your off-course income, I'd be honored to work with you."

Not long thereafter I got a call from Ben. "I've been having those thoughts," he said, "and it's time to do something." He signed with us and we did several major deals for him, including an equipment contract with Yonex, a company that had just entered golf, and an upmarket affiliation with De Beers Diamond company.

With Strange, Wadkins, Floyd, Graham, Jacobsen, and Crenshaw, I was feeling good, but in 1981 the golf headlines came from a second-tier client in the IMG stable, Bill Rogers.

A native of Waco, Texas, and member of an NCAA Championship team at Houston, Rogers had played on the 1973 Walker Cup team and qualified that fall for the Tour, but had done little to distinguish himself until 1978 when he'd won the Bob Hope Desert Classic. It was then that I began courting him, and signed him late that year, another poach from Vinny Giles's firm.

One of the special opportunities I'd dangled before Bill was the possibility of playing in the Suntory World Match Play tournament in Wentworth, England, an elite twelve-player event created and run by IMG, and the following year we got him an invitation. Bill was unquestionably one of the lesser lights in the exclusive field that year, but that didn't stop him from blitzing through a quartet of future Hall of Famers—Sandy Lyle, Hale Irwin, Fuzzy Zoeller, and Isao Aoki—in a gauntlet of grueling thirty-six-hole matches to become the champion.

Then in 1981 all hell broke loose: in a little under nine months Bill won seven times on four different continents. It began with the Sea Pines Heritage Classic. Then, after finishing second to David Graham at the U.S. Open, he broke through for the biggest victory of his career, the Open Championship at Royal St. George's.

I have three vivid memories of that week. First, on Thursday Bill almost cost himself the title before he ever hit a shot. He had a late tee time and was on the range warming up when a gentleman came by, pairing sheet in hand, and said, "Hey, Bill, aren't you supposed to be on the tee?" The 2:51 time Bill thought he had was actually 2:15. Sprinting to the tee, he found his two playing companions already halfway down the fairway, but he'd arrived just inside the grace period and after a hurried first swing went on to post a 72, tied for ninth place after eighteen holes.

On the Saturday evening before the final round, I had dinner with Bill, Ben Crenshaw, and Bill's Houston roommate (himself a three-time winner that same 1981 season), Bruce Lietzke. The evening began a bit quietly, for a couple of good reasons. Twenty-four hours earlier Bill and Ben were at the top of the leaderboard, Bill in first place after a 66/138 and Ben just one stroke back, but on Saturday Ben had staggered to a 76, while Bill, playing alongside him, had held form with a 67 to open up a five-stroke lead. I feared that Ben, a devout golf historian who wanted nothing more than to win an Open Championship, might be justifiably glum. And as excited as I was for Bill at that moment, it would be inappropriate to dwell on what had happened that day or might happen the next. To Ben's eternal credit, he became the life of the party, entertaining the rest of us with an esoteric talent—the ability to mimic the voices of golf's greatest players while simultaneously duplicating their autographs.

But the final memory is the happiest one, that Sunday evening after Bill's victory. His wife, Beth, hadn't joined him for the trip across the pond ("I had no idea the British Open was such a big deal," she later said. "Now I know!"), so the only one he had to share in the joy of victory was yours truly. Back at one of London's finest hotels, IMG had reserved the penthouse suite and sent up a magnum of champagne along with a small banquet of delicacies to enjoy. So there we were, just the two of us, looking out over the lights of London, placing giddy phone calls to friends and family, and slurping Bollinger out of the Claret Jug into the wee hours of the morning.

A month later Bill's blitzkrieg continued with a victory in the World Series of Golf in Akron. By this time he'd become the game's hottest property, a player the rest of the world wanted to see more of. He was thirty years old, but looked younger with his blond mop top and boyish smile. Although an unpretentious Texas boy, he was bright and articulate, comfortable conversing with anyone. Most of all, he was hungry—and practical. Bill Rogers knew, better than most players who find themselves suddenly at the center of the universe, that it could all end in the blink of an eye—and he was ready to take full advantage of his fifteen minutes of fame.

My job was to present him with income opportunities, and that I did. The first order of business was a major renegotiation of his equipment contract with Wilson, but the big payoffs back then were appearance fees to play tournaments all around the world. The first of those came in September at the Suntory Open in Japan, where IMG had an affiliation through its Wentworth partnership. Suntory was quite happy to pay Bill handsomely to join the field, and he not only accepted but won the tournament for victory number four. Back in the states a month later he made it five with a victory in the Texas Open, winning in a playoff over fellow Texan Crenshaw. By that time we'd set him up for a two-week trip to Australia with big appearance fees at the New South Wales Open and Australian Open. What

happens? He goes Down Under and wins them both, completing a season
of dominance that ranks among the best in history.

There were many more opportunities, large and small, domestic and
international, that Bill pursued over the ensuing months. All of them called
for days of his time—time that he would normally have spent practicing
and focusing on his game. The result was that, after that 1981 season, he was
never the same, winning only one event over the rest of his career.

Many saw Rogers's demise as burnout, pure and simple, the consequence
of being overworked by IMG, specifically by me. I won't try to defend myself, but I will let Bill speak. In a recent interview for a golf podcast he said:

> IMG created opportunities in a way no other management company
> could, and I went after them. There was a lot of benefit and there was
> a lot of sacrifice, but at the end of the day it's the player's choice to
> say yes or no. I've always been a "yes" guy, and I'll admit I loved the
> almighty dollar. As a result I got out of my comfort zone, and worst
> of all, I sort of lost the desire to play. I blame no one but myself. But
> I can also look back and know that I did exactly what I wanted to at
> the time and had a lot of fun doing it.

Bill shared another insight with me. The one Tour event he won after
his big year was the 1982 New Orleans Open, and it was at the same
event one year later that a pivotal moment occurred. "I'd finished my
morning round and played well. I probably should have just gone back to
the hotel," he said, "but I knew that would be boring so instead I went to
the range, as much out of habit as anything else, and for no sound reason
started fiddling with my swing. That was the beginning of the end."

This was in the days before every top player was working closely with
a teacher, someone constantly either at his side or a video call away. It
reminded me of a passage from Mark's *Arnie* biography. On the subject of post-round practice, Arnold Palmer said, "I may think I need

to hit some balls, but I won't do it if it's going to harm my endurance, or maybe get me into some bad habits. The worst thing you can do is practice when you don't feel like it."

Whatever the cause may have been, the collapse of Bill Rogers brought some negative focus on IMG—and me—and at that moment it was probably justified. I had begun to make more than a few mistakes.

THE WORST WEEK OF THE YEAR

"April is the cruelest month," said T. S. Eliot, and I couldn't have agreed more, at least when it came to the first week of April and the Masters. I realize that sounds obnoxious to any reasonably constituted golfer, for whom a spring trip to Augusta is the stuff of dreams. But I have my reasons.

For my first year or two, the only tournament credential I got was a grounds pass, which gave me no access to the clubhouse or locker room, where a lot of my work typically was done. So I came up with a solution. The morning-drive guy at Cleveland's biggest radio station was a big sports fan and friend of mine named Larry Morrow, and I proposed a deal. If he could get me a press credential, I'd do a live radio report from Augusta on Thursday and Friday mornings and Monday morning after the tournament. Larry went for it, and I got a Working Press badge: "Hughes Norton, WWWE Radio, Cleveland."

People in the golf business will tell you Masters week is a huge networking opportunity, as everyone who's anyone is there. True enough, but that can also present problems. Mark loved to tell the story from one of his first Masters when he walked into the grillroom to find Arnold and Winnie Palmer sitting at a table. Two tables over were Gary and Vivienne Player, and at a third table were Jack and Barbara Nicklaus. What did he do? He turned on his heel and went back out the door. "No matter where I sat down," he said, "I was screwed."

I sometimes felt the same way, especially after our client list had grown to the point where we had twenty or more players in the field. If I were seen spending more than a few minutes with any one of them, I worried that numerous noses would get out of joint. In general, I disliked meeting with clients at tournaments, much preferred going to their homes, hotel rooms, or at least somewhere far from the golf course. Unquestionably the worst meeting place was Augusta.

Wally Uihlein, the brilliant CEO of Titleist and Foot-Joy, felt the same way. At Augusta each year he would meet me only on a small bench near the grillroom, secluded from view and well removed from the famous big tree under which the golf industry gathered daily.

The yellow pad was crammed: meetings to schedule; calls to make; dinners with clients and wives; international tournament promoters to negotiate with; players to recruit; IMG staff in from around the world to direct, mentor, and motivate. (Oh yeah, and a wife who needed to hear once in a while that I loved her and missed her on my perpetual treadmill to achievement.)

Conscientiousness—meticulous attention to detail and obsessive follow-up to ensure things got done—was a big reason for my success. But it was simultaneously a highway to neurosis. Never did I savor the moment, appreciate the dogwood or azaleas. I was always worrying about the next thing on my list. So many times I wondered, *How the hell does McCormack do this, times ten, without losing his sanity?*

Mark, in recognition of my landing Watson, Lopez, and Strange, had given me fairly broad discretion in terms of choosing players to add to our client list, so when I got wind of a hotshot I followed up quickly—sometimes too quickly.

The classic example came when I received a phone call from one of our broadcast clients, the redoubtable Bob Rosburg, or "Rossie," as he was known to everyone. It was a Saturday evening in September of 1976 and Rossie was phoning from Los Angeles, where, as a member of ABC-TV's announce team, he'd been covering the U.S. Amateur Championship at Bel-Air Country Club.

"Hughes, I've just spent the afternoon watching the most impressive young golfer I've seen in a long time," he said. "This is a kid you've got to sign fast, before someone else does."

Now, Bob Rosburg was not someone whose golf opinions I took lightly. A Stanford graduate, he'd played the Tour for two decades and won six events, including the 1959 PGA Championship. Rossie also knew what it was like to be a young phenom. He'd played as a junior at the Olympic Club in San Francisco, where at the age of twelve he'd faced then-retired baseball Hall of Famer Ty Cobb in the first round of the club championship, and had blown him away, 7 and 6.

More important, Rosburg wasn't given to frivolous praise. Indeed, in the course of his career as a "foot soldier" for ABC, following players along the fairways, his trademark catchphrase had become "He's got no chance," referring to a player whose ball was in any sort of predicament (after which the player invariably would pull off a miraculous recovery). Ironically, Mr. No Chance had called me to deliver a breathless endorsement.

The player in question was Bill Sander, a twenty-year-old out of Seattle who in his semifinal match that Saturday afternoon had played the first nine holes of Bel-Air in 31 and dispatched his opponent by a score of 8 and 7. The next day, Sander took the U.S. Amateur title, winning the thirty-six-hole final match by 8 and 6, the largest victory margin since Jack Nicklaus in 1961.

I was sold and we signed him.

But there was a difference this time. Sander needed some financial backing. He had no family resources, and since his record other than the U.S. Amateur victory was mediocre, he didn't command the kind of signing bonuses from club and apparel companies that could finance a year or so on the Tour.

Sander, like all Tour rookies, had the option of assembling a syndicate of backers to advance him, say, $50,000. Typically, such investors were repaid as soon as the player began to bank some real cash, after which they would take a percentage of the player's earnings for an agreed-upon period. Sadly, that arrangement rarely worked. Either the player failed to deliver and his backers lost money and friendships became strained, or he delivered big-time, immediately paid everyone back, but then had to pay his backers additional thousands of dollars for years, income that would otherwise have been entirely his.

To sign Bill Sander I came up with another option no competitor could match: IMG would advance him the money he needed, with no interest. "Just go and play," I told him. "When you're successful we'll get some contracts going, and that's when we'll get our money back."

This was revolutionary for a management company, even one as large and established as IMG, and conceivably put us on the hook for a large loss. Yet, when I ran it by Mark he was supportive: "If you think signing this kid is worth the risk, go for it." This was typical of how McCormack encouraged his trusted top execs to go down new roads and pursue innovative ideas.

It seemed like a good idea at the time. In the end, however, Bill did not play to a standard that allowed us to recover our investment. He stayed on Tour for fifteen years and never finished better than a pair of seconds. During the same period I made similar bad investments to sign two other promising young players, Canadian Jim Nelford and John Fought, the latter of whom became a successful golf architect after falling short as a player. These three misjudgments cost IMG well into six figures and reminded me painfully of my own fallibility. After a fast start as an agent, I was demonstrating clearly that I was no Mark McCormack.

Signing players who fail to pan out is a letdown, but it happens. At least there's a measure of solace in being able to point to underperformance by the player. A far more serious flaw for an agent is the failure to recognize and pursue talent staring him right in the face—and I did some of that as well.

Curiously, just as Seattle-born Bill Sander was the poster boy of the former flaw, another Seattleite personified the latter: Fred Couples. I can't say I wasn't aware of Fred. He was a 1979 All-American out of Houston and had won the Washington State Open as a nineteen-year-old, defeating PGA Tour veteran Don Bies in a playoff. But he was emerging at the same time

I was wooing Crenshaw and stealing Rogers and placating already stolen Wadkins. There was enough on my plate that I'd begun to hire and train additional people to work in the golf division.

HIRING THE MASTERS CHAIRMAN

In the late 1970s I had what I thought was a brilliant idea. Vinny Giles had been recruiting clients to his new management firm by virtue of the friendships he'd formed with them as a top amateur player himself. Why couldn't IMG find a way to do the same thing?

What we needed was a successful young amateur willing to launch a career in the golf business. As I scoured the landscape, Fred Ridley stood out. He'd been a member of the University of Florida golf team that had won the 1973 NCAA Championship, and in 1975 he'd won the U.S. Amateur, defeating his Florida teammate Andy Bean and Curtis Strange in match play along the way. Following graduation in 1974, Fred had decided against pro golf, enrolling instead at Stetson law school in Florida. He is to this day the last U.S. Amateur champion never to have turned professional.

So one day in 1977 I called him out of the blue and made my pitch. "I know you've graduated from law school, and you're probably planning on a great legal career in Florida," I said, "but how about this. Stay involved in golf, keep playing the top amateur events, and also work as a sports management lawyer—come and do it all at IMG." To say that the call caught Fred by surprise would be a major understatement. But he was intrigued and accepted shortly thereafter.

I thought we had hit a home run, and it worked for a while, but I'd made one basic mistake. Never have an employee start work in Cleveland during the winter, particularly someone from the South. Fred and his wife, Betsy, never adjusted to midwestern life and, a couple of years later, he returned to Florida to join a Tampa law firm.

The rest is history: Ridley captained two U.S. Walker Cup teams, was elected president of the USGA in 2004, and in 2017 became chairman of the Augusta National Golf Club.

My sense is that Fred had always had some misgivings about the agency business. It just wasn't a fit for his personality, style, or career aspirations. Throughout the rest of his career, with each significant achievement in golf administration, the media has chronicled his history to that point—but never has his first job out of law school been mentioned. It's almost as if Fred is embarrassed to have been an aspiring agent at moneygrubbing IMG. And I get that. Such is the perception I wrestled with for my entire career.

One of them was Dustin "Dusty" Murdock, a PGA Tour official whom most players seemed to like. He had lots of "inside baseball" knowledge from his years on Tour, so I figured he could hit the ground running. When he joined us, I made signing Fred Couples his top priority. Remembering how quickly I'd learned when Mark had thrown me out into the cold six years earlier, I figured Dusty could do the same.

Well, he didn't. Our competitors quickly took advantage, making sure Couples realized IMG was courting him with a rookie instead of McCormack or Norton. Each of them assured Fred that their top man would manage his career. He ended up signing with Lynn Roach at Advantage International, an offshoot of an agency that had represented tennis players. Lynn went out on his own a few years later and has represented Fred ever since. I give Fred high marks for his loyalty.

We also tried and failed to sign one of the hottest LPGA prospects, Juli Inkster, but the "miss" in this case was more Juli's than IMG's. Juli won three consecutive U.S. Women's Amateurs in 1980 to 1982 and was better positioned at that moment to commercially capitalize on turning pro than any woman player since Nancy Lopez. I didn't think we had to sell her on IMG. Anyone could see in 1983 that we were in the midst of making fortunes for Lopez and Baugh off the golf course. What rational player wouldn't want to take advantage?

Besides, like any client, Juli could have called the shots. I assured her and her husband, Brian, that there was no need to travel as much as Laura or do as many commercials as Nancy.

No dice. Could not get through to them.

Juli won thirty-one times on the LPGA Tour including seven major championships. There is no doubt in my mind that under IMG's management her $15 million in career earnings could have been augmented by that much or more off the course with little effect on her golf game.

As if those recruiting gaffes weren't enough, at about the same time I also managed to wreak havoc with my number one client, Curtis Strange. In what I'd thought was another stroke of genius I'd gotten him a deal to become the national spokesman for Nevada Bob's golf stores. The money was very attractive, but I'd neglected to consider how an affiliation with Nevada Bob's might sit with Curtis's equipment company, Taylor Made. Technically, the deals didn't conflict—one endorsement was for golf clubs, the other for a chain of retail stores. But in those days Taylor Made, like most of the leading club manufacturers, sold exclusively through on-course pro shops, who hated the idea of competition from a new distribution channel, especially Nevada Bob's, which undercut the pro shop prices.

So the folks at Taylor Made weren't happy. CEO Gary Adams called Curtis moments before he was about to tee off in the Doral Open and threatened to sue him. So Curtis wasn't happy, and his ire only increased when he found himself the target of outrage from PGA professionals nationwide, especially sensitive given his father's history as a club pro. I had no choice but to call Nevada Bob's and ask out of the deal. So that made it unanimous—Nevada Bob's wasn't happy, either. It was an embarrassing blunder for an experienced agent, who should have known better.

What a turn my career had taken. In my first few years I could do no wrong; now suddenly I was a serial fuckup—and the worst was yet to come. In the space of a few months, two of IMG Golf's biggest clients— Raymond Floyd and Lanny Wadkins—would leave. And that buck stopped at my desk as head of the golf division.

Floyd's departure came for one reason: his wife. Maria Floyd was one of the smartest, most complex, seemingly dual-personality people I ever dealt with. One moment she could be warm and caring (she sent baby gifts when my daughters were born), and the next moment an absolute terror on wheels.

Before her marriage to Raymond she'd been a successful businesswoman, and she measured performance like a hawk. I give her full credit for reinvigorating Raymond's career. When he won the PGA Championship in 1969, the champion still received a lifetime exemption on Tour. Raymond was naturally talented, but from that moment on, especially during the years he was single, he'd been on cruise control. Maria kicked his butt—made it clear he was wasting his talent and she wasn't going to put up with it. It was the best thing that ever happened to Ray. He won seventeen of his twenty-two career titles after their marriage, including a Masters, a second PGA, and a U.S. Open.

IMG may have been Ray Floyd's agent, but Maria was his manager, and her attitude was, the squeaky wheel (loudest client) gets the grease. She complained to me often that Ray didn't get enough respect or enough deals as one of IMG's top clients—and her complaints were, shall we say, colorful. Every so often like clockwork Maria would phone me, hurling F-bombs and disparaging me, IMG, and McCormack at great length and volume. These rants were truly spectacular.

When I described these calls to colleagues at the office, no one believed me. So after a while when she'd start in like this, I'd put the call on speakerphone and quietly have my assistant round up anyone nearby to hear for themselves. She would literally go nonstop for five or ten highly entertaining minutes. Her favorite description of IMG: "In the land of the blind, the one-eyed man is king." In other words, IMG sucks—but there's nobody else competent to go to.

Well, in 1982 they found someone else, Donald Dell at Pro Serv, the same fledgling tennis agency whose offshoot had snapped up Fred Couples.

The departure of Ray Floyd, someone I'd been working with for over a decade, was very tough to take. Then at almost the same moment, we lost Wadkins, who had also been with IMG for ten years. We'd done some good work for Lanny, but frankly he was not an easy guy to sell or an easy guy to work with, always had a chip on his shoulder about something. Dan Jenkins knew Lanny pretty well and told me once that Lanny had left because he felt I was paying too much attention to a newly signed young client, Bobby Clampett.

If that was the case, it was for a good reason. Early on, I'd learned from Mark there are two points in a player's career when you can maximize his or her outside income. The first one, which you can pretty much control, is when they turn professional, and the second is the moment they peak. Mark always cited what he called the tragedy of Ben Crenshaw: "He had lots of charisma, but he failed to realize the importance of timing. You either capitalize on someone when they first come up or you have to wait until they make it. In between is no good. By choosing to do nothing, Crenshaw blew the first stage."

As for the other moment of opportunity, the height of a player's career, that's much harder to identify. If there was one player for whom IMG had taken full advantage at that stage, it was Tony Jacklin—yet later Jacklin felt we'd overworked him, citing it as the reason behind his career slump following a devastating loss in the 1972 Open at Muirfield. Tied with Lee Trevino at the par-5 seventy-first hole, Tony was just short of the green in two, while Lee had hit his fourth shot over the back of the green. Trevino chipped in for a 5, a shell-shocked Jacklin staggered to a 6, and it was over for him, a blow from which he never recovered.

When asked about it years later Tony said, "I was burnt out. I had been running myself ragged. Mark McCormack was representing me, and he was always pushing for more. I was traveling between the U.S. and Europe six or seven times a season. I was going to Japan and South Africa, always chasing deals and tournaments. I wasn't living life on my own terms. It was never about what was best for me, it was about Mark and IMG. It took me a long time to realize I was just a pawn in a much bigger game." A bitter assessment if ever there was one. It was also an overstatement. Tony approved every one of those opportunities, the income from which assured him a comfortable retirement.

Bobby Clampett was heralded at the time as the Next Nicklaus. Growing up in Carmel, California, he'd graduated from high school at sixteen and enrolled at Brigham Young, where he was twice named the Collegiate Golfer of the Year. He'd won several major amateur events and was low amateur at both the 1978 U.S. Open and 1979 Masters. But this kid had more than just golf talent, he had a lively intelligence and an infectious personality along with a Harpo Marx–like mop of curly blond hair.

From an early age Bobby's father had not been in the picture. His mother's companion was a colorful character named Fletcher Jones, the most successful car dealer in Las Vegas. As had been my experience with Strange (Jordan Ball) and Lopez (Domingo), I determined that Fletcher was the key influencer.

Via long phone calls and in-person discussions we forged a great relationship. (The phone chats were particularly entertaining, as Fletcher had an expression, "onaccountabecause," that he used liberally. Once I heard the first "onaccountabecause," it was hard to think about anything except when the next one would drop.) Bobby deferred completely to Fletcher, presumably onaccountabecause of Fletcher's business savvy. He turned pro after the 1980 U.S. Open and signed with IMG the next day. From the start, Mark referred to Bobby in-house as "The Man of Destiny."

In the case of Lanny Wadkins, when he left IMG in 1982 he was past his prime. He'd already notched more than half of his career victories including his only major, the 1977 PGA. A bit like Floyd, however, Lanny felt undervalued—lost in the shuffle between the Big Three era and the youth movement that had followed him—and maybe he was. In the end I think we produced for Lanny what his achievements and reputation warranted.

That said, as was the case with Raymond, Lanny's departure was something IMG hadn't experienced for a decade—a major loss. At the end of that 1982 season, no IMG client was in possession of a major championship trophy, and three of the four titles were in the hands of players who had left us, the PGA Championship going to Raymond Floyd and both Opens to Tom Watson.

AN ODYSSEY UNLIKE ANY OTHER

Bobby Clampett was always up for an off-the-wall adventure and there was one day that topped them all. Among the first contracts we got for him was as a playing editor for *Golf* magazine, where my coauthor, George Peper, was then editor in chief. One day George called me with a wild idea he'd cooked up.

"Hughes," he said, "I'd like you and Bobby to join me and photographer Brian Morgan in an attempt to do something no one has ever done—play fifty-four holes in one day on the Old Course at St. Andrews, Winged Foot, and Pebble Beach."

How? With the aid of the Concorde. Peper wanted to make a statement about pace of play, and he'd somehow secured four seats on the Monday-morning charter flight that would be returning PGA Tour players from the 1983 Open Championship at Royal Birkdale.

On Sunday evening after the Open ended the four of us flew up to St. Andrews. The next morning we teed off on the Old Course in barely daylight at 4:15. By 6:45, we'd taken a puddle jumper from nearby Leuchars airport to Manchester and were walking sheepishly down the aisle of the Concorde, getting dirty looks from the likes of Palmer, Nicklaus, Watson, Miller, Trevino, and their wives for having delayed their departure.

As the plane took off, I said to George, "You realize, if this baby goes down, you and I will be listed under 'Other Scores.'"

During the flight Arnie asked George how we were getting to Pebble. When George said we had a Falcon jet, Arnie said, "You're not gonna make it. Tell him, Ray." Across the aisle, Ray Floyd leaned in and said, "They're fast, but they don't last."

Sure enough, after helicoptering to and from Winged Foot, which we played in two hours and twenty minutes, we had to make a pit stop in Cheyenne, Wyoming, before landing in Monterey and completing the fifty-four holes in just over twenty-three hours. Following a champagne toast at sunset on Pebble's eighteenth green, the three of us exhausted elders collapsed into bed, declining twenty-two-year-old Bobby's invitation: "Anybody want to play hoops at my house?" He was serious.

But the most painful moment for me personally that year had come in the Open Championship at Royal Troon, where after two rounds Bobby Clampett had raced to a five-stroke lead. Playing in his first Open, he'd shot rounds of 67–66, and had begun Saturday with two early birdies to extend the margin to seven with thirty-one holes to play. Our "Man of Destiny" was on his way!

And then, just like that, the fairy tale turned into a nightmare. At the par-5 sixth, the longest championship hole in Britain at 577 yards, Bobby found three bunkers and took a triple-bogey 8, leading to a round of 78. After fifty-four holes he still had a one-stroke lead, but a 77 on the final day dropped him into a tie for tenth.

Inexplicably, Bobby then changed his swing, and was never the same again. It was one of the saddest chapters in my tenure as a golf agent. Such talent, on the verge of greatness, such a great kid. After one PGA Tour victory and nine top three finishes those first two years on Tour, no one could have imagined Bobby struggling as he did. Unlike the media pundits, Bobby never attributed his decline to that calamitous fold at Troon, but there were only two more top three finishes the remainder of his career and he never won again.

How could this happen? Why wasn't I there urging Bobby to stay the course with that indomitable swing his coach, Ben Doyle, had nurtured so expertly? Not that Bobby would have necessarily listened. ("You worry about the endorsements, Hughes, I know what's best for my game.") But golf history is replete with pros who, with the best of intentions, changed what was working in an attempt to get better and instead got worse (see Hubert Green, Ian Baker-Finch). I so regret not asking Arnold or Mark to counsel Bobby before making such a consequential decision. But, preoccupied with all the other things on my plate, I stayed in my lane, and have faulted myself for doing so ever since.

Blessedly, thanks to his engaging personality, we were able to get Bobby a tryout as an on-course reporter for CBS-TV and he became a stalwart member of the announce team there, and then at Turner Sports for two decades.

MARATHON MAN

By the late 1970s I'd quit my Tuesday-at-midnight hockey sessions and was getting no exercise at all. Instead I was giving my knife-and-fork skills an intensive workout through endless client dinners and corporate sales-call lunches. Without realizing it, I'd gained twenty pounds.

While on a trip to New Zealand in the fall of 1980, I walked into an airport bookstore, where Jim Fixx's *The Complete Book of Running* was prominently displayed—and so began an obsession. In Christchurch the next morning I ventured out of the hotel and tentatively jogged a few blocks. Despite my trepidation, it felt pretty good—I'd nearly forgotten the exhilaration of sweating.

Things escalated quickly thereafter—from jogging a mile to running five to six miles at 5:30 nearly every morning. The weight came off quickly, I felt better, and, counterintuitively, expending energy on the roads seemed to give me more stamina for the long workdays and constant travel. It was also one of the few things in my day that I could control—get up early, shoes on, out the door—nothing could interfere.

Eventually, someone talked me into a 10K race, which went better than I'd expected, so I tried another. Then, while on a mini-vacation with Candy in Vermont, I impulsively entered a half-marathon, a typically clueless move (see you in a couple of hours, honey) at an important moment when we'd needed some time together away from the kids.

Who knows, maybe that's why I continued to run—from the pressures of work and my faltering marriage. Running became my stress relief, my escape—running away.

There were memorable runs in the deserted early-morning streets of Tokyo, along Sydney Harbor, in London, Paris, Johannesburg, and one ill-advised jaunt outside the protective gates of a Jamaican resort during the Johnnie Walker Golf Classic, following which I was sternly admonished for having run through the most dangerous part of town ruled by gangs whose specialty was kidnapping unsuspecting Americans.

Finally came the ultimate challenge: the 1982 New York Marathon (26.2 miles), which I ran in two hours and fifty-eight minutes, just under seven minutes a mile. A photo of the finish line hangs in my basement. Surrounded by fellow runners excitedly celebrating having beaten the holy grail sub-three-hour mark, I look exactly as I felt at that moment: totally exhausted from half-killing myself at an overachieving, excruciating pace, vowing on the spot never to do it again. And I never did.

At the close of that 1982 season I felt a bit like Clampett had at the end of the Troon Open. After a dream start, my skills as an agent seemed to have unraveled. Despite my best efforts, nothing seemed to be going right, including my family life.

The long work hours and constant travel, much of it international, had detracted from time with my wife and kids. It was that same eternal co-nundrum of balance (rest and practice vs. off-course financial success) that plagued my clients, now applied to my world. Work and family—spend more time on one and the other suffers. Successful executives figure it out. I was having trouble, particularly with a boss like McCormack, who re-lentlessly monitored everything I was doing. It was particularly hard on Candy, so often left as a single parent. When she couldn't take it anymore she insisted we go into counseling.

My growing pains, professional and personal, paralleled a pervasive un-ease with regard to IMG, the mounting perception that our fast-expanding company had become three things: too big, too entangled, and too greedy. We were the 1927 Yankees—nearly everyone hated us.

Since its founding twenty years earlier IMG had exploded, now with hundreds of athletes in all sports under contract along with at least another hundred entertainers, associations, and corporations, a range of clients that included everything from the Nobel Foundation to the Grammys, violinist Itzhak Perlman to Hertz Rent-a-Car.

We'd even struck up a relationship with the pope. In 1979 Pope John Paul II had made a three-day visit to Ireland and it hadn't gone well. The big issue was the unbridled profiteering that had gone on by vendors selling an array of pope-themed mementos and tchotchkes, with none of their profit going to the Roman Catholic Church. Determined to rectify that, the Vatican approached Mark, and three years later IMG orchestrated the papal tour of Great Britain. I still remember the jokes flying around the office about the marketing possibilities: "Give us this day our daily Wonder Bread," Vatican-sanctified Popecorn and Popesicles, papal skullcaps embroidered with the Lacoste crocodile.

IMG in partnership with the pope . . . Who next, Jesus?

MUCH ADO ABOUT NOTHING

In 1982 Mark got a letter from a guy asserting in a very intelligent and convincing way that William Shakespeare never existed and Sir Francis Bacon was the actual author of Shakespeare's works. Of course, that notion had been postulated for centuries, but this chap insisted he could prove it beyond a doubt.

Mark was sufficiently intrigued that he dispatched one of our associates, an extremely bright young woman, to visit the fellow and check out his story. She returned and said, "I think this guy's got something." Apparently, hidden within the Shakespearean oeuvre is a cypher, a code that reveals to the satisfaction of many that Bacon is the author of all those plays and sonnets. But this chap claimed he'd discovered that the same code revealed where many of Shakespeare's original texts were buried. If those texts could be unearthed, the long-standing debate presumably would be settled in favor of Bacon, not to mention a priceless treasure would be found!

IMG became involved. The fellow shared with Mark the exact spot in London where he believed the ancient manuscripts lay. Mark, always looking for a way to turn a profit, then approached his friend newspaper mogul Rupert Murdoch with an offer. "Pay us a hundred thousand pounds and you can have the exclusive story of the excavation. Should the manuscripts be found you can have first look at them for an additional two million pounds."

Well, the mystery endures, because the papers turned out to be buried directly beneath a church, and while the Catholic pope may have been willing to engage with IMG, the church of England was not.

The view of many within the golf industry and beyond was that IMG had become so broad-reaching and diffuse, any new client (Jesus possibly excepted) would get lost in the crowd. Mark was sensitive to that criticism and had a clever answer—actually a question: "If you had a serious medical condition, wouldn't you seek out the best doctor you could find? And once you did, if someone said, 'You don't want that guy, he has a hundred patients,' would that stop you?"

He also prided himself on being choosy when it came to clients, and the list of rejects he divulged in a *Sports Illustrated* piece was impressive:

Wilt Chamberlain: "It's hard to relate to someone who's seven feet tall. What do you do with him? Maybe put him in a Volkswagen to show legroom. But what after that?"

Bobby Fischer: "I told him I could get him $2 million for doing a syndicated newspaper column, but he wasn't interested. Fischer was a very shortsighted man in everything but chess."

Mickey Mantle: "His financial affairs, part ownership in bowling alleys and that sort of thing, were a total disaster. Beyond rescue."

Muhammad Ali (back when he was Cassius Clay): "It had to do with image. He was not the kind of guy Singer Sewing Machine would want to sign up."

Mark Spitz: "He thought our 25% fee was too high. Besides, I wasn't all that sure what we could do for him. After all, there was nobody for him to swim against."

Willie Mays: "He came around too late in his career."

But another issue had emanated from IMG's spreading tentacles— ever-present conflict of interest. A classic example arose in the tennis world at Wimbledon in 1973 when thirteen of the top sixteen players boycotted the event over the banning of Croatian player Nikki Pilic because of his ongoing dispute with the Yugoslav Tennis Federation. At the time IMG (1) represented many of the boycotting players, (2) represented Wimbledon itself, (3) had a contract to film the matches, (4) represented the BBC, which televised Wimbledon, (5) represented both the World Championship Tennis tour and the U.S. Lawn Tennis Association, and (6) represented Bud Collins, the TV commentator tasked with explaining the situation to a global audience. Yet somehow, it all worked out.

Mark's way of handling such situations was simple: full disclosure to all sides. As long as everyone understood the potential conflicts, it usually sorted itself out—except when it didn't. Olympic figure skating client Dorothy Hamill once sued IMG, saying the company had used its size and pervasiveness to create a "company town" in which she and other athletes were manipulated and exploited for IMG's gain, citing an instance when her agent had failed to disclose IMG's 50 percent ownership of an event, where he'd negotiated a lower than normal fee for her to participate. The lawsuit was settled out of court.

The same sort of thing had become rampant in golf, where IMG owned and operated dozens of events around the world. In seeking sponsors for those events, we went first to our own corporate consulting clients—Colgate, Rolex, etc.—offering title sponsorships as well as participation in our production company's film of the competition for distribution on broadcast television and video. We then filled the field of competitors with as many of our clients as possible, paying the players a competitive but low-as-possible fee, since it was IMG's own money we were spending—and of course we then reclaimed 20 percent of that fee as our commission. We didn't just double-dip, we quadruple-dipped, but, just as Mark had predicted when he created this scheme, working all sides of the street, we got away with it, as the federal regulators either didn't see us as big enough to pursue or simply chose to look the other way.

Admittedly, IMG's web of interests occasionally trapped clients in the middle, but those who signed with us knew what they were getting into, and most of them realized that the benefits we brought our clients were unmatchable by smaller agents. Indeed, Mark never portrayed himself simply as an agent. "An agent is a fat, bald guy with a cigar in his mouth and a phone to his ear, booking bands," he said. "We're managers of careers."

As *Sports Illustrated*'s Ray Kennedy wryly put it, "When a new client comes in one door, he will go out the other greased, tuned, and buffed like a showroom model. Beyond the usual merchandising and contract negotiating, IMG may pay an athlete's bills, supervise his investments, answer his mail, direct his publicity, handle his insurance, put him on a budget, plan his estate, arrange his itineraries, sell his book, buy his wife's birthday present and lend a sympathetic ear at two a.m. to hear why his coach doesn't love him anymore."

If that meant we were aggressive and greedy, then guilty as charged. In my experience, IMG's full-service approach more often meant we could be fair-handed with our clients. We didn't need to overbook to keep the company afloat, and the commission we earned on any particular deal was never that significant a factor. The agents to be wary of were the smaller guys with only a few clients—they needed every commission dollar possible to stay in business.

And business—big business—is what professional golf surely had become. Tour commissioner Beman, always a step or two ahead of everyone except perhaps Mark McCormack, had formulated a blueprint for the growth of his operation, and within a few years of taking office, he'd laid much of the groundwork.

But Beman's deft renegotiation of the Tour's television contracts had turned out to be a short-lived win, as the 1979 ratings revealed viewership of golf events had dropped more than 10 percent. It sent him the clear message that the Tour needed to diversify its sources of income. "We were almost completely dependent on TV revenues," he told his biographer,

Adam Schupak. "We weren't in control of our own destiny. Ratings and television revenue were driving the bus."

His first move was to assign a consulting firm to gauge the public perception of professional golf—and the results were eye-opening. The fan base was small, with virtually no viewers under eighteen. Most concerning was the revelation that pro golfers were perceived as selfish, aloof, and unappreciative of the big money they were making, and the Tour itself lacked a positive brand identity.

Late in 1979 Beman put together a blue book packed with ideas big and small, aimed at raising both the profile of the game and the income of his Tour. The list included everything from kid-friendly golf courses called Wee Links to the introduction of electronic tournament scoreboards, a computerized statistics program that identified the Tour's best players in various categories, to an annual awards banquet that honored them. Central to his plan was a branding strategy featuring the Tour's new logo on a line of PGA Tour apparel and a trio of corporate deals announcing the official credit card, airline, and cruise line of the PGA Tour.

As for his big ideas, they were very big: the creation of the Senior Tour, which extended the competitive careers of players over fifty, capitalized on the enduring popularity of Palmer and Nicklaus, brought professional golf to many more cities, and gave the Tour a whole new product to sell; the creation of PGA Tour Productions, the Tour's dedicated film and television production company; the birth of the game's "fifth major," the Players Championship; the purchase—incredibly for one dollar—of 415 acres of Ponte Vedra Beach swampland, which became the Tournament Players Club (TPC) at Sawgrass, a championship course owned by the Tour and permanent home of the Players Championship; the expansion of the TPC concept to dozens more spectator-friendly courses across the nation, all designed in collaboration with Tour players; and the creation of a retirement plan for Tour players that became regarded as the most lucrative in sports, with many players reaping far more from their pensions than they ever made playing golf.

At the same time he was launching all this, Beman was working on an inventive revamp of the delicate four-way alliance among the Tour, television, corporate America, and charities.

Before 1980, there wasn't a lot of golf on TV—three or four hours each on Saturday and Sunday afternoons. The reason? Golf was a very expensive sport to broadcast, due largely to the cost of laying cable over hundreds of rambling acres—and changing the playing site each week—versus a single ballpark or arena. "Until we could find a way of underwriting the networks' productions costs, we couldn't get substantial rights fees," said Beman. "We had to solve the networks' financial problems."

He did that by introducing the notion of title sponsorship—corporations attaching their names to golf events. Tournaments long named after celebrities or cities made room for companies. The Bob Hope Desert Classic became the Bob Hope Chrysler Classic; the Greater Hartford Open became the Canon Greater Hartford Open. Title sponsorship entitled a company to 60 percent of the television commercials on the broadcast.

But Beman quickly realized that when corporations became title sponsors—and by extension became involved with charities—they got much more than just commercials and an image boost, they reaped a bonanza in additional national exposure through leaderboard mentions, on-camera CEO interviews, and frequent repetition of the tournament name in the electronic and print media, not to mention a hefty tax deduction associated with the charity connection. On top of all that, they got to do some serious corporate entertaining by inviting their best clients and prospects to play in the pro-am. When all that was quantified, the dollar figure came to something much higher than what advertisers had been paying in the pre-title sponsor days. So Beman raised the fees dramatically, and the sponsors did not flinch.

In addition, Beman allowed the TV networks to sell the other 40 percent of ad spots for their own gain, which reaped them enormous profits, as corporate America continued to fall in love with golf. The dramatically increased revenue easily covered the networks' production costs and of course brought a very healthy hike in the rights fees. During the Beman era the rights fees paid by the networks to the PGA Tour would increase from $2.8 million in 1974 to $69 million in 1994, with a large portion of that income shared with the individual Tour events.

It was a brilliant plan, leading to dramatically increased golf coverage—all four rounds of every event beamed out on both network and cable, including a newborn Golf Channel. Perhaps most important, the Tour escaped its dependency on TV ratings. The sponsors, most of them purveyors of high-end goods and services, were quite happy with the targeted golf audience—class rather than mass.

But then the same sort of early-1980s growing pains that had afflicted me and IMG also throttled Deane Beman and the PGA Tour, nearly costing the commissioner his job. In March of 1983, a secret meeting took place when Jack Nicklaus traveled to the Bay Hill Club in Orlando to pay a visit to Arnold Palmer. Also in the meeting were Mark McCormack and Alastair Johnston, who had by that time become Arnie's understudy agent. The subject: discontent over Deane Beman's handling of the Tour.

The two titans of golf, who to that point had been constant rivals but never allies, now agreed on a couple of important points. First, Beman's marketing of the Tour, with its barrage of official merchandise and commercial affiliations, had become unwanted competition. Jack and Arnie saw their own entrepreneurial opportunities being sabotaged. Second, Beman's restructuring of the television revenues had impinged on their ability to profit fully from their own tournaments (Palmer's Bay Hill Classic and Nicklaus's Memorial Tournament). Finally, by getting into real estate and golf architecture through the network of TPC clubs, the Tour was competing with Arnold's and Jack's own golf design firms.

At one point in the meeting Nicklaus said, "I'll do everything in my power to stop that man." Over the next few weeks Nicklaus gained the backing of many of his fellow players. Foremost among them was Tom Watson, who told *Golf Digest*, "I think the basic problem is that the tour is competing with its own players. It's marketing the tour for the players but at the disadvantage of the successful ones who could go out and market their own image."

Such a statement was a bit out of character for Watson, one of the least aggressive self-marketers of his time. I suspect the Tour's board chairman at the time, E. M. "Del" de Windt, had it right when he cited Watson's brother-in-law Chuck Rubin as "the guy who stirred the pot."

Curiously, after the clandestine Bay Hill meeting, Mark McCormack had stayed out of the fray. According to Adam Schupak, "Beman saw IMG as a major rival, considering its rapidly growing influence in golf, and regarded McCormack as a clever strategist. He often said that if McCormack had been more actively involved in the rebellion, he 'might've been a dead duck.'"

Ultimately a three-page letter rejecting Beman's vision and policies was sent to Chairman de Windt. It was signed by Nicklaus, Palmer, Watson, and ten other prominent players: Andy Bean, Ben Crenshaw, Ray Floyd, Hale Irwin, Tom Kite, Johnny Miller, Craig Stadler, Lee Trevino, Lanny Wadkins, and Tom Weiskopf.

They felt betrayed and, although the letter did not say so in as many words, what they wanted was Beman's dismissal. It was an eerie foreshadowing of what would occur precisely forty years later when, in the wake of the announced LIV Golf/PGA Tour merger, an angry gathering of players confronted Commissioner Jay Monahan at the 2023 RBC Canadian Open, calling him a hypocrite for suddenly and secretly making a deal with the same Saudis he had just weeks earlier vowed to battle to the end. A week after that meeting, Monahan stepped away from his job for several weeks, citing a "medical situation" that he later admitted was stress.

Deane Beman, however, was not one to back off, and he unearthed a secret weapon, the Tour's original charter, agreed upon by the players (including Nicklaus and Palmer) fifteen years earlier when the Tour had separated from the PGA of America. Its bylaws stated clearly that the PGA Tour had the right to run tournaments, build and own golf courses, and participate in the selling of licensed products.

When Nicklaus and Palmer saw that document they knew they were beaten. Like it or not, the Tour would be continuing to expand, more dramatically than ever, and Jack and Arnie would be among the biggest beneficiaries.

5

Landing a Shark

I'd now been at IMG for ten years. Suddenly I felt as if I'd lost the hop on my fastball. My trial arrangement with Tom Watson had died after one year. Curtis Strange was on his way to being the best player in the U.S., but through no fault of his own he had not generated major appeal in the marketplace, and Bobby Clampett had failed to blossom into the singular talent I'd expected him to be.

"What have you done for me lately?" was a question I often heard from my clients, but now I was asking myself, *What have you done for IMG lately?* Mark had not said anything—the pressure I was feeling was self-imposed, but it was there nonetheless. The only relief came in the rare moments when I could escape the office madness and spend some quality time with Candy and the girls. Candy would say later that I seemed devoted more to Stevie and Mandy than to her, something I was completely unaware of. I wish someone had hit me over the head with that. But I did love my little girls, and hanging out with them was serenity itself.

Plain and simple, I needed—IMG needed—a big win. We needed to find and sign a global star. We'd regained our stature as the game's leading management firm, but we hadn't signed a certifiable golf icon since the Big Three. And the dispiriting truth was, within the ranks of the PGA Tour—indeed within the entire American golf ecosystem—no such player existed.

But there was one on the other side of the world.

Australia's Greg Norman had been on the fast track for three years. As an assistant pro at a club in Queensland he'd entered local tournaments, immediately scoring high finishes, and then, at the age of twenty-one, had won the 1976 West Lakes Classic by ten strokes over a field that included Australian stars Bruce Crampton, Bruce Devlin, and David Graham. From there he'd gone to Asia and had huge success, winning ten events by the age of twenty-five. Next stop was the European Tour, where he'd continued his winning ways, emerging along with Seve Ballesteros as the game's next young stars.

I'd been tracking Greg since his first days in Australasia but he'd signed with James Marshall, an English businessman who'd gotten to him first. By the early 1980s, however, trouble had developed between the two over Marshall's management of Greg's finances. (Greg would end up suing Marshall for financial mismanagement, settling out of court.)

I met Greg for the first time at the 1981 Masters, where in his debut appearance he finished an impressive fourth. Truly, everything about this guy was impressive—good looks, the broad shoulders of a football star, the Aussie accent, a swagger that bespoke confidence but not cockiness. Plus a world-beating talent.

He'd been quite vocal about his dissatisfaction with Marshall. I began speaking with him in detail about a relationship with IMG. Over the next several months, Mark and I met with Greg and his wife, Laura, on several occasions.

If there was ever a golfer who needed a worldwide organization behind him, it was Greg Norman in the early 1980s: playing full-time in Europe, occasional forays to the U.S. PGA Tour, returning to compete in Australia several times a year, with the odd junket to Japan thrown in as well. That was where Mark and I focused our pitch.

James Marshall, one guy, couldn't be in four places at once; IMG had offices, support staff, and local expertise in every one of these markets. I emphasized the financial management services we could offer a world player like Greg: tax expertise and fiduciary competence in each geographic sector. (Marshall, familiar only with UK regulations, was already screwing up with an illegal approach in Australia.) And we made sure it wasn't lost on Greg and Laura that IMG's worldwide presence meant more income opportunities for him in each market than any one-man band or small agency could generate. Separate clothing contracts, for example, in Australia, Japan, the UK, and the U.S. I said, "While you guys are sleeping each night our people are going down to the office in Sydney and Tokyo working for you."

Another selling point. Greg's eventual home tour was destined to be America. It would not be ideal to be playing the PGA Tour full-time with your agent in London. I would be at most tournaments with him and at other times only a two-hour flight away. And I think the contrast between James Marshall, an older, more reserved Brit, and myself, someone closer to Greg's age and energy level, was a factor in IMG's favor.

In early 1983 I signed him to a contract and he immediately became my number one client.

We had a couple of immediate priorities when Greg came on board. Job number one was to undo some of James Marshall's handiwork. Marshall had invested a large portion of Greg's income in a company he claimed was a tax haven. Well, it was, but the haven was from taxes in the UK, not Australia. As a result Greg owed the Australian government a huge sum.

James Erskine, IMG's outstanding managing director in Australia, hired an ace tax accountant in Sydney named Bill Baillie. He negotiated for months with the Australian tax authorities and eventually got Greg a settlement that saved him millions of dollars. It was yet another instance of the value added that only IMG could bring to clients—and not one dollar of the millions in potential back interest/tax penalties we saved Greg was commissioned by his new managers.

Job number two—my job—was to generate some *serious* income for Greg. I relished that opportunity. Greg's good looks, swashbuckling style, and Australian charm, combined with prodigious talent, were a marketer's dream. In a very short time I was able to renew his contract for Spalding clubs and balls at a much higher number, while securing new deals for apparel and shoes, a major affiliation with Qantas Airways, a spokesman role for Epson computers, and a playing editor affiliation and instruction book contract with *Golf* magazine.

The apparel contract was particularly fruitful. Greg's existing deal had been with Lyle & Scott, and it was not a particularly good one for our rising young star. At the time, Reebok was becoming a strong competitor to Nike, and IMG's tennis agents had done some endorsement contracts there. I visualized Reebok as a potential worldwide partnership that could grow with Greg. I worked out an arrangement that positioned him as the company's spokesman, the only golfer wearing their brand. The relationship worked so well that a few years later we persuaded Reebok to develop a signature line with Greg's own logo. Collaborating with them, we found an artist, who developed the multicolor shark logo that quickly became one of the most recognizable commercial trademarks in the world.

Meanwhile in Australia James Erskine negotiated big increases in Greg's appearance fees at the Australian Open and Australian Masters, which Greg loved, as it enabled him to return home to play twice a year. Major endorsements down under with Swan beer, Daikyo, and Nissan soon followed.

James also created a whole new business for Greg, a fifty-fifty joint venture with IMG, to design golf courses in Australia and the Far East. James hired a local architect, Bob Harrison, gave him workspace in the IMG Sydney office, and soon Greg Norman Golf Course Design was busy with projects throughout Australia and Asia. Bottom line, we quickly made Greg the highest-paid player without a major. Between all the agreements we were able to secure, Norman very soon would be earning over $1 million in annual endorsements.

But the mid-1980s marked not simply the beginning of the Greg Norman era on the PGA Tour but the start of a much bigger movement—the blossoming of international golf. Of the forty major championships held between 1975 and 1984, only seven had been won by non-Americans, and those seven were spread among just three players—Seve Ballesteros, David Graham, and Gary Player. In the ten years that followed, however, internationals won twenty of the forty majors (including nine of ten Open Championships and seven of ten Masters), and the victories came from eleven different players representing eight nations: Greg Norman, Ian Baker-Finch, and Wayne Grady (Australia); Seve Ballesteros and José María Olazábal (Spain); Nick Faldo (England); Bernhard Langer (Germany); Sandy Lyle (Scotland); Ernie Els (South Africa); Ian Woosnam (Wales); and Nick Price (Zimbabwe).

The Asia Golf Circuit, for decades a loose confederation of national Opens, had organized itself into a proper schedule (including a couple of tournaments created and managed by IMG); the PGA Tour of Australia had produced several strong home players, while also attracting hopefuls from Europe and the U.S.; and the European Tour—where IMG was running nine of the thirty-four events—had followed the path of the PGA Tour, separating from the European PGA to form an independent circuit controlled by the players, and had begun to reach beyond its borders with events in Africa, East Asia, and the Middle East. All three Tours had enjoyed several years of increases in sponsorship and annual prize money. All of which had produced a windfall for the world's top players, who followed the money, playing in the tournaments that offered the highest appearance fees. Of course, IMG was quite happy to help make those arrangements, taking its standard 20 to 25 percent commission for the effort.

At the same time, the suddenly inflated purses on the U.S. Tour had raised eyebrows and aspirations around the world, and a growing number of talented young players from Europe and Australasia were choosing to finish their educations at American universities, particularly those with strong golf programs, as incubators for the PGA Tour.

The clearest reflection of this globalization was a dramatic boost in the stature of the Ryder Cup. The biennial competition pitting America's best pros against those of Great Britain and Ireland had begun in 1927, and the first four matches were split, two victories for each side. Between 1933 and 1977, however, the U.S. had lost only once and in most years had overpowered the Brits. The Ryder Cup had become an obligation for the U.S.

players, an embarrassment for GB&I, and a nonevent for everyone else. Rock bottom was reached in 1977 when Tom Weiskopf opted to skip the matches in favor of a big-game hunting trip.

But that same year things changed when Jack Nicklaus approached Lord Derby, then president of the British PGA, and proposed expanding the GB&I team to include players from mainland Europe. Nicklaus reasoned that this would at minimum improve the level of competition and might even save the Ryder Cup.

He could not have been more right. In 1985 at the Belfry in England, Team Europe, led by Ballesteros, Faldo, and Langer, won for the first time in twenty-eight years, and two years later they won again, this time in America, in fact in Jack Nicklaus's own backyard, Muirfield Village. A new era was born. Eight of the last eleven matches have been won by the European team and the Ryder Cup has become the most electrifying event in golf.

Equally electrifying has been the financial reward the event now brings to those who host it. For decades the Ryder Cup produced nothing but losses—big ones—for both sides, but the intense rivalry spurred by the modern matches has stirred both fervor and commerce on both sides of the Atlantic. Ryder Cup tickets are like gold and television viewership has soared, as have the rights fees paid for the broadcast. Recent Ryder Cups have brought more than $200 million of income to the communities and nations in which they've been played. The net profits, while a closely guarded secret, are estimated at $50 million, with 84 percent going to the hosting team, 16 percent to the visitors. The big payoff thus comes only once every four years. Nonetheless, in the case of the PGA of America, that quadrennial bonanza is surely salve to the self-inflicted wound the association incurred in 1968 when they gave the seceding Tournament Players Division the rights to every competition except the Ryder Cup and the PGA Championship.

The other major beneficiary of pro golf's emerging global era was the Open Championship. Despite being the world's oldest championship, the

British Open, as it was then known, was not on the radar of most play-ers from this side of the Atlantic. Arnold Palmer became its savior when in 1960, having won both the Masters and U.S. Open, he mused that victories in the British Open and PGA Championship would give him a sort of grand slam. Palmer narrowly missed winning the third leg at St. Andrews that year, but did win the title the following year at Royal Birkdale, and for the next several years the British Open took on a bit more prominence. Then in the 1970s it began to sag again, as several top American players felt that the prize money, about 25 percent less than in the three other majors, wasn't worth the hassle and expense of a trip across the pond. (First prize in 1975 paid just $16,500, so any American player not finishing among the top ten would be struggling to break even for the week, especially if he chose to take his family along for the ride.) More and more players opted to stay home.

Then a few things happened. Number one, a succession of marquee champions—Tom Watson ('75 and '77), Johnny Miller ('76), Jack Nick-laus ('78), and Seve Ballesteros ('79), future Hall of Famers all—added luster to the title Champion Golfer of the Year.

Number two, a burly, gravelly voiced, mustachioed fellow named Keith Mackenzie took over as secretary of the Royal and Ancient Golf Club, and made it his number one priority to cajole as many top Americans as possible into playing the Open each year. Vivid is my memory of Keith standing under the big tree at Augusta, florid-faced and perspiring heavily in his blue blazer in the Georgia heat, while doing his charming best to sell Hale Irwin or Craig Stadler on the delights of a week in Blackpool. And he was very good at it.

Number three, and most important, the R&A enlisted the services of Mark McCormack. A decade earlier Mark had established an association with the All England Club that had reaped immediate financial benefits for Wimbledon, and the same happened with the R&A, as he used his marketing magic to increase the rights fees from American television ten-fold. Up went the prize money and back came the American players.

TV'S RICHEST GAME SHOW

As more and more corporations aligned themselves with golf, the PGA Tour schedule became fully booked with sponsored tournaments from January through mid-October. But both viewers and advertisers wanted more, so the last ten weeks of the year became the repository for "unofficial events," made-for-television sideshows with a variety of formats—team play, match play, shootouts, skills competitions. It quickly became known as the "Silly Season."

The first and most successful of these was a brainstorm of IMG's television executive Barry Frank in partnership with former NBC Sports executive Don Ohlmeyer called the Skins Game. It began in 1983 with the foursome of Arnold Palmer, Jack Nicklaus, Gary Player, and Tom Watson.

The format was one played often by weekend golfers, a hole-by-hole competition where each player competes against the others. If, on a given hole, one player scores lower than everyone else, he wins the agreed-upon stake that has been anted up. It may be a quarter, a dollar, whatever. If, however, two or more players tie for low score, everyone gets a free ride to the next hole, when everyone antes again and the stake is doubled.

In IMG's version there were two big differences: number one, the money being played for was not the players' own cash, it was provided by the tournament organizers, and number two, it was big money—in year one, $360,000: $10,000 for each of the first six holes, $20,000 for each of holes seven through twelve, and $30,000 for each of the last six holes.

Since every hole was a mini-tournament, all four players went all out all the time, firing boldly at every flagstick, which made for plenty of drama. The show was a hit from the beginning and quickly spawned a spin-off on the Senior Tour, just in time to accommodate Messrs. Palmer and Nicklaus. An LPGA Skins Game followed, as did successful versions on the European and Australian Tours.

It was ironic that the inaugural Skins Game showcased the three players who had complained most vehemently to the commissioner about being deprived of moneymaking opportunities—and likewise fitting that none of the whiners was the winner, as Gary Player took home the most skins and $240,000.

But it was Fred Couples who earned the nickname Mr. Skins, in eleven appearances winning seventy-seven skins and $4,405,000. The Skins Game ran every Thanksgiving weekend for a quarter century, a longevity record for special events sports programming.

In short time the Open became a big attraction, so big that the R&A needed a way of determining which players around the world deserved invitations. Once again, Mark came to the rescue. In the mid-1960s he'd created a system of ranking the world's best professional golfers, and had published the year-end list in his annual book, *The World of Professional Golf*. By the early 1980s, however, the high level of competition worldwide called for an ironclad, independent ranking. In collaboration with the R&A, McCormack tweaked his mathematical model to become the Official World Golf Ranking.

The OWGR awarded points to players based on their performance over a rolling three-year period across all accredited international tours—the more points a player accrued, the higher his ranking. McCormack being McCormack, he immediately sold the idea to Sony, which became its title sponsor and paid for the weekly numbers-crunching. The OWGR was launched in April of 1986, and by the end of that year all four major championships had endorsed the system. Nearly forty years later it remains the standard.

Of course, as with anything proposed by Mark McCormack there were critics, and chief among them was the commissioner of the PGA Tour. "One of McCormack's goals was to get more of his international players into more tournaments so they could make more money so he could make more money. It wasn't altruistic," said Deane Beman.

Sorry, Deane, that potshot was unfair. Mark may have done a lot of things out of self-interest, but the OWGR was not one of them. Yes, he got

Sony as a commercial sponsor, but that barely paid for the staff required to compile and operate the system. Mark, a lifelong golf fan, simply believed there should be an objective, statistics-based way to rank the best players in the world. Tennis had such a ranking system, why not golf?

That said, it was serendipitous, when the first rankings appeared, that IMG client Bernhard Langer sat atop the list as the number one player in the world. By the end of that first year, it would be Greg Norman on top, a position he would maintain for most of the next ten years—331 weeks in all.

With Norman on board, my anxiety and self-pity from the loss of clients Ray Floyd and Lanny Wadkins had pretty much subsided. I was now back in aggressive prospecting mode. First on the list was a young man from Louisiana who, in 1983, his second year on Tour, had won a pair of big events—the Players and the PGA Championship. He'd also topped the money list and been named Player of the Year: Hal Sutton.

Enter—or I should say reenter—Fred Ridley. During his brief stint with IMG, Fred had played in the major amateur events as a way of scouting the top college talent, and one of the players he'd gotten close to was Sutton, who in 1980 was named *Golf* magazine's College Golfer of the Year despite playing for unsung Centenary College in his hometown of Shreveport. When a year later Sutton turned pro, he hired Ridley, back in private legal practice in Tampa, as his lawyer/agent. Fred soon realized he couldn't do for Hal the kinds of things IMG could, and he kindly steered Hal our way.

A few chats with Hal made it clear that he deferred all major decisions to his father, Howard, a hard-driving multimillionaire oilman who micromanaged his son's life. One day Hal approached me and said, "My dad would like to have a meeting with Mark McCormack."

In January of 1984 Mark and I flew to Shreveport and had a meeting with Howard and Hal. They were interested in what we could do, but didn't like the commissions we charged and thus were reluctant to commit to any sort of binding contract. Mark, as always, had a creative way to handle the situation and made them a Godfather proposal, an offer they couldn't refuse. A few days later I put it in writing in a letter to Hal from Mark:

January 17, 1984

Dear Hal:

I enjoyed seeing you and your dad in Shreveport.

We have agreed, rather than formalize anything at this time, that we will work for you as described below and will hope to formalize something more definitive toward the end of 1985 which will cover the future.

We confirm that we will undertake your exclusive worldwide business and career representation from now through the end of 1985. At the end of each calendar year, you will determine the fair value of the services that we have performed for you and will pay us what you reasonably feel these services have been worth.

You are aware that we generally represent our top golf clients on a basis of 20% across the board or, in some instances, 10% of prize money and 25% of merchandising and contractual income. I don't have to tell you how important it is that this arrangement be totally between you and ourselves, and that its uniqueness is the result of the rather unusual circumstances that you are in. I look forward to a long and mutually beneficial relationship between us.

Sincerely yours,
Mark H. McCormack

It wasn't the first time Mark had made such a proposal and it wouldn't be the last. He knew two things: (1) No other agent could afford to make such an offer and (2) IMG would deliver mightily from its end, and nine times out of ten the client was sufficiently honorable to reciprocate.

Hal eventually signed with us, and we did some good work for him, but the relationship was always strained because of his father. On one occasion Howard called and ordered me to report to Shreveport immediately for a sit-down. I flew down there, but didn't appreciate the way he was treating me or IMG. If the Suttons were going to constantly second-guess our management recommendations, why hire us in the first place?

After Hal's big 1983 season it would be more than two years before he won another tournament. That unexpected slump along with Howard's regular intrusion made for a difficult ride, and our relationship lasted only a few years.

Another player of interest was Jerry Pate. After turning pro in 1976 he had signed with Vinny Giles, but I'd heard he had grown restless, was looking to increase both his profile and his income. Dusty Murdock had struck up a friendship and had been wooing him, so when I got involved, I tried to stay in the background and keep things light.

Jerry was a character, a combination wise guy and free spirit. Although he'd won the U.S. Open as a rookie and then half a dozen other events, he was best known for winning the first Players Championship at the TPC Sawgrass—and then tossing both architect Pete Dye and Deane Beman into the lake beside the eighteenth green. He liked to have fun and could also laugh at himself, so that was the tone I took when dealing with him.

In one of our meetings, after he started boasting about something, I said, "Jerry, you are so full of shit. Face it, you got lucky, yanked a 5-iron at Atlanta Athletic Club, and won the U.S. Open." (On the seventy-second hole he'd famously struck a 196-yard 5-iron to within a couple feet.) "You were aimed too far right and pulled it tight to the pin. If you'd hit that shot where you were meant to be aiming, you'd have gone straight into the water!" Jerry was the rare kind of guy who could laugh at that sort of kidding and acknowledge that I wasn't far off in my analysis of his celebrated shot.

Toward the end of our courtship I skipped the hard-line pitch, just said, "Jerry, when the hell are you gonna smarten up and come to IMG!" He signed with us and remained a client for years before a series of injuries curtailed his playing career.

The only other player on my radar—and that of every other manager in the game—was Seve Ballesteros, the charismatic Spaniard who had burst on the scene in 1976 at the age of nineteen, finishing second to Johnny Miller in the Open Championship at Royal Birkdale. He went on to win the European Tour Order of Merit that year, and by 1983, his first season on the PGA Tour, had won an Open and two Masters titles with a daring, take-no-prisoners style that was part Arnold Palmer, part Zorro. Other than Greg Norman, he was the hottest attraction in golf.

Sadly we'd missed the chance to sign Seve on day one. Mark admitted it was probably his fault, part of his loss of focus while expanding the company. In those days he'd been spending a good deal of time in Spain at La Manga, a resort whose owner, Greg Peters, was a good friend of Mark's. Peters had alerted Mark about the young Spanish kid who looked like a future star, but Mark had not pursued it.

Rival Ed Barner had, and he'd represented Seve from 1975 until 1983, when the relationship soured and Seve had turned to fellow Spaniard and hometown friend Jorge Ceballos, who was not much of a businessman but had Seve's trust. Ceballos basically fielded proposals and did his best to protect Seve from profiteers.

Through a series of meetings with Ceballos I was able to get IMG a one-year trial with Seve for 1984. To launch things, I had what I thought was a great idea: "Seve across South America," a fall exhibition tour through five or six countries. Seve had never appeared on that continent and I was convinced the reception there would be rock-star level. With IMG's contacts throughout South America we could have put together a week of enormous appearance money in a language-friendly environment that I felt certain Seve would have enjoyed. But the timing conflicted with commitments he had at the end of '84 and I never got enough enthusiasm from Ceballos to schedule it for '85. Our deal ended after one year.

The relationship remained friendly, however, and we could still bring proposals to Seve on an ad hoc basis. At that time Nike was beginning to get into golf and I'd been able to get Strange and Jacobsen apparel and shoe deals, wearing the Nike Swoosh logo. Knowing Seve didn't have a hat deal in the U.S.—he generally avoided hats—I proposed to Nike a one-off, just for the Masters. They bit, and I got Seve $25,000 to wear a Nike visor for one week at Augusta, which I thought could lead to a full-blown relationship with Nike.

Well, for some reason, the visors Nike sent featured a logo never seen before or since—a weird-looking double Swoosh—one on top of the other. Check out an online video of the 1986 Masters tournament and see for yourself. A mistake by someone at Nike or purposely distinctive to draw attention?

Ninety-nine percent of the golf world remembers that Masters as the year Jack Nicklaus won the last of his six titles. What is generally forgotten is that Seve was leading the tournament until the fifteenth hole on Sunday, when he snap-hooked a 4-iron into the pond fronting the fifteenth green, making a bogey from which he never recovered.

I'm not sure why, but that hat deal was the last one we did with Seve. He was a notoriously superstitious guy, and like a lot of great players he believed his playing errors were caused by myriad things, but never himself. Maybe Seve reasoned, "It was that IMG deal for the stupid visor that made me hit the ball in the water." For whatever reason, shortly after that Masters Seve turned his business management over to his brother Manuel, and generally receded from the whole world of endorsements and commercial opportunities.

AN AGENT'S TEN COMMANDMENTS

1. Under promise, over deliver. Do what you say you're going to do. And more.
2. Sweat the details. If your client sees the small things taken care of, he/she develops confidence that you'll handle the big things well.
3. Be accountable. Take ownership of your mistakes. It builds your client's trust.
4. Tell your client what he needs to hear, not what he wants to hear.
5. Disclose conflicts of interest. Always.
6. Don't take it personally. If you're effective at what you do, 95 percent of the things said about you will be negative. Take the heat and, as best you can, ignore it.

7. Figure out the influencers in each client's life. Whom do they trust, listen to the most?

8. Let the person on the other side of the table talk before starting your pitch.

9. Always let the person you are selling to give you the number first. It often will be higher than what you have in mind.

10. And oh yeah—write everything down. The smartest guy I ever knew taught me that.

We may not have hit home runs with Messrs. Sutton, Pate, and Ballesteros, but we got in our licks and continued to reaffirm IMG's preeminent ability to attract and serve the game's best players. Despite an ever-growing number of competitors, our client list remained the strongest in the game, and with Greg Norman now at the top I was riding high again.

Then Candy told me she wanted a divorce.

I should have seen it coming, particularly since our marriage counseling sessions had been less than encouraging. The most sobering moment had come when the counselor said to us, "Given your radically different perceptions of marriage, you two had almost no chance." Expectations of married life, she told us, are formed from observing your parents—it's a subliminal thing, but very powerful—and Candy's home life could not have been more different from mine.

Her parents, artsy theatergoers, were madly in love for forty years. Mom Violet waited patiently for husband Al to return each weekday evening from his nine-to-five job as an Exxon engineer and they enjoyed their cocktail promptly at 5:30. Each was the most important part of the other's life. As for my parents, when I was born they were both forty years old. Dad was immersed in his work. They slept in different bedrooms. After my sister was born, they actually split up for a while before reconnecting and bringing me into the world. The classic "Let's stay together for the sake of the kids."

So I had that going for me. Adding to my dysfunction, I believe, was the almost exclusively male environment I'd inhabited for the first twenty-five years of my life. Exeter was all male. I was in the last all-male class admitted to Yale, and Harvard Business School was about 95 percent male. On top of that I'd spent several summers in the Army Reserves and had joined a company where virtually all the employees except the secretaries were men. I had no trouble relating to guys, but in the company of women I tended to be tentative, clueless, insecure, and awkward. My dating relationships, pre-Candy, had been few, brief, and shallow. Women were sex objects, probably because I never really had any as friends.

And then there was my job. Candy, to her eternal credit, had hung in there, done her best to raise two little girls while I was constantly on the road. Even when I was in Cleveland it was often difficult. Many was the evening I'd come home, settle down to dinner hoping to have a nice chat with my wife, and what happened? The phone rang—Curtis Strange or whoever needing to talk. I could have said I'd call him back in the morning, but often that client had an 8:15 a.m. tee time, so that wouldn't work. The hard truth was, when I was at the office my clients were on the golf course—their time to speak to me was frequently at night. So my workday never ended at a normal hour—and that took a toll. Candy's perception was that I loved my job more than her.

"You're a great father and a great provider, but you're a lousy husband," she said.

"Guilty, guilty, and guilty," I said, still hoping we could talk things out.

But Candy had made up her mind. That morning, when I realized she was serious about ending things, I got up from the breakfast table, walked out the front door, and ran—ran for ten miles. I guess I was running away.

Candy kept the house and I moved into a nearby home owned by McCormack. A nondescript place, it was often made available to new employees until they found permanent lodgings, but it was also sort of a safe house for the lost boys of IMG. It seemed that at any given moment someone in the office was going through marital strife, and it was especially pervasive among the top executives, all of whom were in the same sort of lifestyle I was. The marriages of Bob Kain, Ian Todd, Peter Johnson, and Alastair Johnston all ended while they were at IMG. Hell, even Mark got divorced, about a year after I did.

I'd like to say I handled my divorce well, but I didn't, and there was one particularly childish moment. The alimony agreement called for me to make an initial payment of $50,000. I actually took the time and trouble to write one hundred $500 checks for Candy to individually endorse. Then I took them over to her place. When she opened the door, I said, "Have fun with these," and tossed a wad of them into the air so they blew all over the front yard. She just stood there incredulous, laughing.

But the story wasn't quite over for me—there was insult to add to the injury. About a year later my direct report, Dusty Murdock, invited me to dinner. After an hour or so of small talk about work he cleared his throat and said, "I want you to know, I'm seeing Candy."

I was flabbergasted, unable to speak. He, of course, had a right to date my ex-wife and she him, but somehow it didn't seem right, coming from a guy I'd hired and mentored. I shoved my dinner plate across the table at him, got up, and walked out. (Leaving rather than facing moments of personal conflict had become my go-to way to cope.)

Dusty wisely left IMG shortly thereafter and married Candy in 1987, divorcing decades later. (Their new stepfather's demeanor troubled my young daughters from day one.) He and I remained members of the same golf club in Cleveland and unavoidably our paths crossed, neither of us giving so much as a nod to the other. One year we could have faced each other in the finals of the club championship. When Dusty learned I had won my semifinal match, he defaulted his before teeing off to avoid an ugly thirty-six-hole confrontation in the final.

In the nearly forty years since my divorce I've never remarried and have had few serious relationships, although there have been a couple that could be characterized as semi-comical. The first was with Sally Jenkins. If you recognize the name you're likely a sports fan or at least a fan of good sports-writing. Sally is the daughter of legendary writer and author Dan Jenkins and herself an award-winning writer for the *Washington Post.*

I'd known Sally casually from her years covering golf's major championships and we began dating in 1989. She was smart as a whip, knew golf as well as I did, and we hit it off immediately, seeing each other in Washington and at tournaments. The relationship reached its peak at the 1990 Open Championship at St. Andrews, which the two of us enjoyed mostly from my room at the Old Course Hotel.

Of course, I had known her father for many years, and at some point I felt the need to be open with him about Sally and me. One day I approached Dan and said something like "If you never speak to me again, I understand. I mean, among the aspirations you have for your daughter, I suspect dating a sports agent isn't among them." Dan, somewhat uncharacteristically, had no rejoinder, witty or otherwise.

In any case, the relationship with Sally lasted only a short time, just sort of fizzled out, and it was later rumored that she'd left me for a woman—further testimony, I suppose, to my chronic ineptitude as a paramour.

In 1986, not long after my divorce was finalized, IMG colleague Andy Pierce set me up with his wife's college roommate, Olwen Weatherhead. Our first date did not go well. My beloved Red Sox were playing in the World Series and I spent most of the evening with one eye on the television over the bar. Olwen also told Andy that I'd come across as too bitter over my just-concluded divorce. So I'd blown it again, a big blunder because Olwen was a knockout, super smart, and fun to be around.

We had a second date, but it didn't come until twenty-five years later, when a friend took another stab at matchmaking. By that time, Olwen had been married to the son of Cleveland Browns owner Art Modell. When the Browns left Cleveland for Baltimore, so did Olwen, following which David Modell, executive VP of Art's new team, left her for a Ravens cheerleader.

I made the trip to Baltimore, was one hundred percent attentive this time, over (almost) my divorce, and we clicked. Although we lived in separate towns, Olwen came back to Cleveland regularly to see her mother and two sisters and I made my way often to Maryland to see her and also play golf at Caves Valley, conveniently less than three miles from her house. Long story short, she eventually tired of living apart (and probably of me) and broke it off, saying she needed someone in her life full-time (although she didn't ask me to come live in Baltimore). It was sad, because I really liked her, and it was the first exciting relationship I'd had in forever.

Anyway, once she'd given me the news I sent her a couple of things. First, an email titled "Top 10 Reasons Olwen Dumped Hughes," which she said made her laugh so hard she nearly peed herself. Second, to make her feel better about giving me the ax, I wrote her a note: "Olwen, no big deal. I've been fired by the best in the world, I'm used to it."

6

Blond Ambition

Greg Norman won five events his first year with IMG and another five in 1984, including his first PGA Tour event, the Kemper Open. But it was the week after that win that he burst to worldwide prominence in the U.S. Open at Winged Foot, holing a forty-five-foot putt at the seventy-second hole to force an eighteen-hole playoff the next day with former Masters champion Fuzzy Zoeller. On that Monday morning I rode with Greg and Laura to the course. When we arrived, very few spectators were around, and workers were busy dismantling the tournament paraphernalia. Greg rolled down the window to get a better look and said, "This feels like a pro-am, not a major championship playoff."

Uh-oh, I thought, *I don't like the sound of that.*

Greg came out flat that afternoon, fell behind Zoeller early, and shot 75 to Fuzzy's 67. It was the first of many agonizing disappointments he would suffer in the major championships.

Reflecting a few days later on that morning at Winged Foot, I remembered a story Mark McCormack had told me about a similar situation. In 1965, Gary Player had faced an eighteen-hole playoff with Kel Nagle for the U.S. Open at Bellerive. At breakfast with Mark that morning, Player felt the same sort of day-after doldrums and decided he needed to get himself mentally pumped for the battle.

"Say something to make me mad," he said to Mark.

Ever prepared, Mark obliged: "Did you see that newspaper article that said you'd never win another major title?"

"Yes," said Gary, "that's a good one. Now make me madder."

"Okay," said Mark, "what about that guy who said you'd never win anything with those fiberglass-shafted clubs you're using?"

"That's a good one, too," said Player. Suitably incensed, he rose from the table, marched out the door, surged to a five-stroke lead after eight holes, and won the playoff by three.

At times, being a good agent requires much more than just drumming up deals. On that day at Winged Foot, I'd sensed Greg was a bit off, yet I hadn't said or done anything to help him get his head back in the game. On that day I hadn't done my best for my client.

The best I could muster was some postmortem consoling. "Look at it this way," I said. "You shouldn't have been in the playoff to begin with." He looked at me funny. "Listen, you made one of the great pressure putts in major championship history on eighteen green yesterday just to tie Fuzzy. That's what I'm going to remember, Shark." And I meant it.

I consoled myself with the knowledge that I had worked my tail off to maximize Greg's off-course income, and at times it seemed that making money—lots of it—was what really drove him.

In 1985 Greg had his first-seven-figure year, earning $1 million from endorsements, appearances, and licensing income. At the time, that threshold was unprecedented—only Palmer was in the same neighborhood. To commemorate the achievement, Greg gave me an expensive leather briefcase. In a business where such genuine appreciation from clients is rare, that gesture meant a lot to me. But as always when things were at their best, I had a foreboding: with a volatile guy like this, there was nowhere to go but south.

In 1986 Greg had the best year of his career—and the worst. His eleven victories—four in the U.S., three in the UK, and four in Australia—were arguably the finest single-season performance since 1945, the year of Byron Nelson's incredible eighteen wins, eleven of them in a row. Greg topped both the U.S. and Australian money lists, became the first player to win a million dollars worldwide in a single season, and finished the year ranked number one in the world. A dream season for any golfer.

But what Greg Norman is *really* remembered for in 1986 is his "Saturday Slam." In each of the four major championships he held the lead after fifty-four holes—playing in the final group on Sunday in the Masters, U.S. Open, Open Championship, and PGA Championship, perhaps the best chance since Nicklaus in 1972 of winning the single-season grand slam— but he won only the Open at Turnberry.

At Augusta, a birdie at the seventy-second hole would have won it for him, and although he'd faltered early in the round he'd roared back with birdies on fourteen, fifteen, sixteen, and seventeen, only to push-block his approach to the final green and make bogey to lose to Jack Nicklaus. In the U.S. Open at Shinnecock Hills, he'd staggered in with a 75 and finished six strokes behind Ray Floyd. And in the PGA at Inverness it was an even worse collapse—a 76—to finish second to Bob Tway. Tway had sealed his victory dramatically by holing a greenside bunker shot for birdie at the final hole. Half an hour later, sitting in front of his locker, Norman looked up at a handful of journalists, shook his head ruefully, and said, "And this is the game we all love . . ."

Bobby Jones once described golfers as "dogged victims of inexorable fate," and there was no more dogged a victim than Greg Norman. Despite his outward brawn and bravado, he became a tragic figure. Surely no professional golfer was ever thwarted more cruelly or repeatedly by one-in-a-million shots.

There was the Bay Hill Classic in 1990, where he was in the clubhouse, poised for a victory handshake from Arnold Palmer, when the last man with a chance to catch him, unsung rookie Robert Gamez, impossibly holed a 7-iron from 167 yards for an eagle to win by a stroke. A month later, on the final hole of the New Orleans Open, it happened again as South African David Frost blasted fifty feet out of a greenside bunker and into the hole, edging Norman by one.

But the most brutal moment came at the 1987 Masters—incredibly the first major following the Saturday Slam that had climaxed with Tway's killer bunker shot—when on the second hole of a sudden-death playoff, Larry Mize holed an inconceivably difficult pitch shot from 140 feet, depriving Greg of the title he wanted more than any other.

Predictably the press had their fun.

"Ever seen a Great White Shark eaten by an anchovy? Twice?" asked *Sports Illustrated*'s Rick Reilly. "Another catastrophe and you can look for Norman on the cover of *Psychology Today*."

"Greg Norman will lose the next U.S. Open when Joe Bob Zilch holes out a wedge from the top of a eucalyptus tree on the third extra hole in San Francisco," wrote Dan Jenkins. "Norman will lose the British Open when Sam Sausage holes out a wedge on the fifth extra hole from ten fathoms beneath the Firth of Forth hole at Muirfield. Norman will lose the PGA Championship in Palm Beach when Rex Shank holes out a wedge from a jewelry store on the seventh extra hole. Norman will then retire and autograph straitjackets for a living."

On a couple of occasions, after a few beers with Greg, I made my own feeble attempt to lighten things up.

"Well, at least you've made people forget about the only other guy in history to lose playoffs in all four majors . . .

"Larry Mize, Bob Tway, Mark Calcavecchia? C'mon, Shark, if this is going to keep happening, at least get some Hall of Famers on that list . . ."

My gallows humor didn't go down very well.

I'm not sure whether it was to Greg's credit or detriment, but he never admitted to any responsibility for the defeats he suffered, at least not to me. I think he took welcome refuge in his bad breaks, embraced the victim role, and thereby avoided the truth. Some great players do that—absolve themselves of any blame in order to keep themselves positive; others confront their mistakes and try to learn from them.

And if Greg chose to disavow his errors, so in time did just about everyone else. Everyone remembers Jack Nicklaus's stirring Augusta charge to victory at age forty-six; few recall Greg's fatally flared 4-iron from the middle of the fairway on eighteen that Sunday to make bogey and lose by one. Everyone remembers Bob Tway's bunker shot; few recall that Greg's score on the final nine at Inverness that day was 40. Everyone remembers Mize's miracle chip; few recall that Greg would have won that Masters in regulation had he not bogeyed two of his last three holes.

But if Greg will not take any measure of blame for his missed opportunities, I will, because once again I failed him.

When I renegotiated Greg's contract with Spalding, it was literally a huge deal. A five-year agreement, it called for him to carry the Spalding bag, play Spalding clubs, and along with two other Spalding staff players— Johnny Miller and Craig Stadler—introduce a brand-new product, the Spalding Tour Edition golf ball.

Spalding had for years dominated the market for weekend golfers with its Top-Flite ball, a two-piece (cover and core) model that produced maximum distance for those with lower swing speeds and also cost significantly less than the three-piece wound ball (cover, elastic winding, and core) made by Titleist, which was the preference of better golfers. The Tour Edition, constructed with new materials, was Spalding's attempt to break into that higher-end market. They predicted it would make the three-piece ball obsolete within five to ten years.

Greg began playing the ball in 1986 and immediately noticed it produced much more backspin on his iron shots, but felt it was something he could handle. He was a tinkerer, always fiddling with shafts, lofts, and lies, and he believed he could lessen the spin by tweaking his clubs.

Well, that didn't happen. Go back and look at video highlights from those painful major championship losses. Over and over again you'll see his second shots into par-4 holes land on the green, take a hop forward, and then zip back twenty or thirty feet, sometimes clear off the front of the green.

"How do I play to a back pin?" Greg complained to me. "If I throw it all the way back there and go a little long, I'm over the green and short-sided. If I play it safe to the back third of the green, it spins too much and I'm left with a twenty-five-footer!"

Curiously, neither Miller nor Stadler seemed to have the same problem with the Tour Edition. Maybe Greg's club tweaking had somehow exacerbated the spin thing, or more likely, his higher clubhead speed and steeper angle of attack were the cause. In any case, the ball was doing him harm, particularly on the firm, fast greens of the major championships.

At that moment, it was my duty to step in and do something, but I didn't. At first I told myself, *This guy is so much better than everybody else, it won't make a difference.* But when the problem persisted I continued to do nothing. What I should have done was get him out of that ball contract.

An agent's job begins with a solemn obligation that's akin to the physician's Hippocratic oath: above all else, do no harm. Every move you make for your client must be in the best interests of his competitive career, especially when it comes to the clubs and balls he's playing. It's hard enough for a player to succeed at the highest level of professional golf without being saddled with equipment that's inferior or doesn't properly fit his game.

It would have been difficult to walk away from Spalding, and it certainly would have been costly for both Greg and IMG, but we could have done it. I could have gone to Titleist and made a similar deal, or found an equipment company that didn't require him to play their ball, or better still, let Greg play the golf clubs of his choice with no compensation involved. That would have meant forsaking his most lucrative endorsement contract, but Greg had plenty of offsetting outside income thanks to the other deals I had concluded for him. Spalding might have sued us, but I doubt it, because the last thing they would have wanted was a high-profile legal battle over the alleged inferiority of their golf ball.

We simply should have walked away from the Spalding deal. As his agent I should have insisted on it. Now, had we done so, would Greg have won more majors with a ball he was more able to control? Maybe, maybe not. But greater success would, I think, have been inevitable, and that would have dwarfed many times over the loss of income from Spalding.

Mind you, Greg did not suffer while he was my client. For most of the eleven years he was with IMG he was the number one player in the world, with prize winnings of nearly $11 million. Over the same span we generated $50 million off the course for him—nearly five times what he earned playing golf, and far more outside income than any other golfer of that era.

GREG NORMAN'S INCOME WITH IMG

Year	Prize Money	Off-Course Income	Total Income	In Today's $
1983	$366,819	$439,765	$806,584	$2,475,557
1984	$533,405	$639,674	$1,173,079	$3,451,393
1985	$392,720	$906,572	$1,299,292	$3,691,281
1986	$1,146,584	$1,655,395	$2,801,979	$7,815,144
1987	$715,838	$3,653,850	$4,369,688	$11,758,577
1988	$957,497	$5,884,135	$6,841,632	$17,678,997
1989	$1,351,761	$6,909,626	$8,261,387	$20,366,387
1990	$1,457,378	$7,388,777	$8,846,155	$20,690,053
1991	$503,755	$7,463,711	$7,967,466	$17,882,398
1992	$1,240,771	$7,674,187	$8,914,958	$19,424,251
1993	$2,227,268	$7,363,676	$9,590,944	$20,289,725
TOTAL	**$10,893,796**	**$49,979,368**	**$60,873,164**	**$145,423,663**

Source: International Management Group 1993.

Over the same period, I became a close friend of both Greg and Laura. Greg and I traveled all over the world together, partnered twice in the AT&T Pebble Beach Pro-Am, and on many occasions he and Laura welcomed me and my daughters at their Florida home. My two girls were about the same age as their daughter, Morgan-Leigh, and son, Gregory, and the four kids got along well. In the wake of my divorce, being able to escape Ohio for Florida with the girls every now and then was truly a blessing. I'll never forget the kindness Greg and especially Laura showed us.

There were many good times, but a particularly happy occasion was the Sunday evening following Greg's victory at Turnberry. IMG had a great relationship with the Turnberry Hotel, and we were able to get rooms for most of our clients, as well as one for me, a suite for Mark, and a first-floor parlor, where we entertained all week. It was there that we held a champagne celebration for Greg, which was followed by dinner in the main dining room overlooking the course and the Irish Sea beyond. The partying went on past midnight, at which point Greg, drunk as much on happiness as champagne, felt the urge to return to the scene of his triumph. And so a small band of us—Greg, Laura, myself, and Lawrence Levy, a British golf photographer and close friend of Greg's—made our way down to the course, champagne bottles in hand, and plopped ourselves down on the surface of Turnberry's eighteenth green, staring up at the final scoreboard with Greg's name at the top. It was a magical moment. I don't think I've ever seen anyone enjoy a victory as much as he did that one.

OUT FOR A QUICK SPIN

Greg was the most flamboyant, self-confident, larger-than-life individual I ever met. He lived every day at full speed—overdrive, actually. Race cars, boats, surfing, cave diving, helicopter piloting, punishing workouts on the StairMaster. It was as if he always needed something to prove.

At the Memorial one year I asked *Sports Illustrated*'s talented golf writer Rick Reilly to join Greg and me for dinner. On the way there, Greg driving, his love for sports cars came up—specifically a recent experience he'd had with Formula 1 pal Nigel Mansell doing U-turns on a racetrack at high speed.

"Yeah right, Greg," Reilly and I responded.

With that, Greg accelerated our tournament courtesy car (not exactly designed for high-performance maneuvers) and—before it dawned on Reilly and me what was about to happen—in the blink of an eye we were going 180 degrees the other direction. Reilly, stunned, couldn't speak. I nearly threw up in the back seat. Neither of us could believe what had just happened. That was life with the Shark.

With a major championship finally under his belt Greg was more marketable than ever, and with professional golf continuing to grow in popularity around the world with both fans and sponsors, the timing was perfect. Every event on the European and Australasian Tours wanted him in the field, and I did my best to capitalize.

When David Inglis, the promoter of a tournament called the Australian Classic, found out our asking price was more than the first prize of 180,000 Australian dollars ($120,000 U.S.), he went public with it. "Norman Doesn't Come Cheap" read the headline in a Melbourne paper, and the story was picked up around the world. When I told Mark about this, he said, "I hope you didn't lower your price." I didn't. Inglis paid and Greg played.

When I told another Australian promoter there was no way Greg could play his event, that he wanted that week off, the promoter said, "What would it take to get him?"

"Half a million Australian dollars [$333,000 U.S.]," I said, assuming that would be the end of the conversation.

"Done," said the guy without batting an eye. When I called Greg, his reaction was "How can we turn that down?" We didn't.

No client in my experience loved making money more than Greg. As time went on I sensed the dollar becoming Greg's way to keep score, particularly as his major championship performances kept falling short of expectations. Money validated him, as did the things he bought, among them seven Ferraris, three successively larger airplanes, a 218-foot yacht, and a twelve-thousand-acre ranch.

Back when things were really rolling for him, he'd be in a tournament locker room and call out to a player, say Payne Stewart, "Hey, Payne, you with IMG?" Stewart would then grumble something derogatory about IMG or me. There would be a pause, after which Greg would say in a loud voice, "Guess you don't like money, huh?"

Another time, a player in the locker room observed that he'd never seen anyone hit so few practice balls before a tournament round. Greg's response: "It doesn't take much to warm up a Rolls-Royce, mate!" Such swagger made Greg less than popular among his peers, and he did little to undo their perception. As Fred Couples said recently, "Greg has been hated for 25 years."

Couples was referring to Greg's role as CEO and commissioner of LIV Golf. Looking back, it was almost inevitable that Greg would find his way to such a position. He was a polarizing figure from the start of our relationship. Ultra-aggressive with no second gear, constantly needing an adrenaline rush. Little concern or tolerance for others, always convinced he was right. Confrontational, loved a fight, never backed down. And on top of all of that, a consuming need to be visible and relevant.

By the end of the 1980s Greg's superstar status was such that I thought we could build an entire tournament around him. Beating the corporate bushes, I stirred interest from a prominent if unlikely sponsor— McDonald's. It ended up being one of my most productive negotiations—a lucrative endorsement deal, with the famed Golden Arches logo on Greg's apparel, and a multimillion-dollar commitment from McDonald's as title sponsor of a new limited-field event in California, the Shark Shootout, which quickly became a highlight of the PGA Tour's fall calendar, generating significant annual contributions to Ronald McDonald Children's Charities.

The last piece of that puzzle was finding the site for the event, and Greg and I secured it in a meeting with David Murdock, the billionaire chairman of Dole Foods. Murdock was also the owner/developer of Sherwood Country Club, a lavish new golf community in Thousand Oaks, California, with a championship-caliber course designed by Jack Nicklaus, and it was there that we got together. Murdock instantly saw the value of the television exposure the Shark Shootout would bring to his property and signed a multiyear agreement to host the event.

Following that meeting Greg and I took a short helicopter ride down the Pacific coast on a gorgeous California afternoon to LAX, where we caught a nonstop Qantas flight to Sydney. We had side-by-side seats in first class, and both of us were ready to sleep, but for whatever reason we drank beer, watched movies, and laughed the entire eleven hours. At Sydney Airport, Australian media mogul Kerry Packer's driver whisked us to Packer's spectacular flat, where he graciously let Greg and me stay whenever in Sydney.

It was all pretty heady stuff, and I will admit to being seduced, both by the Greg Norman lifestyle and his jaunty brand of hubris, an attitude that he deserved it all. Indeed I sometimes started to think I deserved similar treatment. On one level, I knew I was nothing more than a glorified caddie, a gofer to the stars, but it was hard not to delude myself that I was also more than that. I was a rainmaker, the guy who crafted images and made fortunes for players. It was not for nothing that *Golf Digest* had twice included me among the thirty-six most powerful people in the game.

That was more or less my state of mind on the day, not long after the Australia trip, that Greg proposed to me—asked me to leave IMG and work exclusively for him. Equally shocked and flattered, for a brief moment I envisioned myself as the chief operating officer of Great White Shark Enterprises. But that fantasy quickly gave way to the reality that this was a bad idea, especially for Greg.

"You're doing much better with me at IMG than you would with me as your in-house guy," I said. And I meant it.

Fundamentally, Greg was feeling insecure. "Your loyalty is not to me," he said, "because McCormack's the one signing your checks."

Actually, I'd been totally loyal to him—in one instance, loyal to a fault.

During his worldwide travels Greg had become enamored of a twenty-two-year-old Australian model named Kirsten Kutner then living in Hong Kong. He couldn't use his home phone or cell phone to call her, lest Laura find out, and one day he said to me, "Huey, lend me your phone," and told me why.

Talk about agent conflicts of interest. If I give him the phone, I become complicit in his cheating on Laura, a wonderful woman whose friendship I greatly valued. If I don't give him the phone, he'll question my loyalty to him, maybe even fire me.

Reluctantly, I handed him the phone, and later gave him my billing information as well so he could charge calls to my number—thousands of dollars of calls for which I would never be reimbursed.

I have regretted that decision, that betrayal of Laura, since the moment I made it. For years it haunted me, as Greg continued the affair with Kutner, then began another one, even more egregious, with tennis star Chris Evert. Greg had become great friends with former pro skier Andy Mill, Chris Evert's husband, and the two couples socialized often and spent a lot of time together. When in 2007 Greg dropped the divorce bomb on Laura to run off with Chrissie, Andy was every bit as devastated as Laura, having been betrayed by both his wife and his best friend.

The Norman-Evert marriage lasted only fifteen months, as Greg continued seeing Kirsten Kutner, who eventually became his third wife. It was not until years later, when the internet gossip site RadarOnline went public with the story of Greg's philandering, that I opened up and apologized to Laura.

She could not have been more gracious. "I know you were sorry," she said. "I kind of thought you knew what he was doing and were caught in the middle. All is forgiven."

So when Greg had asked me to come work for him, the notion of loyalty was just as front of mind for me as it was for him. Over the ensuing months he would repeat his proposal more than once, and each time my answer was the same: "Thanks but no thanks."

My ultimate loyalty was to IMG. I loved my job, and although Greg was my number one client, there were always other prospects on my radar, and as Greg was making his mark, two future Hall of Famers became our clients. The first was Mark O'Meara. A Southern California kid, he was an All-American at Long Beach State, and in 1979 had won the U.S. Amateur, defeating John Cook in the thirty-six-hole final by a score of 8 and 7. Back then I'd made an overture to him, but he'd already been lured by another management agency. By 1985, however, he'd lost his confidence in them and we were able to lure him to IMG, which turned out to be great timing for us, as Mark won both the Bing Crosby and the Hawaiian Open that year.

I assigned him initially to another IMG exec, but O'Meara later insisted that I handle him personally—it was important to him that the top agent be his guy—and despite having my hands full I was happy to comply. Mark was liked by just about all his peers and was also vocal in the locker room, and I figured if I could do a good job for him, IMG would reap the benefits when he spoke positively about us to other players. He was also someone who didn't mind doing a lot of international travel, so we kept him running, with the result that he not only banked a boatload of appearance money, but notched several victories in Europe, Asia, Australia, and South Africa.

A BIG MISS

During the height of the Greg Norman era I heard about a wild character on the Nike (now Korn Ferry) Tour who allegedly hit the ball miles farther than anyone in pro golf. Back then my old stomping grounds, Portland, Maine, had a Nike event, and one summer when I'd gone back there on vacation I decided to drive over to the tournament site, The Woodlands Club, to have a look for myself.

I went to the range, hoping to catch this kid bombing a few tee shots. Not there. Next I went to the first tee to watch his group tee off. No show. I asked an official why he'd missed his tee time. "We haven't heard from him," was the reply. I didn't think much of it, as that happens every once in a while on all the pro tours.

The next morning I found out why. A headline in the *Portland Press Herald* read: "Pro Golfer Arrested after Late Night Bar Altercation, Jailed Overnight for Drunk and Disorderly."

That sort of diminished my interest in ever signing this guy. My bad. A couple of years later, John Daly made history, winning the 1991 PGA Championship at Crooked Stick after squeaking into the field Wednesday night as the eighth alternate—something that never happens. (Typically at major championships, only two or three alternates are lucky to get in—often it's zero.)

Daly was not at the tournament site when he got the call, so he'd hopped into his car and driven all night from Arkansas to Indiana, arriving Thursday on no sleep, with no caddie, and no familiarity with the golf course. He then posted a seventy-two-hole total of 12 under par to win the title by three strokes.

Most frustrating of all, he had just signed with another agent. I'd dropped the ball big-time, forgetting something McCormack had said to me years earlier. "Going back to George Bayer in the 1950s or even earlier, the game's longest hitter has always been marketable."

The other star who joined IMG in the late 1980s was Colin Montgomerie, although—hard as this may be to believe—I first met him the day he came to my office in Cleveland to interview for a job.

Colin was from Ayrshire, Scotland, where his father, James, was the longtime club secretary at Royal Troon. Like a lot of talented young international golfers of the time, he'd sought his education in the U.S., enrolling in Houston Baptist University, where he'd played solid if not eye-catching golf while earning a joint degree in business and sports management law. His father, not keen on seeing another member of the family toil in the golf world, had encouraged Colin to seek a real job.

Colin phoned IMG's London office and they suggested he come and see me. So one morning at the door of my office there he stood in his coat and tie, a big cherub-cheeked lad with curly blond hair. He was well spoken, well mannered, a smart young man with a good sense of humor, and I liked him instantly. Back in London, IMG's European managing director Ian Todd was looking for some help with the management of newly signed young clients Nick Faldo, Sandy Lyle, and Ian Woosnam, and this kid seemed like the perfect fit.

I made a call to Ian, who arranged to meet with Colin the following week at Turnberry, where IMG was running a pro-am. The plan was for Colin to come down and play in the event with Ian and a couple of other IMG guys. Well, somehow signals got crossed regarding the tee time, and by the time Colin arrived, Ian and the two others had already finished the front nine, having drafted one of the Turnberry staff pros to fill in. Colin quickly put on his shoes and raced to the tenth tee just in time to catch them. He then proceeded to play the back nine of Turnberry in twenty-nine strokes—7 under par—all the while chatting merrily with his prospective employers.

In the clubhouse afterward, word got around quickly about the chubby kid who'd shot lights out. At one point, Ian leaned in to Colin and said, "Honestly, lad, I think we should be talking about working for you instead of you working for us." To this day, Colin cites that as the moment he decided to turn pro.

Less than a year later Colin Montgomerie was named the European Tour's Rookie of the Year. Then in 1989 he won the Portuguese Open by eleven strokes, launching a career that would produce fifty-four tournament victories around the world. Colin played on eight Ryder Cup teams and finished number one on the European Tour Order of Merit a record seven consecutive years. Bottom line: as fine an agent as Colin surely would have become under my brilliant tutelage, I doubt that a career at IMG would have come close to the one he had as a professional golfer.

Greg Norman's single biggest contract was with Spalding. I'd negotiated a pair of five-year renewals in 1983 and 1988, and as a third renewal approached I'd been going back and forth with Spalding's senior executives. We'd finally reached an agreement on a groundbreaking deal, starting at $1 million a year—three times the previous renewal and more than any other golfer in the world was making on golf equipment—with escalators and performance bonuses to ensure Greg remained the highest paid. Then, at the eleventh hour, came the oddest phone call I ever received.

"Sorry, Hughes, the deal is off," my Spalding counterpart announced.

"What are you talking about? We've reached an agreement on every point!"

"I know," he said, "but George just vetoed the deal." George was George Dickerman, Spalding's president.

"On what grounds? We've been finalizing this for months!"

"George decided he just can't have one of our athletes making more money than he does."

Beyond bizarre. Wouldn't that have occurred to the guy way earlier in the process?

When I passed the news on to Greg, he was far less disappointed than I was. For one thing, no Spalding contract meant no Tour Edition ball to deal with. For another, Greg was always looking for a bigger, better deal, the next big opportunity, the next jackpot, and as arrogantly self-confident as he'd become, I think he may have seen the collapse of the Spalding deal as an omen, a sign that it was time for him to make something happen on his own.

Instead, he just got lucky. Out of nowhere one day Greg got a call from an old Aussie friend, Tom Crow. A former Australian Amateur champion, Crow in 1973 had started the golf equipment company Cobra, which had made its mark with the introduction of one of the first utility clubs, the Baffler, essentially a 3-wood with two bars on the sole that helped weekend golfers escape from thick grass and rough. Crow and his partner, car dealer Gary Biszantz, were now looking to take Cobra to the next level and they saw an alliance with Greg as the key.

Cobra couldn't come close to matching the Spalding endorsement money. In fact they wanted money from Greg—a $2 million investment in exchange for a 12 percent stake in the company. Greg would also become a director of the company and its national spokesman.

I recommended against it. I thought it was too big a risk on a company that hadn't proved itself, but Greg, always a risk-taker, was determined. This was the guy, after all, who as a young $32-a-week assistant pro back in Australia had regularly bet as much as $1,000 on himself against all comers. I then proposed that IMG contribute some percentage of his investment—share in the risk as well as any profit that may result—but the Cobra guys wanted none of that.

Well, I'll be the first to admit, Greg made a great move. In 1992, Cobra introduced the King Cobra oversized irons, which became the bestselling iron set in golf. That success attracted the attention of American Brands, owner of Titleist and Foot-Joy, which bought Cobra in 1996 for $700 million. Norman's $2 million thus returned $44 million for five years of work.

When the news of that windfall reached me I suggested to Greg that, in fairness to our relationship, he make a payment to IMG of $1 million in recognition of the commissions we'd lost out on because of the unorthodox nature of the Cobra endorsement contract, but Greg refused, citing a general animosity toward Mark and IMG. I then suggested that if he didn't want to pay IMG directly he could pay me the $1 million (which I would then have quietly redirected to IMG). Greg misunderstood this overture and accused me of personally trying to profiteer. How dumb would I have had to be to try to pull off something like that!

The Cobra experience had sent a message—Greg was taking a stronger hand in his own affairs. A few months earlier there had been a foreboding of that message during a meeting with another one of his biggest contracts—Reebok.

Greg and I were at Reebok headquarters in Boston for the type of review meeting I encouraged clients to do annually with their major licensees. After presentations from Reebok personnel on upcoming apparel/golf shoe plans and promotions, the last of which was attended by CEO Paul Fireman, we were done for the day.

As we left the meeting and headed down a hallway, Greg approached Fireman and said, "Can I have a word with you?" I continued walking alongside until Greg turned to me and said, "Hughes, this is just me and Paul." Boom, it hit me. The handwriting was on the wall. When your client starts meeting with companies on his own without you there, he has clearly lost trust in his agent—the most important element of a relationship.

Greg's contract renewal with IMG was up at the end of 1992 and he chose neither to renew nor terminate it. Instead we proceeded in a sort of contractless limbo. We continued offering him opportunities, and he continued considering them, and things proceeded that way for a year. Then in December of 1993, during the week of another tournament we'd developed with Greg's name on it—the Greg Norman Holden Classic—in Australia, Greg asked to have a meeting with me, IMG's Australia chief James Erskine, and Frank Williams, the manager of our Melbourne office.

The four of us assembled in his suite at a downtown hotel in Sydney. Greg, characteristically, got straight to the point. "As you all know, I've not been happy for some time, so I've decided to cut my ties with IMG. Frank has accepted a position with me and he will also be leaving."

Those words hit me like a cannonball. I was speechless, just sat there and stared at him. The guy who had been not only my number one client but my close friend for more than a decade—the guy for whom I'd produced $50 million of income—had just fired me. Granted, there had been warning signs—the tension over the Cobra deal, the brush-off with Paul Fireman—and I suppose I should have been expecting a bomb to drop, but I just couldn't conceive of Greg ever leaving IMG.

Sensing it was over, but desperate to come up with something brilliant to change Greg's mind, I finally spoke up. "Greg, think about a couple of guys you respect. Nicklaus left IMG with the best intentions. A couple of near-bankruptcies later, does Jack now think he did the right thing? And you saw what Lee Trevino said to a reporter the other day? 'The biggest mistake I ever made was not signing with Mark McCormack when I had the chance.'"

It made him stop for a second, but not for long. Shark's mind was made up. Sayonara.

In the years since, I've gained some perspective. It becomes almost inevitable in our business that players at the very top consider going solo. When athletes reach the pinnacle, they tend to become victims of their own success, developing a sense of empowerment and entitlement. They say to themselves, "I can do this. I've sat in the meetings, read the contracts. I can run my own empire and save millions in management fees."

Mark had seen it happen with Jack Nicklaus. I'd seen it with Tom Watson. Did either of them make the right decision? Who's to say? For some players, the freedom to call their own shots is what matters. In the case of Nicklaus, however, the financial history suggests that he made a huge mistake. In addition to barely skirting bankruptcy Jack became embroiled in litigation with various associates and business partners. By contrast, Arnold Palmer remained with IMG his entire career, had little business stress, and banked several hundred million dollars. As for Watson, as I've said earlier, few if any golf stars of the modern era have been less successful in capitalizing financially on their playing achievements.

I guess my real problem with Greg's decision to leave was the way he handled it. "Let's make this friendly" were the last words he said to me in that Sydney hotel, but not long after that he sent a scathing letter to Mark complaining about how he'd been treated by IMG—not by me personally, but in general. Mark was incensed by the tone of that letter. I remember him drawing the parallel to Nicklaus's departure, how Jack had conducted himself with class all the way through the process. It prompted Mark to write a return letter to Norman, essentially telling him that he ought to be ashamed of himself.

In his autobiography, *The Way of the Shark*, Greg wrote, "I could see early on that IMG was not interested in building equity in somebody else's brand. They did a commendable job presenting me with income-generating opportunities, but weren't helping me build equity in my own brand." In an interview with *Golf World* he was even more brazen: "Even Joe Soap from down the street could have made me a lot of money. Quite honestly, I was the hottest property in golf."

Norman also saw himself—still does, as evidenced by his LIV role— as a brilliant businessman, but there is little evidence to back that up. He once said to me, "Huey, if it flies, floats, or fucks, rent it." So what did this budding business tycoon do? He bought several Gulfstream jets, built a humongous oceangoing yacht, and is now on his third wife. What, after all, is Greg Norman's legacy as a businessman—peddling Wagyu beef and the wines of other vintners? Designing overly difficult courses that often needed to be redesigned? Getting fired as a commentator for Fox Sports because, in their words, "he didn't prepare adequately for the broadcasts"? No, surely it will be his ill-conceived, megalomaniacal obsession with the notion of an elite world golf tour.

Earlier in this narrative I referenced Mark McCormack's Second Tour idea, first proposed in 1964 and documented in his biography of Arnold Palmer, and then raised again in 1976 at a meeting with me and a handful of IMG colleagues. The idea had been killed, certainly the first time and as nearly as I can surmise the second, by Arnold out of his loyalty to the PGA.

Several times during the course of my eleven-year relationship with Greg, I shared with him the details of Mark's idea—the elite field, the limited number of events, the huge purses, the TV and sponsorship aspects—all of it. As someone who loved playing golf around the world—and for lots of money—Greg was mesmerized by the concept every time we talked about it.

At the time, a voice in my head told me I probably shouldn't be sharing all this, and as it turned out that voice was right, but not for the reason I then thought—that I was betraying Mark's confidence. All of us in that 1976 IMG meeting had been sworn to secrecy. I guess I justified my loose lips with the conviction that the world tour idea would never fly—if McCormack couldn't make it work, no one would.

Imagine my surprise in 1994—one year after Greg left us—seeing him pontificate about "his" concept for a world tour. "I had this idea, how do we get the best players to play against each other on more of a regular basis and give them an annuity into the future. I just thought there was a better way, a World Golf Tour where they could have ownership. That's thinking outside the box. Like an entrepreneur. Understanding the marketplace."

Except, of course, it wasn't his idea, it was Mark's as conveyed by me. The blueprint Greg laid out, in alliance with tournament operator John Montgomery, could have been photocopied from Mark's manifesto.

And just like Mark's idea, it never happened. In his haste to launch the idea, with a press conference at his Shark Shootout tournament in November of 1994, Norman made a major strategic error by trying to blindside the PGA Tour. At the last minute Tour officials got wind of what he was up to and preempted him, holding a player meeting the day before his press conference during which several players spoke up against the idea. The overall tone was "This is a bad idea, a Greg Norman idea that is about Greg Norman and for Greg Norman."

The *New York Times* ran a poll showing that not one of the top thirty players supported it. In *Shark*, a biography of Greg, Lauren St. John wrote, "The reaction of the golf community to Norman's World Tour was outrage. While it was generally agreed it would provide a much-needed wake-up call to the smug complacency of the other tours, most people believed that greed lay at its heart. Any way you painted it, it perpetuated the wealth and success of an already elite minority, glorified Norman, damaged the other tours and the image of the game, and cheapened the majors and the competition."

But it was the man who spoke last and most passionately at that 1994 player meeting who ultimately killed the idea—just as he had twice before—Arnold Palmer.

At age 65 Arnie was still fit enough to be included in the exclusive Shark Shootout field, albeit as a largely ceremonial figure. More important, he held the deep respect of every player in the room.

"Greg," he began, "have you ever heard of the Big Three? How many times do you think we were approached with a plan like this? More than I can count. Do you know why we always said no? Because it would have been bad for the game and bad for the fellas. You guys are young and have a lot of golf in front of you. You can do what you think is best, but I don't want any part of this."

And with that he rose and walked out of the room.

Norman claimed to be stunned by Arnie's remarks. "I had never had a conversation with him about any of this prior to his speech. It was one of the most disappointing moments of my life," he wrote in *The Way of the Shark*. Clearly he'd forgotten, or more likely chosen to dismiss, my telling him years earlier of Arnold's long-standing opposition to the World Tour—such would have been consistent with Greg's arrogance.

It was an embarrassing setback for Greg and he would harbor a bitter animus toward the PGA Tour for more than a quarter century before resurfacing with "his idea" three years ago, this time under the guise of Saudi-backed LIV Golf. And this time he would enjoy eighteen months of fleeting, artificial success before suffering the greatest public humiliation of his life, when during a Congressional hearing it was revealed that his dismissal as CEO of LIV Golf would be a mandatory condition of any PGA Tour agreement with the Saudis.

Incidentally, I don't know whether it was Greg who came up with the name LIV—the three roman letters standing for the fifty-four-hole format—whether he did or not, a delicious irony lies therein: had professional golf tournaments been contested at fifty-four holes instead of seventy-two, Greg Norman would have won five more major championships.

Back when he severed his ties with me, someone who knows him intimately reminded me that Greg's history is moving on, with no regard for the people who have supported him along the way.

"He feels that everything he's done, he's done completely on his own," this person said.

"Look up narcissistic personality disorder: *a mental condition in which people have an inflated sense of their own importance, a deep need for excessive attention and admiration, trouble with relationships, and a lack of empathy for others.*"

That, sadly, is the true way of the shark—a word, incidentally, that is widely agreed to have come from the Dutch *schurk*, meaning villain or scoundrel (as in card shark, loan shark), applied only later to the sea creature because of its predatory behavior.

As damaging as Greg's abortive World Tour fiasco was to him personally, it served a purpose for his Tour-playing brethren by suggesting that more could and should be done to capitalize on the growing global popularity of professional golf by providing additional high-profile playing opporunities. A number of such intiatives had begun, and one of them had come from IMG.

Our proposal was to pit the holder of the Ryder Cup (but not necessarily the same twelve players as on that team) against a team from the Southern Hemisphere (Australia, New Zealand, South Africa, South America, and the Pacific Islands) in a biennial competition tentatively titled the Hemisphere Cup. The idea was to showcase the likes of Norman, Zimbabwe's Nick Price, and Fiji's Vijay Singh, who were ineligible for the Ryder Cup, not being native to either the U.S. or Europe. We lined up television partners in ABC Sports, Sky TV in Great Britain, and Star Television in Hong Kong, but the idea never got off the ground because PGA Tour commissioner Deane Beman beat us to the punch with a few ideas of his own.

Beman, like Mark, had seen the growing popularity of the Ryder Cup and he wanted to enlarge it into a three-way competition with a third team comprising the best players from the rest of the world. In order to make that work, however, he needed to secure the American rights to the Ryder Cup, and they were held firmly by the PGA of America, which had no interest in relinquishing them, so the idea never gained traction.

What did emerge was Beman's other idea, the Presidents Cup, a biennial match between teams from the U.S. and the rest of the world (excluding Europe) played in alternative years to the Ryder Cup. In a matter of just a few weeks, Beman got Presidents Ford and Bush to back the idea, then got the approval of his policy board, and in April of 1994 announced that the event would be held that September. It was an extremely tight time frame for such an event. As one Tour executive quipped, "All we were missing was a golf course, a sponsor, the format, and the field." But it all came together at the Robert Trent Jones Golf Club in Virginia, where the U.S. won, 20–12, the first of many American routs in what has sadly become a competition as lopsided as the early Ryder Cup.

On the final day of that inaugural Presidents Cup came the announcement that a federation had been formed among the world's five PGA Tours—U.S., Europe, South Africa, Japan, and Australasia—for the purpose of conducting major competitions involving the world's top players. What ensued was the World Golf Championships, five $4-million tournaments, one of them a match-play event, that were staged mostly in the U.S. from 1999 to 2023. The stated purpose of these championships was to help grow the game around the world, but there is little evidence they did anything beyond swell the bank accounts of the game's stars.

THE PERFECT MARRIAGE

I was out running early one morning at the 1989 Shark Shootout when a car pulled up alongside me, the window rolled down, and the driver said, "You are my hero. I've got to get out and do more of that."

Behind the wheel was Jim Nantz. He'd been an IMG broadcasting client for several years, but I'd met him for the first time only the night before. That morning, I was surprised he'd remembered my name let alone stopped to say something so gracious, but I've since learned that's exactly who Jim Nantz is. The brief chat we had that morning was the beginning of a friendship that endures to this day. I don't think there's anyone in the world I'm prouder to call a friend.

A few years after that first encounter I phoned Jim with a deal I'd put together with Titleist CEO Wally Uihlein.

"Jim," I began, "we have an offer for you to become the voice of Titleist, do all their commercials . . ." and was about to explain why I thought it would be such a good thing, when he said, "Are you kidding me? The number one brand in golf? How could I say no to that! What are we talking about?"

"They want you to do two recording sessions a year, each of which will require about two hours of your time—just simple voice-over stuff—and an occasional sales meeting appearance."

"And what's the number?"

"Two hundred and fifty thousand dollars a year."

There was a long silence. I'll never forget Jim's next words.

"Hughes," he said, "I can't do that."

"What are you talking about?"

"It's not fair to them. It's too much money."

It was the first and only time I ever heard those words from a client. But that's Jim Nantz.

He was honestly reluctant until I said, "Jim, you are worth every cent of it. Wally is the smartest guy in the golf business and the truth is they're getting a bargain because just as they're number one in their field, so are you—it's the rare perfect marriage of two leading brands."

Jim Nantz and Titleist recently marked their twenty-fifth anniversary. Don't be surprised to see the relationship continue for a few more decades.

Mark McCormack's Hemisphere Cup may have been beaten by Deane Beman's Presidents Cup, but during the 1980s there weren't many business competitions McCormack lost. In 1990, *Sports Illustrated* annointed him the Most Powerful Man in Sports. The opening paragraphs of E. M. Swift's eight-thousand-word profile provide a vivid snapshot of just how far IMG had come since Mark's handshake with Arnie.

It is, quite simply, the most powerful, farsighted, far-reaching (some would say grabby) corporation in the world of sport: International Management Group, the company that people love to hate.

Not its clients, of course, who would never refer to IMG with any four letters other than R-I-C-H. Not the Chris Everts and Greg Normans and John Maddens, whom IMG has helped make as wealthy as sheiks by arranging their commercial endorsements and managing their finances. Not the Wimbledons and USGAs and Albertville Olympic Committees, whose coffers are overflowing thanks in large measure to IMG's handling of their licensing, merchandising, and television contracts. Not even the Hertzes, Rolexes and Nestlés, corporations that fork out small fortunes to sponsor IMG-run events, rent IMG tents, and have outings with IMG clients. Nope, all those folks will turn blue in the face telling you how honest, innovative, and dependable IMG—specifically, Mark Hume McCormack, its founder and chief executive officer—is to deal with.

But many members of the business community who have never made a deal with McCormack are wary of his reputation as a shrewd negotiator, and vaguely mistrust the personal style and motives of the man who six years ago wrote the best-selling business advice book *What They Don't Teach You at Harvard Business School.* "My stomach tells me that McCormack is the ultimate hustler, that he will use you to the nth degree," says the head of one Fortune 500 company, whose misgivings about McCormack have kept him from taking the IMG plunge. "There's something shady and unattractive about him—he doesn't give much eye contact. I wish I could be more specific. It's just a feeling I have."

Many in the media are similarly antagonistic toward IMG. The company's agents, like all sports agents, vigilantly shield their biggest clients from all but a handful of interviews. What sets many IMG agents apart is the supercilious manner in which they often deal with the press and public relations people, expending an absolute minimum of courtesy. "The worst thing about being represented by IMG is always having to defend it," says one former client, Greg Lewis, a sportscaster for NBC. "It's like having a tattoo."

And just about everyone vilifies IMG for being, well, too all-encompassing and powerful, with tentacles that reach into the backwaters where sport and the dollar meet. Whose idea do you suppose it was to spread the Olympic Games, Summer and Winter, over three weekends instead of two, as was first done at Calgary in 1988? Who invented the corporate tent for major sports events, those portable entertainment centers just off the 10th tee or just beyond center court, which have been sprouting like mushrooms after a rain ever since the '74 Wimbledon championships? Who made commonplace the practice of paying golfers appearance fees—sums that are often greater than the first-place money at the tournament in which the golfer is to play—to lure American stars to the European, Japanese, and Australian tours? The answer to all these questions is IMG.

IMG employs more than 1,000 people in 43 offices in 20 countries. Its revenues have increased from $25 million in 1975 to a projected $707 million in '90. IMG revenues grew 430% during the '80s, and while IMG officials expect, even want, that expansion to slow—they only recently lifted a six-month hiring freeze—their company is so well positioned internationally that a significant cooling-off period is not in the forecast. "The company is growing in immense leaps, almost too fast," says McCormack, 59 and still very much the man at the helm, although he has passed much of the day-to-day operating decisions to his top level of managers. "But it's hard to stop it, because if there's an opportunity and you don't fill it, someone else will, and you're creating unnecessary competition."

Mark loved expanding IMG. He never really cared about big annual profits. Since his company was owned by him, with no quarterly reports to shareholders, he figured profit didn't matter, especially since he never planned to sell the company. Revenue is what mattered on his scorecard—revenue to spend on more offices and new projects to further build his legacy.

To that end, the late eighties and early nineties brought several major expansions and acquisitions, beginning with the Nick Bollettieri Tennis Academy, which gave us access to rising talent and further solidified IMG Tennis, which under Bob Kain's capable leadership enlisted a stable of top players, including Andre Agassi, James Courier, and Pete Sampras.

We expanded our relatively small presence in team sports, not by trying to sign the top players, but by hiring top agents in each of the major sports. By 1990, IMG managed the careers of seventy-five baseball players, forty football players, twenty-five basketball players, and three hockey players. At the same time IMG became a sports team owner, acquiring a French soccer club and a Chinese basketball team. No sport and no corner of the earth was beyond our reach; we even got into Indian cricket and Indonesian badminton.

On the non-sports side, Mark's Anglophilia came to the fore—IMG represented Oxford University and in 1992 enlisted a distinguished new client, former British prime minister Margaret Thatcher.

While all that was going on our TV production division, Trans World International, was producing more than one hundred sports shows each year, everything from traditional competitions to made-for-TV events like the *Skins Game* to trash sport spectacles that appealed to the lowest common denominator of viewer: *The Superstars, Survival of the Fittest, American Gladiators*, and the *World's Strongest Man*.

By the time IMG had entered its third decade, however, the division that had started it—golf—had in Mark's eyes lost some of its luster. In an interview with *Brandweek* he said golf was "peaking a little bit. I don't see it growing at the same levels."

When I read that line, I took it personally. It was, I felt, a reflection on my job performance—and an accurate one. Pure and simple, I hadn't produced as well as in earlier years, and the loss of Norman was only part of it. At around the same time I'd had one other top priority—signing Phil Mickelson—and once again I'd failed.

Phil had been on my radar, and that of every other agent, for years. A four-time All-American and three-time NCAA individual champion while at Arizona State, he'd won sixteen events during his collegiate career, including the U.S. Amateur. Most impressive of all was his victory at age twenty in the 1991 Northern Telecom Open, a PGA Tour event he won while still a junior in college, one of only six players in history to win a pro event as an amateur. He was the number-one-ranked amateur in the world, and whoever was in second wasn't even close.

LEFT: Phillips Exeter Academy radio station. "Stacks of wax...a golden nugget 'cause you dug it!"

BELOW: Portland Country Club 1970 Champion. Somehow I defeated Ray Lebel, one of New England's greatest amateur players.

LEFT: Laura Baugh wall clock (Japan). A marketing phenomenon years before the Shark and Tigermania. My first client at IMG.

BELOW: IMG Golf Committee 1984. Colleagues referenced in the book: Front Row: Bev Norwood, HN, Mark McCormack, Alastair Johnston, Barry Frank, John Simpson 2nd Row: Andy Pierce, Hans Kramer (striped shirt), Bill Carpenter 3rd row: (starting 5th from left) Dusty Murdock, Ian Todd, James Erskine

ABOVE: Medinah Country Club (Chicago). George Peper and I played a practice round with Curtis Strange, who was going for three consecutive U.S. Open championships.

LEFT: *Golf Digest,* "36 Most Powerful People In Golf." I never believed that "most hated man in golf" stuff.

26

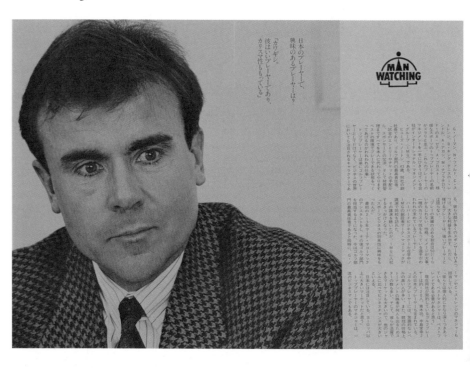

ABOVE: Quality time on the beach in Florida with Norman and Norton kids

BELOW: Interview at IMG Tokyo office with *Weekly Golf Digest Japan*. No country was more bonkers about golf.

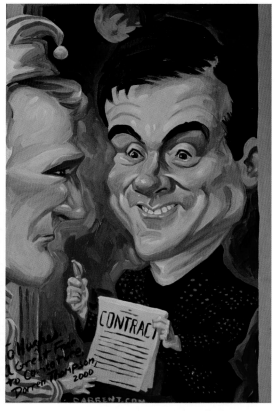

ABOVE: The joys of my life: daughters Stephanie and Mandy

LEFT: Caricature of me bringing client George Burns a contract to sign in the middle of the night. Never happened, but you get the idea: a good agent never sleeps.

ABOVE: Stomach-churning demo flight in Melbourne courtesy of the Royal Australian Air Force. Greg perpetually in search of a new thrill.

LEFT: Pouring the boss a glass of champagne in London at IMG's World Match Play Championship.

THE AGENT

ABOVE: Presented to me by the guys at Nike right after we concluded the deal for Tiger. No wonder Mark McCormack bristled at the term "agent".

RIGHT: IMG executive Clarke Jones helped me manage the Tiger maelstrom.

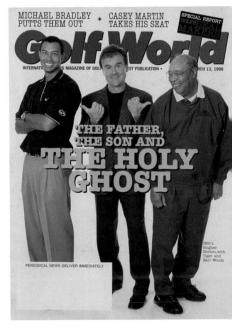

ABOVE LEFT: Harvard Business School 25th Reunion. Ten graduates from the class of 1972 were profiled. A huge honor to be included with classmates like billionaire Steve Schwartzman.

ABOVE RIGHT: *Golf World* cover story. One of my biggest regrets in three decades as an agent.

BELOW: Hughes Norton, 2023, at the Country Club of Cleveland

The competition to sign Phil was intense and I decided we needed to come at him with everything IMG had. That led me to cross over into our Team Sports Division to a talented guy named Mike Barnett. Mike was our hockey man, the agent for Wayne Gretzky and many other NHL stars, but he was also into golf and was based in Los Angeles, thus within relative easy reach of Mickelson's home in Scottsdale, and I thought he'd be a great fit with Phil.

Mike and I had a couple of meetings, then brought Mark in for some final strategizing, and came up with a pitch: I would be Phil's overall agent and Mike would be his exclusive manager with no other golf clients. Mike was a wizard at marketing, had done creative work for Gretzky, and we would show Phil a few of the cool commercials Wayne had been in. We'd wrap it up by saying, "Phil, you can be golf's Gretzky and we're ready to help you get everything you'll deserve from that role."

In June 1992, Mike and I flew to Arizona for a meeting with Phil at one of the clubs where he played. Here, from my files, is the one-page document that was the basis of our pitch.

IMG'S OFFER TO MANAGE PHIL MICKELSON

- IMG will advance Phil money for expenses to play the Tour when he first starts (vs. taking out a bank loan or signing with a sponsor). No interest charge, Phil pays us back as we go along.
- In the first 3½ years of Phil's professional career, IMG will guarantee him income opportunities totaling $3,500,000.
- IMG offers Phil the best management team in the world:
  - Hughes Norton, the most experienced agent and negotiator in the business, will personally represent Phil.
  - Mike Barnett, based in Los Angeles, who has generated millions for his hockey clients and is one of the most creative marketing agents in sports, will work with Phil as his only golf client.
  - Mark McCormack, the man who invented sports management and

has represented the best athletes in the world for 30 years, will stay in touch with Phil by telephone and meet with Phil at least twice per year to review all of Phil's activities. Mark's role will focus on the strategic planning of Phil's career as it develops in stages from Tour rookie to proven tournament winner to major championship elite level.

- Executives in IMG's offices worldwide will generate income opportunities for Phil and personally take care of him wherever he travels to play golf throughout the world.

- IMG financial management experts will work closely with Phil to develop a comprehensive program to enhance his net worth: tax strategies, insurance, accounting, legal services, and investment advice.
  In naming IMG as one of the top financial planners in the country, *Money* magazine stated: "IMG's resources are arguably the most extensive in the financial planning field."

When we walked into the room for our meeting, sitting there with Phil was his brother, Tim, along with a big burly guy who was our worst nightmare—Steve Loy. Phil's golf coach at ASU, Loy had been rumored to be the one who'd be managing him. We were toast. Their only intention with the meeting was to use us, learn from our presentation how IMG would manage Phil.

That's always a risk in our business. I couldn't blame Phil for the direction he'd chosen to go—he and Loy had been bonding for four years. Still, it hurt, as I knew we could have done so much more for Phil than Loy, who at that point knew as much about the intricacies of sports management as I did about coaching college golf.

Shortly after losing Norman, we'd also lost another major client, Nick Price, who like his good friend Norman decided to go on his own. I could have—should have—been on top of that. I knew Nick and Greg were close and agreed about a lot of things, but if I'd been more proactive we might have been able to hold on to Nick.

Or maybe not. Maybe I wasn't the superagent I thought I was. Maybe I'd spent so much time in the company of Norman, I'd become as self-centered, toxic, and polarizing a figure as he was. No wonder I was shocked when, at the end of 1993, Mark told me he was relieving me of my title as head of IMG's golf division and replacing me with Alastair Johnston, the second part of that news even more stunning than the first.

A guy who worked for Alastair for 20 years once described him this way: "He knew nothing, and did nothing." Why did Mark tolerate such mediocrity? The only explanation: Alastair took the day-to-day management of Arnold Palmer off McCormack's hands, giving him critical breathing room to grow and expand IMG into all the other areas besides golf. Forever grateful, Mark gave Alastair a pass, holding him to a lower standard than the rest of us.

It was the lowest point of my life. I'd alienated my wife, my clients, my boss, and who knows how many other people. As Mark McCormack had risen to become the most powerful man in sports, I'd gone in the opposite direction, identified in a *Golf World* article as "if not the most powerful agent in golf, if not the most hated agent in golf, certainly the most powerfully hated agent in golf."

The holiday season, in the years since my divorce, had become the emotionally toughest time of year for me, as it is for so many people, but that year was particularly difficult, as I just sort of shut down and recoiled from the world. I later learned that more than one person who knew me well had been afraid I might think about taking my own life.

Well, thankfully it was never that bad. But I was down, deeply hurt for several weeks, before finally deciding to stop feeling sorry for myself and get back to work. I guess I knew, for someone whose self-esteem stemmed from his job performance to the extent mine did, that what I needed to do was get back on the horse and start producing again.

At the time, there was one kid out there who seemed to be the next can't-miss player, and I set my sights on him. David Duval had won the 1989 USGA Junior Amateur, and was a four-time All-American at Georgia Tech and the 1993 Collegiate Player of the Year.

He wasn't an easy sell—a bit quirky, a bit skeptical, but very intelligent and a voracious reader. At Pebble Beach one year, when I stopped by his hotel room to pick him up for dinner, I noticed on the bedside table a novel by Ayn Rand (a writer known for her ultraconservative views—yet David was one of the PGA Tour's few registered Democrats). But that wasn't the only book, there were two others, each with a bookmark. While most Tour players spent hotel time watching TV or putting on the carpet, David was simultaneously reading three books.

Probably because he was bright and perceptive, he had some initial doubts about me. I later learned he'd seen the *Golf Digest* article listing me among golf's thirty-six most powerful people, and that had changed his mind. He decided to take the plunge with me and IMG. Within a short time we got him an apparel contract with Tommy Hilfiger that, we learned, was four times what Polo Ralph Lauren was paying major champion Justin Leonard, and a huge equipment deal with Titleist that I knew paid more than Tom Watson was getting from Ram and Maxfli—pretty good for a Tour rookie.

It took David a couple of years to get going, but once he did he turned it on with thirteen victories between 1997 and 2001, including a Players Championship, a Tour Championship, and the Open Championship at Royal Lytham. In March of 1999 he rose to the number one spot in the Official World Golf Ranking.

One of the coolest perks of my job was getting the opportunity to play in the AT&T Pebble Beach Pro-Am. I was lucky enough to play nine times, but the 1995 partnership with David was a special one. They'd given me nine strokes that year and David and I meshed beautifully, finishing in second place with a better-ball net score of 254, 34 strokes under par, thanks in large part to David, who finished second in the tournament proper at 15 under, two strokes behind another IMG client and friend, Peter Jacobsen. Playing the final round at Pebble Beach in their company—and with a young Stanford kid named Notah Begay as my caddie—remains the greatest thrill of my competitive golf life.

We finished three strokes behind a team featuring professional Bruce Vaughan, who had shot one under par for fifty-four holes and actually missed the cut in the pro event by ten strokes, but he nonetheless played on Sunday because his partner, an alleged 15-handicapper from Japan named Masashi Yamada, had improved the team score by forty-five strokes, a performance that a handicap expert later deemed "statistically impossible."

An investigation showed that Yamada was actually a 6 handicap, not to mention a former Japan Senior Amateur champion. His handicap had been verified by Tokyo's Mangijo Country Club, which the seventy-two-year-old Yamada not so coincidentally owned.

Two months after the tournament, when the truth was learned, the tournament organizers disqualified Yamada and awarded first prize in the pro-am to David and me. I'll never forget the phone call I got from tournament director Lou Russo: "Hughes," he said, "I'm afraid we have to ask you to return the second-place prize you won." A couple of weeks later the champion's prize arrived: a twenty-four-piece set of handcut Waterford crystal.

As I beheld all that glassware, and considered the circuitous path it had taken to my door, it struck me how life so often takes strange turns, but then when you least expect it things tend to right themselves. The delayed gratification I had received from AT&T, that remarkable reversal of fortune, seemed both an omen and a kick in the ass. There was still time to turn myself and my career around and get back on top.

Besides, I was pretty sure I had an ace up my sleeve.

7

Finding (and Funding) Tiger

Cypress, California, was as nondescript a town as you could imagine. Roughly twenty-five miles south of Los Angeles, it came into being in the late nineteenth century as a center of dairy farming. By the 1950s, the population numbered 1,700 humans and 100,000 cows. In the decade that followed, however, a housing boom in Orange County drove the bovines out as Cypress became a middle-class dormitory suburb. In 1989, it had roughly 40,000 residents—and one of them had attracted my full attention.

It was a balmy afternoon in September. I'd been on a West Coast business trip with a couple of IMG colleagues. That morning, after an abbreviated meeting in L.A. with the marketing people at Mazda, my two associates had hoped to catch an earlier flight back to Cleveland, but I'd cajoled them into dropping me off in Cypress before doubling back to LAX. Less than pleased, they'd taken the opportunity to give me some grief about what I was doing.

"How old did you say this wunderkind was—thirteen? What are we talking about here, Hughes, miniature golf?"

"Yeah, what are you two planning to do this afternoon, watch some cartoons, play Super Mario Brothers?"

I couldn't argue with them. Stalking young kids was not my thing, although it had actually become common practice in IMG's tennis division, as the prodigies in that sport were turning pro as early as age fifteen. (Current world-number-one ranked Carlos Alcaraz signed with an agent when he was 13!) Golf was another story. Nearly all the top prospects finished college (or at least high school) before trying for the

Tour, and the teenagers who did go for it were usually flameouts. The lone exception had been Seve Ballesteros, who'd turned pro at sixteen, becoming the finest player Europe ever produced.

Besides, it wasn't as if IMG Golf was hurting for clients, particularly at that moment. In June, Curtis Strange had won his second consecutive U.S. Open, and for the better part of seven years Greg Norman had been world number one. Meanwhile, the guys in IMG's London office, led by John Simpson, were killing it, having signed a powerhouse quartet of European Tour players—Nick Faldo, Bernhard Langer, Sandy Lyle, and Ian Woosnam—who collectively would win eleven major championship titles between 1985 and 1996. The truth was, IMG Golf was on a roll, and my own stock in the company had never been higher. We were back on top as the management firm uniquely suited for every major player, but always in my mind was the lesson Mark had learned from his own experience: "Never get complacent!"

Those words rang especially true now, since the landscape of our business had continued to evolve. Eight major agencies were focusing on golf, with more than seventy players managed by firms other than IMG. Pro golf had grown into a high-stakes game, and the competition to represent elite players was intense.

That's why I was on my way to meet a thirteen-year-old. That and the fact that this particular thirteen-year-old, with the curious name Eldrick "Tiger" Woods, was clearly something special. I'd been tracking him for about five years, clipping newspaper reports of junior tournaments he'd won by several strokes while competing against boys two or three years older than he.

Back then, one of the major championships for kids was the Optimist Junior World held in San Diego. It attracted competitors from around the globe. Woods had won it four times at various ages. But the event that had spurred me to find a Cypress phone book was the Big "I" Insurance Classic, where each year more than eight thousand boys ages thirteen to eighteen competed in local qualifiers to earn one of the 108 spots in the final, a seventy-two-hole stroke-play event. That summer—standing five foot five and weighing one hundred pounds—the thirteen-year-old Woods had not only qualified for the final but finished second, bettered only by Justin Leonard, nearly four years his senior.

In those days, the junior qualifiers who made the thirty-six-hole cut got to play round three in the company of a PGA Tour player. Woods's group drew a husky twenty-three-year-old rookie named John Daly— and on that day, after the first nine holes, Daly found himself three strokes behind Tiger. Only a birdie barrage on the second nine enabled Big John to save face. This kid truly seemed to be another Ballesteros, a once-in-a-generation freakish talent.

I arrived at 6704 Teakwood Street. A low-slung suburban ranch house, typical of that tasteful era that brought us lava lamps and bell-bottoms, it sat within a tract of several hundred similar homes, all one-story, none larger than two thousand square feet, no two of them separated by more than fifteen feet.

The Woods's front yard was 80 percent driveway with a patch of grass about the size of a living room rug, and the home's most salient architectural feature was its entry, where the A-line roof swept down to frame a facade of faux fieldstone evocative of a 1960s diner.

I hadn't quite known what to expect that day. Earl Woods had welcomed my call, but I wondered whether I was the first to make contact or other agents had beaten me to it. One thing I decided I was *not* going to do was make a sales pitch. After all, as good as this kid seemed to be, he wasn't likely to turn pro for at least another five years—nine years if he finished college. I was there mostly to listen. That worked out just fine, as it quickly became apparent that Earl Woods loved to talk, and his favorite subject was his son.

He was a burly guy with an outgoing personality, a former military man who liked being onstage and in charge, while his diminutive Thai wife, Kultida, was reserved. We had barely settled into our seats in their living room when Earl launched into a detailed recitation of Tiger's remarkable path in golf, beginning with what, I would come to learn, was one of his go-to stories.

"I'm in the garage, banging balls into a net, and Tiger's there with me, sitting in his high chair. He's ten months old, but he's watching me wide-eyed, mesmerized, really into it. So I unstrap him and have him come over with me. He picks up a cut-down club I'd made for him as a toy, puts a ball down, waggles, and hits it smack into the net—first time! I shouted to Tida, 'Honey, get out here—we have a genius on our hands!'"

Earl then rhapsodized on what had followed: Tiger at age two hitting balls with Bob Hope and Jimmy Stewart on *The Merv Griffin Show*, making his first hole-in-one at age six, breaking 80 at age eight, breaking 70 at twelve, etc. Tiger had by that time won more than 150 junior and amateur events.

Throughout all this, Tida had remained silent, but when Earl finally took a breath she spoke up. "Tiger a good student, too. He no get good grades, Mom put his golf clubs in closet."

Short and to the point. As I would learn in the years to come, it was Tida Woods who was often the tougher parent, the disciplinarian. Earl liked to project the image of a hard-ass taskmaster, but when push came to shove in the Woods household, it was invariably Tida whose will prevailed.

They were an unlikely couple, Earl and Kultida Woods, two people who had found each other, as many couples had a generation earlier, through the harsh exigencies of a war.

Earl had grown up in Manhattan, Kansas, and attended Kansas State, where he'd played on the baseball team. After graduation he'd spent twenty years in the army, including two tours in Vietnam, where he'd become a highly decorated Green Beret and risen to the rank of lieutenant colonel.

Back then, after doing a stretch in the war zone, soldiers were allowed a week of R&R, which could be spent in any of several locations in Asia. Most of the American troops opted for Australia, and why not, it was a land where English was spoken, the beaches were beautiful, the bars plentiful—the perfect place to let off some steam.

Not Earl Woods, and for a valid reason. In those days, African American GIs were not made to feel very welcome in Australia, as an attitude of white supremacy had sadly lingered. So he opted instead for Thailand, and it was there in 1966 that he met Tida. Three years later they were married.

Every time I think of the way they met, I marvel once again at the power of fate, the almost supernatural force that predetermines how so many aspects of our lives—and the lives of others—play out. Consider that, if Earl hadn't made that trip to Thailand, there would be no Tiger Woods.

I'd been speaking with Earl and Tida for about forty-five minutes, when suddenly the front door opened and in walked Tiger, all five-five and one hundred pounds of him. As we shook hands, he flashed the toothy grin that is now world-famous. He was a polite and respectful little kid, if a bit shy, often looking downward as he spoke. But at the same time there was a quiet self-confidence.

We made small talk for a few minutes and then Tiger took me back to his room. At the threshold I noticed, penciled into the left side of the door frame, the classic series of hash marks and dates parents use to record their child's growth over the years. To Tiger, however, I think those notches probably signified more than that. They were a way of keeping score, assessing his development with a series of irrefutable numbers, like a golf handicap. My bet is that he was watching those ascending pencil marks impatiently, yearning to hit six feet–plus, as he knew a more powerful physique would make him a more powerful golfer.

His room was typical for boys his age with posters on the walls, except that, instead of rock idols or NFL quarterbacks, Tiger's heroes were golfers—Jack Nicklaus, Greg Norman, et al.—and tacked on one wall was a now-famous clipping from *Golf Digest*.

Following Nicklaus's victory in the 1986 Masters, the magazine had compiled a list of his career accomplishments, including his age at the time of each achievement. Tiger back then likely was not thinking about major championships, but he was laser-focused on Jack's feats as a junior and amateur golfer—and on hitting each mark at an earlier age. So far, every box had been ticked.

What surprised me as I looked around the room was a conspicuous absence of trophies.

"They're gone," said Tiger matter-of-factly. "By the time I hit eleven, there were a hundred and thirteen of them around the house. Mom made me give them all away. I don't care."

Wow, I thought, *how many thirteen-year-olds would agree to that?* Then it hit me, this kid was more focused on the process—the grind, the ball beating, the competition. Prior accomplishments meant little to him. The only important trophy was the next one.

My actual face time with Tiger lasted only a few minutes, and then Earl, Tida, and I returned to our seats in the living room. I was sitting by a window, and a few moments later, out of the corner of my eye, I saw Tiger on his bike, pedaling off down the street. Taking that in, I thought, *Welcome to the tennis world*.

As the conversation continued, I gave Earl and Tida a quick history of IMG, and they let me know that no other agents had approached them. That was a good feeling, but at the same time, the situation in which I now found myself was different than with any prospective client I'd ever approached—different in an awkward way. Given the nearly thirty-year gap between my age and Tiger's, most of my future dealings would be not with him but with his mercurial father.

Just before the visit ended, Earl made a couple of emphatic points. "Number one," he said, "this kid is gonna change the world—not just the golf world but the world. Number two, he has something to prove. I can't tell you how many times Tiger and I—as the only two Black people traveling the junior circuit—have walked into country club grillrooms and felt the chilly silence of the assembled white folks. I told Tiger to learn a life lesson from those moments: forgive, but never forget." Earl was counting on Tiger to use those dark memories to fuel his fire to become the best golfer the game had ever seen.

As we walked to the door he said, "The first Black superstar in golf is going to make himself and someone else a whole lot of money."

"That's why I'm here, Mr. Woods," I said. "That's why I'm here."

A week or so later I sent Earl Woods a quick note of thanks, said, "Let's stay in touch, and let me know if there's anything I can do." Thereafter, from time to time, I'd send him something I thought was of interest, often a Tiger press clipping, anything to remind him we were there for him and Tiger. I also did what I could to arrange "playdates" for Tiger with our pro clients, knowing the kid liked to see how his game stacked up against the best. But that was about as far as I could go and still remain within the NCAA regulations.

TIGER MEETS THE SHARK

When Tiger was fourteen or fifteen, I was able to put him together for a game with Greg Norman at Old Marsh Golf Club in Palm Beach Gardens. It was only nine holes, but they got a sense of each other's talent. Greg said he was amazed to see such clubhead speed and distance from such a skinny little kid, while Tiger was impressed with the variety of shots around the green that Greg had at his command.

At the same time, neither was ready to go overboard. Greg, being Greg, needed to continue believing he was and would ever remain unrivaled as the best player on the planet and had no intention of gushing over Tiger. Tiger came away thinking that if Norman was the best in the world, he was also within his reach— or would be within a couple of years.

Perhaps most notable was the fact that, despite both being the best players of their respective generations, neither felt any sort of kinship or chemistry with the other. It was a relationship that from the first day was cool, would never be close, and would end contentious throughout the LIV fiasco to the present.

In 1990, fourteen-year-old Tiger made his debut in the U.S. Junior Championship held that year at Lake Merced Golf and Country Club in Daly City, California. After qualifying for match play he won his first four matches (including a 3-and-2 victory over a kid from Albuquerque who would later become his Stanford teammate and one of his closest friends, Notah Begay), then lost in the semifinals 1-up to Dennis Hillman, who had been the medalist that year.

The loss to Hillman was the last match Tiger would lose in a USGA Junior. A year later at the Bay Hill Club in Orlando, Florida (the same course where, as a pro, he would win eight Arnold Palmer Invitationals), he was the qualifying medalist and won the title on the nineteenth hole over Brad Zwetschke, becoming at that time the youngest champion in USGA history; in 1992 at Wollaston Golf Club in Milton, Massachusetts, he was again the medalist and beat Mark Wilson 1-up at the eighteenth, becoming the first player to win the title back-to-back; and in 1993 at Waverley Country Club in Portland, Oregon, he made it three in a row, defeating Ryan Armour on the nineteenth hole.

Tiger's three consecutive wins in the U.S. Junior were arguably the most impressive achievement of his career. Because of the short age window (a maximum age of seventeen when Tiger played, now eighteen), this is the toughest national championship to win even twice, let alone three times in a row. Since its inception in 1948, only one other player has won the title more than once, Jordan Spieth in 2009 and 2011. Tiger's triple is all the more impressive because in most of his matches in 1991 and 1992, his opponents were two or three years older than he. One kid was six foot one and 190 pounds and outdrove him by thirty or forty yards, an advantage as much psychological as physical, but Tiger wasn't fazed. Even in the context of his eighty-two professional victories and fifteen major titles, winning three consecutive USGA Junior Championships may be his most unassailable record.

By this time, Tiger had won more than two hundred other junior titles to go with his three USGA crowns. That mind-blowing total had come at a significant financial cost to the Woods family, as the yearly travel schedule had taken Earl and Tiger all over the country, driving and flying to tournament sites. Earl was retired, and although he had a pension from the army and another pension from a twenty-year career at McDonnell Douglas, I knew from comments he'd made here and there that he was struggling to keep Tiger's playing schedule going.

One day while driving home from work I had an inspiration. IMG had no one actively scouting junior players. We had a hard enough time in those days scouting the college circuit. *What if we paid Earl to do it?* It would kill two birds with one stone—three, actually. It would provide Earl with significant extra funds to handle his father-and-son travel expenses. IMG would have a set of trained eyes evaluating the top junior players in golf. And, best of all, the arrangement would further solidify my growing relationship with the Woods family.

There was just one big question—how would such an arrangement affect Tiger's amateur status? How would the USGA read it? I didn't want to even broach the idea with Earl before I had a good handle on that.

The next day I took the idea to Mark. He liked my creativity and knew how to move things forward. A few years earlier, as part of a pitch for IBM to become the marketing consultant to the USGA, Mark had gotten to know then USGA president Frank "Sandy" Tatum, a distinguished San Francisco lawyer, low-handicap golfer, and one of the most respected men in the game. Mark called him and explained my proposal. Several days later, after consultation with his colleagues and considerable thought, Tatum called Mark back and gave his blessing— with the condition that there was absolutely no quid pro quo: Earl's acceptance of our job offer could not be linked explicitly or implicitly to Tiger's later signing with IMG.

There was never a formal contract between Earl and me, not so much as a handshake. I simply told him we wanted to confirm our support for him and his son, we needed someone to scout talent on the junior circuit, and we saw him as the ideal person for the job. Before he could object, I assured him we expected nothing in return other than his field reports and told him the arrangement had been sanctioned from the very top of the USGA.

Earl was only too happy to accept our offer of $25,000 a year plus expenses. Looking back, I'm pretty certain he was committed from the beginning to going with IMG and saw my offer as pure gravy, a chance to make some money for himself. Earl served as an IMG consultant from 1992 through the fall of 1994.

Despite having the USGA's approval of this arrangement, both Earl and I agreed to keep our new relationship quiet. My own fear was that once word got out the press would have a field day with it, and our competitors would do their best to discredit IMG while making their own sanctimonious overtures to Earl. I was particularly afraid that a big Los Angeles entertainment agency might go after him with the pitch that someone as special as Tiger deserved more than just a sports agent. To my surprise and relief there was little of that.

Eventually, of course, Tiger's achievements spurred attention from other agents, although not the golf-based ones who were aware of the relationship I'd established. Leigh Steinberg, the big-time L.A. sports agent often cited as the inspiration for the Oscar-winning movie *Jerry Maguire*, is reputed to have parked himself in the Woodses' driveway, and the William Morris Agency sent a proposal, as did a couple of groups of African American businessmen who thought they might have an inside track, but Earl did not respond to any of them.

Instead, he settled into his new job, diligently filing a series of handwritten reports on yellow lined paper and in remarkably beautiful penmanship. Earl's only weakness was his Will Rogers complex—he never met a player he didn't like. Granted, he'd befriended some of these kids and their parents while on the junior golf circuit with them, but nearly every report was a breathless rave that ended in "Hughes, mark my words, this kid is a *player!*" Sadly, none of Earl's can't-miss phenoms made a mark in pro golf. Years later I told him, "Earl, you had to be the worst talent scout in history," and we both had a good laugh.

Three straight USGA Junior titles had brought seventeen-year-old Tiger to a new level. He now had a clear goal and he wasn't shy about expressing it. "I want to be the best golfer ever," he said. "I don't know whether I'll achieve that or not, but it's a helluva goal. I think I'd be more worried if I set too low a goal and achieve it too easily."

Tiger had had the same swing coach since the age of ten, a California instructor named John Anselmo, who had succeeded Rudy Duran, a hometown pro who had nurtured him through his early childhood. Speaking with Earl in the summer of 1993, I raised the notion that it might be time for an upgrade. Earl agreed and wondered whether I had any ideas. Did I ever.

Butch Harmon had rebuilt Greg Norman's swing following a slight slump in 1990 and transformed an already top player into the best in the world. I'd gotten to watch some of their practice sessions and was impressed by Butch's ability to mix camaraderie with tough love. More important, I said to Earl, Harmon had no set "method" he taught to everyone, as did David Leadbetter and so many other coaches. Butch had learned his approach to teaching from his father, 1948 Masters champion and longtime head pro at Winged Foot, Claude Harmon: "Never take away what a player does naturally, just make it better." Butch looked for the one thing in a Tour pro's swing that could cause bad shots under pressure—and focused on fixing that one thing.

Earl was on board. Now the question was, would Butch do it? I called him with a simple pitch: "I have another great player for you, another player who's destined to become number one in the world." He needed no sales job on Tiger, and we set up their first session in late August at Butch's club, Lochinvar, in Houston. When I called him a couple of days later, Butch said: "This kid has the fastest unwind of his hips and body I've seen since Ben Hogan. He doesn't have a go-to shot coming down the stretch when he absolutely has to drive the ball in the fairway, and we'll work on that. But I'm not going to take that speed away from him because I've never seen anything like it."

With a newly "Harmonized" swing, Tiger was ready to take on his next big challenge, the U.S. Amateur. His three Junior Amateur victories had earned him exemptions from local and sectional U.S. Amateur qualifying in 1991 to 1993, but he'd had little success. Age fifteen, in his first appearance, at the Honors Course in Tennessee, Tiger didn't play well enough in the thirty-six holes of on-site qualifying to earn one of the sixty-four spots in the match-play portion. A year later, at Muirfield Village, he opened the stroke play with a 78, but roared back with a 66 on day two to make the field, only to lose his second-round match, 6 and 4, to future Tour player Tim "Lumpy" Herron. The following year he lost again in the second round, this time to Englishman Paul Page.

That would be the last time Tiger Woods lost a match in the U.S. Amateur. Over the next three years—1994, 1995, and 1996—he went 18–0.

In his first win, at the TPC Sawgrass, he came from six holes down with twelve to play in the thirty-six-hole final match to beat Hank Kuehne, at age eighteen becoming the youngest to win the U.S. Amateur. A year later at Newport Country Club in Rhode Island, I was among those who watched him come from behind in the final once again, this time against George "Buddy" Marucci, icing victory on the final hole with an 8-iron approach that stopped two feet from the cup. Then, in the 1996 final at Pumpkin Ridge in Oregon, he found himself behind yet again—five down to Steve Scott after the first eighteen holes—but fought back one more time, winning on the second hole of sudden death, the first and only player to win three straight U.S. Amateur titles, a feat that had eluded even the great Bobby Jones.

I was on-site for that victory as well, this time in a more intensely interested way. Three days later, it would become official: Tiger would be represented by IMG and I would be his agent. And both of us were more than ready to get going.

Tiger had entered Stanford in 1994 and had won the first collegiate tournament he played, two of the first four. By the end of his sophomore year he'd won ten events, including the NCAA Championship. At that point, although he'd never said a word to me, I was getting the strong sense that he had no intention of staying at Stanford the full four years. College competition wasn't enough for him, and a degree was not going to help him pursue his chosen profession. He was wasting both time and money.

Hank Haney, who would later become Tiger's swing coach, clearly saw it the same way. "In college golf there is one big event the players want to win: the NCAA Championship," he told *Golf World.* "When a player is able to raise his game and do it, that shows something special. Tiger is in a totally different league. I believe strongly in academics, but I can't imagine why he's stayed in school. His game may not suffer, but I don't see how it's going to get better."

Tiger was also watching what Phil Mickelson and David Duval, the top two collegiate players just ahead of him, were doing. Neither had stayed in college the full term, and that had to have been an influence. Moreover, I'd shared with him my memory of twenty years earlier when Curtis Strange, facing the same decision, had decided to leave Wake Forest.

I can't recall the precise moment when I heard from either Earl or Tiger that the decision had been made, but it was well before U.S. Amateur number three, because that week at Pumpkin Ridge I had with me a couple of very big contracts for Tiger to sign, the fruit of several weeks of "what-if" negotiations with Nike and Titleist. By the time Tiger raised the trophy that Sunday evening in Portland, his Nike logo apparel had been sized and tailored, his Nike shoes had been tested for comfort, and a Titleist staff bag emblazoned with his name and filled with a set of custom-fitted clubs was as ready to hit the PGA Tour as he was.

The process had begun two years earlier, just after Tiger won his first Amateur. (I was not officially his agent—I couldn't be until the day he publicly renounced his amateur status—but we had a tacit understanding.)

My strategy was a bit unorthodox—instead of stirring interest among several apparel and equipment companies in the hope of creating a bidding war, I decided to put all my eggs in two baskets, Nike and Titleist. It was a gamble, to be sure, but one I thought could pay off.

The two companies had a few things in common. Both were leaders in the sporting goods industry, both had distinctive corporate cultures that reflected the strong personalities of their CEOs, both had built their successful brands around megastar athletes, and most important for my purposes, both had plenty of money to spend.

At the same time, Titleist and Nike were as different as a golf ball and shoe. One was a conservative sixty-year-old company, based in a boxy manufacturing plant in southeast Massachusetts, the other a quirky, cocky upstart, its sleek headquarters sprawling across a three-hundred-acre "campus" in northwest Oregon. One had been centered on golf-and-nothing-but-golf from the moment of its birth; the other had only recently dipped its toe into the game. And going back to those two CEOs, one I knew well, respected more than just about anyone I'd ever dealt with, and trusted one hundred percent. The other I knew only by reputation, had some suspicions about, and ultimately discovered to be someone worthy of no trust at all.

My challenge, however, was the same with both of them: maximize the value of a twenty-year-old kid who had dominated the junior, collegiate, and amateur ranks, but had done almost nothing to show he could beat the pros. Between 1992 and 1996 Tiger had been given exemptions to play in seventeen professional tournaments and had missed the cut ten times. He had never finished better than twenty-second and had compiled a scoring average just south of 74. With those numbers, if he were able to get to the Tour, he wouldn't stay there long. I thus found myself frequently repeating the disclaimer made famous by financial institutions: "Past results are in no way indicative of future performance."

Further impeding my aspirations for Tiger were the efforts of other golf agents. In an interview with *Golf World*, Rocky Hambric, president of Cornerstone Sports, which managed about thirty PGA Tour players, said, "As good as Tiger is, he's not yet ready to be a dominant player, not even close . . . People have tossed out figures that are more than inflated. They expect him to make more money his first year than Arnold Palmer and Greg Norman put together. Twenty million? That's ridiculous." Pros

Inc.'s Vinny Giles was even more skeptical. While admitting Tiger could be "the Michael Jordan of golf," he saw the limit to what he might command initially at "five million dollars a year for five years."

Nike, I suspected, would require more spadework than Titleist, so it was there that I commenced. Thanks once again to the unique resources of IMG, I had a couple of things going for me. A few years earlier our tennis division had established a strong relationship with Nike, bringing them the flamboyant Andre Agassi, who had been the perfect fit for Nike's studiedly edgy image. It was IMG's tennis division head, Bob Kain, who in the early 1980s had introduced me to Nike's director of sports marketing, Rob Strasser.

In the Ben Affleck/Matt Damon movie *Air*, about the creation of Nike's Air Jordan shoe, Strasser was played by Jason Bateman as a sort of reserved, dithering character, but the truth is he was just the opposite, a blustery three-hundred-pounder nicknamed "Rolling Thunder," who loved describing himself as "loud, obnoxious, and fat." Kain told me the story of doing a deal with Strasser one evening in a bar. After multiple beverages, Bob scrawled the terms of what they'd agreed to on a paper napkin. A week later Strasser didn't remember the details but honored Bob's notes on the by then rumpled napkin.

My own dealings with Strasser were far less colorful. At the end of 1983 I sent him a proposal for what I thought would be a dramatic way for Nike to announce they were serious about getting into golf: Seve Ballesteros would wear Nike golf shoes worldwide, Greg Norman would wear Nike apparel, and Curtis Strange would carry a Nike golf bag.

Strasser passed; the company just wasn't ready yet. But imagine how that deal might have changed history—no Reebok affiliation for Norman, no Hertz golf bag endorsement for Curtis, and possibly less interest by Nike in Tiger a decade later. I was probably lucky Rob said no. Eventually I was able to get shoe deals for Curtis and Peter Jacobsen.

Strasser was just one of several colorful characters inhabiting Niketown, beginning with chairman and CEO Phil Knight, a middle-distance runner for the University of Oregon who got a business degree at Stanford, cofounded Nike on a shoestring in 1964, and became one of the richest men in the world (*Forbes* currently ranks him twenty-fourth with a net worth of $47.7 billion).

Among Knight's eccentricities was a penchant to go barefoot in the office, an odd proclivity for anyone, but particularly for the owner of a shoe company. I had little personal contact with Phil Knight, but from what I could glean almost no one was admitted to the sanctum sanctorum that was his office, and even those allowed to penetrate the gigantic outer room where his secretaries worked were required to remove their shoes before entering, presumably in compliance with the boss's shoeless fixation.

As the moment for generating a deal for Tiger approached, I began spending some time in Beaverton, Oregon. I had a gut feeling about what I wanted to propose to Nike, but first wanted to get a better feel for the culture of the place and its people. Happily, Peter Jacobsen lived in Portland, which gave me an excuse to piggyback visits to him with stops at Nike. Of course, I never let on to Peter what I was up to—one of my cardinal rules was never to tell one client what I was doing for another—it could never end well. Plus, at that moment, the fewer people in the world who knew what was brewing with Tiger, the better.

I must say, Nike headquarters was no hardship to visit. Designed to mimic a college campus, it comprised dozens of swooping buildings—most of them named after athletes—sprinkled across a parklike landscape. In addition to offices, there were gymnasiums, tennis and basketball courts, even playing fields for those who signed up for the "lunch leagues." All the food in the employee cafeteria was free, all the items in the company store were half price or less. The only dress code was "Wear Nike." It was hard to get the employees to go home at night.

If there was a downside to the place it was the general and pervasive attitude of superiority, a "We're Nike and you're not" vibe that nearly everyone there projected.

By 1993 Rob Strasser had left the company to become CEO of Adidas America, and Nike's new director of sports marketing was Steve Miller.

Miller had been the director of athletics at Kansas State University, where he'd transformed a losing football team into a perennial bowl invitee by hiring Hall of Fame coach Bill Snyder. It was Steve who became both my Nike campus tour guide and my interlocutor in negotiating the Tiger deal.

As a new guy, Steve was blessedly bereft of Nike arrogance. At one early point he said, "I'm an outsider, I'm not one of the Kool-Aid drinkers, and I realize that may limit my future here, but I'm okay with that." It was an honest admission and it set the tone for the open and frank negotiations we would have.

After three or four visits with Miller, I felt my homework was completed and I was ready to talk Tiger. Here was my thinking:

1. The explosive growth of golf had not gone unnoticed by Nike. The company had made a tentative first move into the game with shoes and apparel and was on the cusp of a bigger commitment into clubs and balls.
2. Nike prided itself on identifying with only the very best players in their respective sports—Andre Agassi, Michael Jordan, Jerry Rice. Stars drove the Nike brand.
3. Those guys now were past their primes, aging out of the picture. Nike had not signed a megastar in years. They needed a win.
4. Tiger would give it to them. The timing was perfect.
5. Phil Knight was a jock sniffer who simply had to sign the best athletes. If he was already paying Agassi and Courier big bucks, I reasoned, imagine what he might pay the best young golfer to come along since Jack Nicklaus.

With all that in mind, I put my cards on the table with Steve: "Here's a generational talent with charisma and global appeal who will instantly rocket Nike Golf into the big leagues. Not only are we coming to you first and exclusively, we will give you the opportunity to own Tiger's identity. The Nike Swoosh on his shirt front and cap will be the only branding he displays—no other company logos on the shirt collar, chest, sleeves, or back of the hat—a pure Nike message, front and center, for all to see. Based on his unprecedented amateur achievements, every other company will want him. Nike can preempt them all, but it's going to cost top dollar."

Then, swallowing hard, I told Steve somewhere in the neighborhood of $50 million over five years would get it done.

No one else in golf—not Palmer, not Norman, *no one*—was earning *anything* like that for apparel and shoes. But through our tennis guys, I knew Agassi's Nike contract was in the neighborhood of five million a year and from Steve I had a pretty good feel for Jordan's compensation, so I thought, why not go for it.

Steve's first response, of course, was "That's ridiculous," but he didn't say forget it. From the beginning he was straightforward about Nike's strong interest. I figured the $50 million, while an overreach, wasn't too far from where I might be able to end up, and that was a huge win not simply in sheer dollars but in the worldwide promotional power Nike would bring to the table. No other company in golf had the advertising budget or clout to help make Tiger a household name. On that score, Nike could have argued that they should pay Tiger less, not more. But they never did.

The other unusual part of my proposal on which they did not balk (and I still can't believe I got it) was all five years of Tiger's compensation was guaranteed, regardless of his performance. I wanted Tiger to have financial certainty no matter whether he failed to get his Tour card, missed Q-School, struggled initially, whatever. Nike would have been entirely within its rights to ask for significant reductions in compensation for years two through five if Tiger failed to live up to the hype, but they never did.

And then there were the bonus clauses—for dollar figures that were unprecedented in golf. I knew that Nike was used to paying bonuses to tennis players, so I checked the contracts of Agassi and other IMG tennis clients and was astonished to see six-figure payments for victories in Grand Slam events.

So again, I went for it with Tiger: $500,000 per major championship win in year one, increasing $100,000 per year to $900,00 per win in year five.

Then I added the same bonus payment related to the Official World Golf Ranking—if Tiger were to reach world number one, same deal: $500,000 in year one escalating to $900,000 in year five. (There were also provisions for ranking second to fifth ($350,000 in year one, increasing to $550,000 in year five) and sixth to tenth ($250,000 increasing to $350,000 in year five). And these bonuses were based not on year-end ranking, as ranking bonuses normally were, but on the highest ranking achieved at any time during the year. Thus, even if Tiger were to reach the number one position for just one week, he'd get that level of bonus.

I guess no one at Nike bothered to check the contracts I'd reached for Strange and Jacobsen a decade earlier—$5,000 for a major championship win in year one, $7,500 in year two. Had someone done so, they legitimately could have laughed my Woods numbers out of the room. But no one did, and those clauses would add $8 million to what Nike paid Tiger between 1997 and 2001.

So when Steve eventually came back to me with a counteroffer of $40 million—$8 million a year guaranteed for five years—well, it was the most delightful compromise imaginable. Delivering the news to Mark and then to Earl and Tiger was the most sublimely satisfying moment of my career.

Then a few days later, as the final contracts were being drawn up by our legal department, something astonishing occurred—an attempt was made to sabotage the deal. By one of our rival agents? No, by Phil Knight.

Knight had a notorious hatred of agents, and on this occasion he decided he'd eliminate me. At the eleventh hour he secretly dispatched a young African American Nike executive to the Woods home in California with an offer for Earl: "You don't need IMG. Deal with us directly, and you'll save the twenty percent commission fee."

To Earl's everlasting credit, he called right away and told me about it. Barely able to breathe, I waited to hear the outcome.

"I told the guy no," Earl said. "I told him to go back and tell Phil Knight, it's important for me to be able to trust someone—and Hughes Norton is that guy." Earl's loyalty in that moment meant the world to me.

Titleist CEO Wally Uihlein, like Phil Knight, had no use for agents and preferred to deal directly with players, but any similarity between the two corporate chiefs ended right there.

Uihlein was hands down the brightest, most highly skilled executive I ever encountered. Like me, he'd spent his entire career in one place, having joined Titleist in 1976 as a regional sales rep, risen within a year to national sales manager, then vice president of sales and distribution, and eventually CEO.

Wally was the very soul of Titleist, the main reason the Titleist ball had achieved and maintained the market dominance it had. No one was more fiercely protective of his company than Wally, and he wasn't afraid to take on anyone, whether it was rival equipment manufacturers, the golf media, Jack Nicklaus, or the USGA, in the defense of his brand.

Titleist's golf clubs had never gained a reputation anywhere near to that of the ball, but during the mid- to late nineties Wally had made it a priority to elevate the Titleist club line, particularly in the eyes of low-handicap players. One of the smartest moves he'd made was to hire two of the best clubmakers in the business—Scotty Cameron and Bob Vokey—to produce putters and wedges, respectively, exclusively for Titleist.

All this made Titleist the perfect home for Tiger. He'd been playing a Titleist ball forever, carried a Cobra (owned by Titleist) driver and Titleist fairway woods, and had no particular loyalty to the Mizuno irons in his bag, confident he could win with any brand of clubs. So the timing was perfect to marry Tiger with Titleist, make him the spokesman for their new era of top-line equipment for better players.

So convinced was I that Tiger and Titleist were the ideal match that I'd mentioned it to Wally on more than one occasion as Tiger was compiling his USGA Juniors and Amateurs. Wally and I had been good friends for years, a friendship I cherished greatly, in part because of the irony that I was one of those dastardly agents he so detested, but also because, by his own admission, Wally had few close friends. I think we had an unspoken mutual respect for each "doing our homework" better than our competitors in the industry.

When the time for negotiation approached, we did most of the back-and-forth by phone and confidential email. I began by making Wally aware that we'd been talking to Nike about some very big numbers. Being the super-prepared guy he was, he parried by reciting the statistics on Tiger's theretofore lackluster performance in pro tournaments. But from the beginning there was a shared understanding that a deal was going to happen, and it didn't take long to reach the numbers: $20 million for five years (with escalating bonuses similar to those in the Nike contract).

All that remained before finalizing the contract was a meeting. Wally wanted to formalize things with a face-to-face with Tiger, and this was a get-together that needed to be clandestine, so it was agreed that Tiger, Earl, Wally, and I would meet in San Francisco. It was June of 1996, and Tiger was just finishing up his second year at Stanford, so he was already there. Wally flew in from Boston, Earl from Los Angeles, and I from Cleveland, all of us converging at a downtown hotel where Earl and Tiger had booked a suite.

I began by going over what the parameters of a deal "might look like if and when Tiger should decide to turn pro." (At this point the decision had been made but not announced, and it was important for all concerned to stay within NCAA and USGA regulations.) Wally asked Tiger several questions about his specs and preferences with regard to clubs, shafts, etc. Then he made a very strong statement, assuring Tiger that there would never be a moment when Titleist would ask him to play a product that he wasn't happy with—the company would not rest until Tiger had exactly the clubs he wanted. I know that resonated with Tiger because I'd shared with him the travails of Greg Norman and the Tour Edition ball.

It was a great way to end the meeting, except that it wasn't quite over. Earl had something he wanted to say. With a twinkle in his eye he looked at Wally and said, "Now let's get to the really important stuff—when do I get *my set of clubs?*"

By late August, when Tiger arrived at Pumpkin Ridge for the 1996 U.S. Amateur, everything was in place. I'd surreptitiously arranged for him to get sponsor exemptions into most of the remaining PGA Tour events, and

Phil Knight had laid on his private jet to take Tiger to the first of those events, the Milwaukee Open, where Nike had also made arrangements at a hotel for a Wednesday morning press conference.

That said, Tiger had given no indication of his intentions. A week earlier he'd assured his college coach he'd be returning to Stanford in the fall, and at Pumpkin Ridge, when USGA president Judy Bell approached him and asked whether he'd be playing in the World Amateur Team Championship scheduled for November in the Philippines, he told her he would. Earl had been less circumspect—two weeks earlier he'd told a couple of golf writers the decision had been made and would be announced immediately after the Amateur, but he'd also sworn them to secrecy, and the scribes had managed to hold their pens.

I was on-site that week at Pumpkin Ridge, but kept a low profile, giving Tiger a wide berth. I was riveted watching the progress of his matches. He'd been pointing to this event and this event alone for months and I knew how badly he wanted to complete a second USGA triple. Selfishly, I also knew that if Tiger could cap his amateur career with an unprecedented third straight victory in the U.S. Amateur, it would add to the already considerable leverage I'd have when I began negotiating with the several companies that had expressed interest in affiliating with him.

Late on Sunday afternoon, when Tiger holed the winning putt to beat Steve Scott on the thirty-eighth hole, it was hard to process what he'd accomplished. This kid won six USGA National Championships in six consecutive years on six different courses—thirty-six straight matches against the highest level of amateur competition. Beyond his own unrelentingly stellar play, there was so much that had to go right. In any of those thirty-six matches he might have shot 66, yet been eliminated by someone who'd had the round of his life. A bad bounce here, a ball in a divot there, and the streak could have ended. The odds were so overwhelming, I couldn't help musing that it was all somehow meant to be. I told myself I knew better, but maybe Earl's bluster was legit: Tiger Woods *is* the Chosen One.

That evening, before leaving the course, there was one bit of business to attend to. The Nike folks had reserved a room in the clubhouse for a brief meeting. When I arrived with Tiger and his parents along with Butch Harmon, we were greeted by a smiling Phil Knight. Along with him was a guy I recognized from a visit to Nike.

"This is Jim Riswold," said Knight. "He's written some ads for me." That was an understatement. Riswold, the creative director of Nike's ad agency, Wieden & Kennedy, was something of a legend in the business, having created several iconic Nike commercials. They included "Air Rabbit," pairing Michael Jordan and Bugs Bunny, and the "Bo Knows" series featuring Bo Jackson.

But the most noteworthy ad Riswold would ever create was the one on the cassette tape he was holding in his hand—the "Hello World" message that would signal Tiger's debut. It would be shown for the first time at the press conference in Milwaukee, and Knight and Riswold were giving all of us an advance screening. At a signal from Knight, Riswold inserted his cassette in a video player and all eyes turned to the television monitor in the room.

As the video played—a collage of images from Tiger's childhood and amateur career—a choir sang in the background and the words "Hello World" appeared on the screen. There were no voices in the entire sixty seconds, just Riswold's script:

I shot in the 70s when I was 8.
I shot in the 60s when I was 12.
I played in the Nissan Open when I was 16.
Hello world.
I won the U.S. Amateur when I was 18.
I played in the Masters when I was 19.
I am the only man to win three consecutive U.S. Amateur titles.
Hello world.
There are still courses in the U.S. I am not allowed to play.
Because of the color of my skin.

Hello world.

I've heard I'm not ready for you.

Are you ready for me?

To say it was unlike any golf commercial I'd ever seen would be an understatement, and my first reaction wasn't all positive. I had doubts about how the "courses I am not allowed to play" line would be received, but I figured Nike knew advertising. Beyond that, there was also Earl's painful history of discrimination—all those country clubs where he and Tiger had been made to feel unwelcome. With respect for that, I kept my thoughts to myself.

When the screen went black there was dead silence in the room as we all tried to process what we'd just viewed. Then Tiger said, "Can I see that again?"

After the second showing it was, surprisingly, Butch Harmon who spoke first: "That's the best fuckin' ad I've ever seen," he said. There was nothing anyone could add to that. The professional career of Tiger Woods was about to launch.

Two days later in Milwaukee I knocked on the door of the hotel suite where Tiger and Earl were staying. It was time to make things official. In my briefcase I had the two contracts from Nike and Titleist, which, when Tiger signed them, instantly guaranteed him $60 million. Tiger signed them both without comment, indeed without reaction of any kind. Curiously, he'd always seemed almost indifferent to the money. Granted, a twenty-year-old just beginning as a professional would have little or no frame of reference for the enormity of these contracts. But even when I'd tried to put the Nike and Titleist agreements in context—"Tiger, do you realize you're now making four times what the current number one player in the game, Greg Norman, earns on golf clubs and balls and more than double what Greg makes on shoes and clothes?!"—his reaction was muted: "That's not bad, right?"

Having worked as hard as I had persuading companies that this as-yet-unproven kid was worth multiples of what top athletes were being paid, I guess I thought a more appropriate response might have been: "Holy shit, Hughes, that's incredible!"

The third contract he signed that evening was his representation agreement with IMG. It differed in significant ways from most of the contracts
I'd done, beginning with the commission structure. Working together with
Tiger's attorney, John Merchant, I'd agreed to adjust our fees to a sliding scale
similar to the royalties on a book contract: IMG would receive 15 percent of
the first $2.5 million in annual merchandising income we earned for Tiger,
20 percent on income between $2.5 and $5 million, and 25 percent on all
income above $5 million.

A second clause related to the term of the agreement. The base contract was for four years, from August 1996 to August 2000, but I'd added
incentives. If in any year IMG were to produce income for Tiger exceed-
ing $16 million, the contract would be extended by two years to 2002;
if we could produce more than $26 million, the contract would extend
another two years to 2004; and if we could produce $38 million, it would
go one more year to 2005, a total of ten years. We would earn all six years
of those extensions by the end of 1997.

And finally there was what's known as a "key man" clause, which
read, "It is understood that the personal involvement of Hughes Norton
is the decisive factor causing you to enter this Agreement. Therefore, if at
any time during the term of this Agreement Mr. Norton is no longer employed by IMG, or, in the event Mr. Norton discontinues the day-to-day
overall responsibility contemplated by this Agreement, you shall have the
unqualified right to terminate this Agreement." Such clauses were common throughout the business world, but IMG always resisted them. I let
it go this time for selfish reasons. Three years earlier, when Greg Norman
left and I was demoted from head of IMG's golf division, I might have
lost my job entirely had it not been for the long-standing recruiting relationship I'd formed with Tiger. This clause, I thought, was important to
Tiger and Earl, but also protected me.

With those contracts signed, Tiger Woods was set for life financially
and free to pursue his quest to become the best golfer the game had ever
seen. He was launched—now we'd see how high he could soar.

8

Managing the Maelstrom

And so, across the entire sports world, "Tigermania" erupted. No rookie in history had been so anxiously awaited or rapturously received. Within hours, "Tiger Turns Pro" became front-page news everywhere, the lead item in every TV and radio broadcast. I remember as a ten-year-old kid being blown away by the Elvis Presley gale force of celebrity in the late 1950s. This was Elvis all over again, only bigger. A tsunami.

Tiger was transcending the game of golf seemingly overnight. Everybody wanted a piece of him: reporters, talk shows, fans, autograph seekers, and the organizers of every professional tournament around the globe. Golf's TV ratings went through the roof, while at every tournament he played, extra shuttle buses, grandstands, and portable toilets were required for the huge increase in traffic, fans, and media. To avoid the huge crowds dogging his every step, Tiger started playing tournament practice rounds at 6 a.m. Even at that hour he had to walk through a gauntlet of autograph seekers. At every place he teed it up, large boisterous galleries jockeyed for position to catch a glimpse of him.

One of my jobs as Tiger's manager was to shield him from as much of this chaos as I could. But even before that I had another task. With the kind of money Tiger was making, both on and off the course, priority number one was to minimize the taxes he'd be paying—and that meant getting him out of California, which had one of the highest state tax rates in the nation. The obvious choice was Florida and its zero state tax. The move would save Tiger $5.5 million on his Nike and Titleist income alone.

With Tiger too focused on his golf game to worry about such things, I chose his new residence for him—Isleworth near Orlando, an upscale community with an Arnold Palmer golf course and an expansive practice area.

Key to that choice was the proximity of a "pair of Marks." Mark McCormack had a lavish home at Isleworth and was spending more and more time there with his second wife, professional tennis player Betsy Nagelsen. More important, Isleworth was the home of Mark O'Meara, who I thought could be valuable to Tiger in a couple of ways. First, as an IMG client he could be a sounding board for Tiger in the early days of our relationship. I also thought having a fellow Tour player and friend nearby would help Tiger adjust to his completely new environment. I ran my idea past O'Meara first and he readily agreed. Tiger ended up spending a lot of time with Mark and Alicia, whose house was just three doors from his, and the O'Mearas became an informal second family to him.

Meanwhile, Tiger's first item of business was to play his way onto the PGA Tour. His amateur laurels, impressive as they were, had gained him nothing in terms of playing privileges as a pro, and now he had to prove himself. There were only eight events remaining on the 1996 Tour calendar (I'd quietly secured him sponsor exemptions in most of them) and he needed to earn about $150,000 to climb within the top 125 money winners and thus secure a player's card for 1997.

"It'll be very difficult for Tiger to make $150,000," Justin Leonard told an interviewer. "That's a lot of pressure riding on a 20-year-old's shoulders." That comment surprised me a bit, coming as it did from someone who, seven years earlier, had come close to losing the Big "I" Insurance Youth Classic to Tiger, who was four years his junior (thirteen years old) and weighed barely one hundred pounds. Justin Leonard of all people should have known not to underestimate Tiger Woods.

Tiger's professional debut at the Brown Deer Park course in Milwaukee was less than auspicious, a tie for sixtieth place, but he did give the Sunday crowd a thrill by making a hole-in-one at the fourteenth hole, foreshadowing the excitement to come. From there, it was full steam ahead—eleventh place the next week at the Bell Canadian Open, then a tie for fifth at Quad Cities, a tie for third in the B.C. Open, and in his fifth start, victory at the Las Vegas Invitational, where he beat Davis Love III in sudden death. The next week came another third place at the Texas Open, followed the week after that by his second win at the Walt Disney Classic.

In seven weeks, Tiger made over $700,000 ($1,356,844 today), finishing the year not simply within the top 125 on the money list, but number 33. He was also named the Tour's Rookie of the Year and *Sports Illustrated*'s Sportsman of the Year.

ON THE ROAD WITH EARL

Earl Woods, I quickly discovered, was a tightwad. During Tiger's first few pro tournaments, Tiger and Earl stayed in a hotel suite and I was in a room elsewhere in the hotel. Tiger and Pop's favorite meal was McDonald's, so every night we'd call down and ask the bellman to go to the nearest Mickey D's and pick up our order. The kid would bring it up to the suite with a receipt, where Earl would pay him at the door. But without a tip! More than once I had to go sprinting down the hall after the bellman with a $20 bill out of my own pocket. I remember thinking: *No tip? Tiger just signed contracts worth sixty million dollars, and no tip?*

Like so many veterans, Earl smoked constantly, but what blew me away was the first time I watched him drink coffee. On active duty with the Army Reserves I thought I'd seen every bizarre combination of cream and sugar, but nothing had prepared me for the concoction Earl created. In a small cup he would stir in seven or eight packets of Splenda along with a copious amount of cream. I never asked to try a sip, but I guarantee the coffee flavor would have been hard to distinguish. I always looked forward to coffee with Earl just so I could watch him diligently go through his ritual of added ingredients.

At the end of that seven-week run Tiger was understandably ready for a rest, and with his twenty-first birthday approaching on December 30 he invited a bunch of his buddies—Notah Begay, one or two other Stanford teammates, and a couple of friends from high school—to help him celebrate in style with a bash in Las Vegas.

This posse had joined him a couple of times before. They were quite a rat pack—as refreshingly sophomoric as you'd expect of twenty-year-olds—and occasionally I found myself among them, reliving my youth. One day, we were in a hotel lobby waiting for Tiger to come down from his room, when the amigos decided to have the front desk page a guest. On my signal, when Tiger emerged from the hotel elevator, an announcement blared through the lobby: "Paging Mr. Heywood Jablomi, repeat, hey would ya blow me." Tiger's pals were laughing so hard they could barely breathe. Me too.

Possibly because of such antics, I'd begun to feel a bond with the lads, and in one regrettably unguarded moment I sort of invited myself to the birthday blowout. After only a few hours into the first night, I could tell someone didn't belong. Tiger made it clear his crew was heading to one of the hot Vegas clubs, and they'd like to do so absent the forty-nine-year-old guy who'd been trying to hang with them. What was I thinking?

Such frat boy interludes aside, Tiger allowed himself little time for light-heartedness, so monomaniacal was his drive to be the best ever to play the game. It was the same when it came to most of his dealings with me. Although every major business-related decision was made by a three-man vote—Tiger, Earl, and me—Tiger had zero interest in business and left 100 percent of the details and follow-up to me. His priorities were to practice and play, as they should have been.

With the Nike and Titleist deals having set up Tiger financially for life, we could afford to be selective about the opportunities to pursue going forward. Foremost in my mind was aligning him with companies whose goods and services were revered as highly as he was. Image had become as important as income.

To that end, among my first targets was American Express. In the *Wall Street Journal* one morning I saw that Amex had appointed a new president and chief operating officer, Ken Chenault, the third African American to head a Fortune 500 company. Chenault was a 1973 graduate of Bowdoin College in Maine, where I'd learned to play hockey, and I knew a couple of the guys he went to school with. I called Chenault's office and set up a meeting.

He was interested, and a deal came together quickly, Amex paying Tiger $25 million to be the company's spokesman for five years. It was exactly the "fit" I was hoping for as Tiger's first non-golf endorsement—the most respected brand in its field aligning with the emerging dominant brand in golf. Did Chenault make the deal because Tiger was Black? I never asked, but I didn't pitch Tiger to Ken on the basis of race.

EYE OF THE TIGER

Tiger's eyesight was terrible. As a kid he wore Coke-bottle-thick glasses, and his teammates at Stanford nicknamed him Urkel after the nerdy high school kid on the TV show *Family Matters*. He then switched to contact lenses, which served him well with one exception.

Tiger's third career victory came in the opening event of the 1997 season, the Tournament of Champions played at the La Costa resort just north of San Diego. In the third round, he'd birdied the last four holes to tie Tom Lehman, the PGA Tour 1996 Player of the Year, and a big battle was expected on Sunday. But heavy rains washed out the round and Tour officials decided to determine the winner with a sudden-death playoff beginning at the par-3 seventh hole.

Tiger was on the range warming up when one of his contact lenses slipped out. As would be the case with another challenge later in his career—a broken leg at the 2008 U.S. Open played just down the road at Torrey Pines—blurred vision wasn't going to stop this kid. After Lehman hit his tee shot into a pond, Tiger stepped up and laced a 6-iron to within eight inches of the hole.

Tiger never mentioned his contact lens issue to the press afterward and to this day no one knows about it. As a lifetime

contact lens wearer myself, I knew exactly how helpless it feels
with one eye 20/20 and the other blurry. So the next day, I got
Tida to give me a couple of spare pairs of Tiger's contacts, which
I carried with me everywhere from that moment on. Happily,
I never had occasion to use them. In fact, I still have them
somewhere in a bathroom drawer.

The other aspect that's important to consider when seeking commercial
affiliations for an athlete—or any celebrity—is authenticity. The endorsement should be credible; the public needs to believe that the product is
something the star actually enjoys using. In Tiger's case, there was one
natural product category—video games—and there was only one place to
go: the industry leader, Electronic Arts.

Tiger was obsessed with video games. When he wasn't playing golf,
practicing, eating, or watching ESPN's *SportsCenter*, he flopped on a couch,
grabbed a controller, and locked in. When I approached EA Sports, however, their reaction surprised me—they were the first company that was less
than champing at the bit to link up with Tiger. The reason? The video game
market was a young one, the golf market was an old one. EA's existing golf
game, licensed to the PGA Tour, was floundering.

"That's exactly why you *should* partner with Tiger," I said. "Beyond his
incredible game and charismatic smile, he's still a kid—any golf game with
his name on it will have instant appeal to other kids."

They understood that, even believed it, but they also wanted to believe
in Tiger—that same element of authenticity. Before they threw a pile of
money at this kid, they wanted to be sure he was a bona fide gamer. And
so it was that several EA representatives made their way to the Isleworth
clubhouse to meet Tiger, their main agenda being to check out his gaming
chops.

"I'm not really into the sports games," he told them immediately.
"I'm more a Mortal Kombat and Need for Speed guy." He then chatted

animatedly with them about what he liked and didn't in the games he played, and made it clear that if he were to associate with EA, he'd want to be very involved in the design of the game. Among his big issues: eighteen holes of video golf should not take more than half an hour to play.

That was music to their ears, and before long we had a deal—or so I thought. There was one major snag—the contract we had with Nike had granted them "interactive rights" to Tiger. I or IMG's legal department should have caught that one, but we didn't. Nike was quite happy to cede those rights to EA, but only if EA paid them a chunk of cash, which EA rightly was not interested in doing. Suddenly I found myself in the middle of a dispute with Tiger's biggest corporate partner. Then Tiger got dragged in—the last thing either Nike or I wanted. "Can't you just work this fucking thing out?" he said.

We could. After a couple of tense back-and-forth sessions with the Nike folks, I reached a settlement with them and a deal with EA—a four-year contract with a minimum guaranteed royalty of $1 million in year one in exchange for Tiger's name and likeness and several days a year of his time for the creation and promotion of the game. When in 1998 Electronic Arts released Tiger Woods 99 PGA Tour Golf, it became an instant hit. Within a year Tiger's EA game accounted for 44 percent of the golf games sold for personal computers and 41 percent of such games on home consoles. Both figures topped the field. Tiger's partnership with EA would last fifteen years and bring him a total income of roughly $100 million. And thanks to his love of gaming, it was the only deal where I don't remember him bitching about the time commitment required.

Another clear fit for Tiger was Rolex, where IMG had a long-standing relationship dating to 1967 when Arnold Palmer became the first Rolex golf ambassador. Our many other Rolex-wearing clients included Jean-Claude Killy, Rod Laver, and Jackie Stewart.

That said, no deal Rolex had ever made with an athlete was quite like the one I got for Tiger. At the time, Phil Mickelson's contract with them was rumored to be for $25,000 a year and a few free watches. Tiger, in year one, received a retainer of $200,000 plus an additional $645,000 in royalties on the sale of a Tiger Woods Signature Tudor watch. Never before had Rolex created a signature timepiece or paid royalties to an athlete. The five-year deal also called for Rolex to make donations to the Tiger Woods Foundation, created to help disadvantaged kids pursue their passions through education. The payments started at $60,000 per year and escalated to $100,000 in year five. All this in exchange for one day per year of his time.

Earl pushed me for such contributions from each of Tiger's sponsors—it was a big ask of corporations already paying the kid millions for his endorsement. Raising this much money for an athlete's charity was unprecedented. I felt proud to help launch something so important to Earl and Tiger. And not one dollar of the $5 million raised was commissioned by IMG.

CONTRIBUTIONS TO THE TIGER WOODS FOUNDATION BY TIGER'S SPONSORS

COMPANY	1997	1998	1999	2000	2001
American Express	$1,000,000	*	*	*	*
Nike	$325,000	$250,000	$250,000	$250,000	$250,000
Titleist	$546,696	$10,729			
CBS Sportsline	$100,000	$100,000	$100,000		
Rolex	$60,000	$70,000	$80,000	$90,000	$100,000
Asahi	$100,000	$100,000	$100,000		
Golf Digest		$300,000	$300,000	$300,000	
All Star Café	$194,000	$70,000			
TOTAL	$2,326,496	$900,729	$830,000	$640,000	$350,000
5-Yr. Total $5,047,225					

Source: International Management Group 1998.

* A percentage of Amex charge card purchases during a three-month span each year

Much of the golf world was aware of Tiger's affiliations with Nike, Titleist, EA Sports, and Rolex, but there were also lucrative deals known to almost
no one. The weirdest one was with Unilever, a multinational packaged goods
company producing a variety of products in the areas of food and personal
and home care—everything from Breyers ice cream to Helene Curtis cosmetics to Vaseline jelly. Senior management really wanted to do something
with Tiger, but they couldn't decide what—sell lipstick? We had a number of
meetings that never seemed to get anywhere. Finally I said, "Look, until you
guys figure out what you want to do we'll give you exclusivity in all Unilever
product categories between now and the end of the year. Price: $2.125 mil-
lion." (Who knows how I came up with that number.) And they went for it!
In the history of sports management, I suspect no athlete had ever been paid
that kind of money simply *not* to endorse that company's competitors.

Then there was Asahi, a Japanese beverage maker that agreed to bring
a production crew from Tokyo to Orlando for a one-day commercial
shoot with Tiger endorsing their canned coffee drink. Payment: $4.6 mil-
lion per year for three years—more than twice what any athlete had ever
been paid for a Japanese commercial—plus another $100,000 a year for
three years to the TW Foundation (which Asahi had never heard of and
got no tax benefit from supporting). They later asked to do a calendar featuring stock photos of Tiger to send to restaurants and bars throughout
Japan. That brought him an additional $450,000. (The deal was renewed
for another three years at a lesser amount—$4.3 million a year—but with
a reduced time commitment by Tiger.)

The last two corporate deals in year one were much smaller, a five-year
contract with *Golf Digest* that paid $320,000 a year ($300,000 of it to the
TW Foundation) for four hours per year of his time, and another with
Wheaties for $250,000 per year to be on the cereal box cover. The money in
both cases was of comparatively little importance. *Golf Digest*'s covers were
the key to that deal, as a continuing way to promote both Tiger and his
affiliations with Nike and Titleist, while the Wheaties deal was a statement.
Only household-name athletes ever appear on a Wheaties box.

Managing Tiger's image and income was one thing; managing his time was quite another. He hated being asked to give days—even hours—of his time. It was one of the few things that got his blood boiling. When I presented him with requests or reminded him of contractual commitments for days of his time, his knee-jerk response was "Fuck 'em." He saw any business obligation outside the ropes as an aggravating burden and quickly adopted a hard-and-fast policy: If the contract called for one hour of his time, that is exactly what he gave them. When the sixty minutes were up, he walked out. You can imagine the pressure this put on, say, the editors of *Golf Digest*, scrambling to interview him for two or three articles while also doing the accompanying photo shoots before the clock ran out.

The way Tiger saw it, the only money that meant anything was what he earned playing golf. The rest was "paper money" earned for him by me, and it really didn't matter whether the contract was for $100,000 or $100 million. If it brought a pain-in-the-ass time commitment, it was more trouble than it was worth.

Bev Norwood and I calculated that in our first year with Tiger we received 1,545 requests for his time, nearly all of which we rejected; managing Tiger had put us in the business of pissing people off. On top of that came the mailbags full of requests from fans, received at the IMG office in Cleveland, at Tiger's home in Florida, his parents' home in California, the PGA Tour headquarters, and his locker wherever he played. These were all funneled to Cleveland, where my tireless assistant Kathy Repeta did her best to deal with them—literally thousands every month.

Most of them were fans looking for Tiger's autograph, but there were always a couple dozen significant requests, and I'd take those on the road with me and slide them in front of him whenever I could, usually pre-personalizing them myself with a "To Ned, thanks for all your support" or whatever, so all he'd have to do was sign them. He didn't love this, but always complied.

Occasionally, the signature signals would get crossed, as I was reminded by my coauthor George Peper. His wife, Libby, an artist, had been commissioned to do a painting of the tenth hole at Augusta National, and as part of her fee she was given several prints, one of which she donated to a charity auction. As a way of increasing the auction action George offered to get the print signed by Tiger, and sent it to the Cleveland office. It came back a couple of weeks later inscribed, "To Elizabeth, all my best, Tiger Woods." Useless (except to bidders named Elizabeth).

The one who really drove Tiger nuts was his caddie, Mike "Fluff" Cowan. Fluff was a memorabilia hound. Almost every time the three of us were together he produced bags of stuff for Tiger to autograph. I presume Fluff hung on to a few of those items; if he did, his retirement is going to be a lot more comfortable.

In a very short time, we realized the only sane way to handle the unending avalanche of autograph requests was to find a way to replicate Tiger's signature. Back then, Jack Nicklaus had a sophisticated printer that did the job, as did many prominent athletes and celebrities. After doing a bit of research we settled on something more basic—a hand stamp. We sent Tiger's signature to the stamp maker, and back it came perfectly reproduced, embossed on the bottom of the same sort of ink pad stamp used by post offices to mark something airmail or special delivery.

It worked simply and was extremely realistic, if a bit time-consuming. Poor Kathy was saddled with most of the bam-bamming from ink pad to paper as we tried to reply to as many fans as possible. (You can imagine the postage bills—something I never brought to Mark's attention, figuring it was one of the costs of doing business.) So fair warning to any of you out there who wrote to Tiger in the late 1990s looking for an autograph. That photo hanging in your den may have been stamped by Kathy Repeta rather than signed by Tiger Woods.

Out on Tour, managing the maelstrom around Tiger was a constant process that required the efforts of a substantial entourage. Tiger was rarely alone, as the IMG traveling squad in any week might include myself, Bev, and fellow agent Clarke Jones, backed up in the Cleveland office by Kathy, staff attorney John Oney, and financial manager Chris Hubman. The on-site golf handlers were caddie Fluff Cowan and frequent drop-ins Butch

Harmon and sports psychologist Jay Brunza. Tiger even had his own unofficial publicist and beat reporter in *Golf Digest*'s Pete McDaniel.

His go-to friends—to the extent Tiger had any truly close friends—were Notah Begay, Mark O'Meara, Mark McCormack (when in residence at Isleworth), and Michael Jordan. And overseeing it all, of course, was Earl (often acting at the behest of Tida), along with the family attorney, John Merchant. By my count that's seventeen people working full- or part-time on Team Tiger.

And there were times when Tiger needed as many friends, family, and fixers as he could get, as he made his share of rookie mistakes. The first of them came just five weeks after he turned pro, when he opted not to play in the Buick Open. Normally that would not have been a big deal, but on this occasion it was the same week Tiger was to be presented the Haskins Award as the college golf player of the year. The place and time had in fact been arranged to fit his schedule.

Having played five weeks straight—the grueling U.S. Amateur (164 holes in six days), followed by four PGA Tour events—Tiger was exhausted. "I can't do it," he told me. "I've gotta take a week off and rest."

I knew there would be fallout if he refused, but the kid was pleading for a break. An agent's conflict: you have to respect your client's state of mind even when you know that acting on his behalf in that moment will cause problems later. I chose to support his wishes.

The press had a field day, and I did sadly little to parry their shots. Truth told, I was terrible at public relations, and it was one area where I'd learned nothing from Mark McCormack, because he was as inexperienced at it as I was. When Mark started out he was just a lawyer improvising his way in the sports marketing business who got extremely lucky when his first client was Arnold Palmer, someone whose unimpeachable character and powerful charisma were all the public relations he needed.

Tiger, for all his appeal, was never Arnie, and when he made mistakes there were consequences. Another major faux pas came in January of 1997 when we granted a request from *Gentleman's Quarterly* to do a cover story.

On the appointed day a limousine showed up at Tiger's parents' home in California. In the back seat was writer Charles Pierce, who would be interviewing Tiger for several hours as Tiger did a photo shoot for the piece. Looking back, this being Tiger's first major interview for a non-golf publication, I probably should have chaperoned him, but as I say, I was clueless at the intricacies of PR, so off Tiger went on his own.

At age twenty-one, he wasn't savvy enough to say "off the record" before telling Pierce a couple of off-color jokes, and Pierce took full advantage, positioning the jokes prominently in his piece. When the magazine came out, Tiger took some hits. We tried to deflect them by drafting an apology from Tiger, but the damage was done.

Tiger was uneasy with sudden fame. Life was getting complicated in ways he'd never envisioned, and he was not happy about it.

Not long after that I invited *Sports Illustrated* writer Alan Shipnuck to a meeting with Tiger, Earl, and me in the hope *SI* would publicize the impressive fundraising work I was initiating for the Tiger Woods Foundation. But that, too, backfired when Shipnuck took some unnecessary shots in his article.

Tiger came away from those episodes concluding, understandably, that the press was looking only for the negative—and therefore was not to be trusted. Thereafter he became arguably the worst interview in golf, answering questions as tersely as possible and revealing virtually nothing of himself. "A lot of things in my life I like to keep private," he told me. "Unfortunately, people can't accept that."

Tiger's enemy number one from the press corps was John Feinstein, a sports columnist for the *Washington Post* and author of several bestselling books, who for whatever reason chose to be an attack dog. The week after Tiger turned pro, Feinstein wrote a piece describing Earl Woods as "a pushy father," comparing him to the notorious tennis father Stefano Capriati as someone "in pursuit of publicity for himself and every possible dollar." That infuriated Tiger—nothing angered him more than attacks on his father—and launched a relationship that would only get worse.

When Tiger skipped the Haskins Award, Feinstein had been the first to pounce: "When you are the game's next Next One and you know your presence in a tournament has been promoted, you really should show up," he wrote. "And when the sponsors of a major golf award have scheduled their awards dinner to suit you at a time and place where you have told them you will be, you don't blow off the dinner and go home."

Feinstein also took a bunch of shots at me as the venal and self-absorbed monster from "IMGreedy," a posture that always struck me as hypocritical, since John himself had an agent—famed literary agent Esther Newberg— who worked hard to get him every possible dollar of advance money for his books. Funny how he never found fault with her.

Within Tiger's inner circle, the individual who was most supportive to him during his early months as a pro was probably Mark O'Meara. When they were both at Isleworth they played together often. Mark, although eighteen years older than Tiger, was still in his prime, as he proved in February at the 1997 AT&T Pebble Beach Pro-Am, holding off a final-round 64 by Tiger to win by a stroke over him and David Duval. It was O'Meara's fifth victory in that event and he followed the next week with a win at the Buick Invitational, his eighteenth career title.

So O'Meara had game, but he was soon to see it was not close to Tiger's. A few weeks later, he and Tiger played a casual round together at Isleworth. (Tiger, having won three of his first nine tournaments as a pro, had risen to number fourteen in the world, but O'Meara, fresh off his two consecutive wins, was above him at number eight.) I happened to phone Tiger that same evening, just to check in with him.

"So I had a pretty interesting round today," he said. "I shot 59."

"What?"

"Yeah, I played with Marko. Started with a par on 10, then birdied 11 and 12, eagled 13, and birdied 14, 15, 16, 17, 18, and one—27 on the back nine and ten under for my first ten holes."

"Holy shit! Then what?"

"Believe it or not, I didn't birdie either of the par fives—had a 5-iron to three and 3-iron to seven and made five on both of them. But I made three more birdies on the front so it was 32-27—59 but it could have been a few lower than that."

This on a par-72 course measuring 7,149 yards and rated 74.4—one of the toughest in Florida. Amazingly it was the only sub-61 score of Tiger's life.

But the story gets even better. The next day he and O'Meara go out again and once again start on the back nine. This time Tiger opens with a birdie—and then on the eleventh makes a hole-in-one. Years later, O'Meara recalled the moment for an Action Network interview.

"He's hitting like an 8-iron. I haven't even gotten out of my cart. It goes right at the pin, one-hops, and goes into the hole. So I go over and take $100 or whatever it was, I can't remember, and I put it on his cart seat. I didn't even hit my shot. I said, 'That was a really nice shot. I quit. I'll see you later on the driving range when you get done.'

"He's like, 'Where are you going?' I said, 'I quit. You shot 13 under yesterday, you just jarred that, you're 16 under for your last 20 holes. I quit. I'm outta here.'"

Those two days were April 4 and 5, 1997—the Friday and Saturday before the most momentous week of Tiger's young career—the Masters. Had I been a betting man, armed with this inside info, I could not have placed a Masters wager fast enough on my young client.

It would be a week to remember for a number of reasons—all of them related to Tiger, most of them positive, but at least one very tragic.

Back then, a limited number of Masters "patrons" were able to buy tickets to the four rounds of the tournament for a total of $100. While most of these patrons did attend the tournament, a good number of them took the opportunity to make a quick profit, selling their badges for $400 to $450 a day or $1,600 to $1,800 for the week to middlemen such as Allen Caldwell, a local liquor dealer who annually purchased dozens of such tickets, building them into corporate hospitality packages that included a rental home. Caldwell's MO was to wait until the last minute, when prices typically dipped a bit, then jump in. In 1997 he had contracts to deliver 250 tickets.

Then came Tiger. As the tournament approached and the buzz around him grew, the market for badges intensified. A couple of weeks before the tournament, the asking price for a four-day badge jumped from $1,500 to $3,000. Then at the last minute things exploded when Phil Knight came into town with a slew of Nike executives and guests and put the word out that he would pay anything to secure badges. By the Wednesday before play began, badges were going for $10,000, the most expensive ticket in sports history.

Suddenly, the 250 badges that Allen Caldwell had estimated would cost him about $300,000 now cost $2.5 million—he was facing financial, professional, and personal ruin. And so, on the eve of the tournament, he walked onto the deck of his home in Martinez, Georgia, three miles from Augusta, and used a twelve-gauge Remington shotgun to take his own life. His story was generally lost amid the circus of that week, a sad footnote to the era of greed and venality that Tigermania had ignited in the world of professional golf.

I was literally an agent of that era, at the center of the money churn. But that week, such thoughts were far from my mind. As always during Masters week, I had deals to do. Under the tree fronting the Augusta National clubhouse, McCormack's good friend Russ Meyer, CEO of Cessna Aircraft, introduced me to Rich Santulli, the founder of a start-up named Executive Jet (now known as NetJets). That week Rich and I reached an agreement for Tiger to become the company's spokesman in return for two round trips to Europe and one to Asia each year in a Gulfstream IV. The ad featuring Tiger ran in *Forbes*, *Business Week*, and the *Wall Street Journal* for two years and used existing photos, so there was no time requirement whatsoever from Tiger. Indeed, this was the one deal that saved him both time and money. Annual retail value at the time of those Gulfstream trips: $1 million. And I didn't commission one dime of it.

I'd also arranged another meeting that did not promise to be a pleasant one—with our dear friend John Feinstein. On an ESPN show called *The Sports Reporters*, he'd been on one of his rants about IMG exploiting Tiger, and I wanted a face-to-face with him to clear the air. At the time Feinstein was writing a column for *Golf* magazine, where my coauthor, George Peper, was editor in chief, and where John had also taken a couple of swipes at Tiger. Since I barely knew John, I asked George if he'd mind setting up the meeting. I figured it wouldn't hurt if George knew about the Woods-Norton-Feinstein situation; if nothing else he might be able to serve as a buffer.

We agreed to meet for breakfast in the Augusta National clubhouse on Wednesday morning. When, the night before, I told Tiger about the meeting, he raised his eyebrows and said, "I think I'll join you." I also asked Clarke Jones and Bev Norwood to join us, and George brought along Feinstein's editor at the magazine, Mike Purkey. Feinstein was there when we arrived and I remember noting how nervous he seemed—his hands were actually shaking.

I thanked everyone for coming and said that we were expecting a surprise guest at any moment—Tiger—but we shouldn't wait for him. Clarke and I then began by asking John a number of questions about the sources for various things he'd asserted both on the air and in print. Something that has always bugged me is the penchant of some journalists to cite unnamed sources. John did his best to stiff-arm us, and the situation only became more tense. Finally, I said, "You know, John, you're not doing *Golf* magazine much good with your vitriol. At the moment they're competing with *Golf Digest* to sign Tiger as a playing editor. Your very affiliation with the magazine is a negative, and when you lash out at Tiger—or me—the way you've been doing, it only makes Tiger less inclined to consider *Golf* over *Golf Digest*."

That set him off. He stood up from the table, looked at Peper and Purkey, and said, "If you want to stay and eat with these assholes, go ahead, but I have better things to do than listen to this crap." Off he stomped, and we were done before Tiger even showed up. A week later, when everyone else in the press was writing glowing stories about Tiger, John started after him again, and as far as I can tell, he hasn't stopped since.

As for the *Golf* magazine/*Golf Digest* contest, when a month or so later Tiger went with *Golf Digest*, Feinstein had comparatively little to do with it. The *Golf Digest* editors, notably Jerry Tarde, Jaime Diaz, and Pete McDaniel, had years earlier worked their way into Earl's good graces (McDaniel was actually cowriting a book with Earl) to the point that, when the time for a decision came, Earl wasn't even interested in looking at *Golf* magazine's proposal, which involved the clout of its parent company, the *Los Angeles Times*; included six-figure donations to the TW Foundation; and was more generous than *Golf Digest's*.

"At least let's use it to better *Golf Digest's* number," I said, but Earl was adamant. I suspect he'd already told *Golf Digest* they had the deal.

When on Thursday it came time for Tiger to tee off, the crowd at number one was six-deep, so I made my way to the balcony of the clubhouse to view from above. All around me were members of the staff at Augusta National—waiters, dishwashers, and bartenders, all smiling and applauding as Tiger strode to the tee. A moment I'll never forget. Also standing on that balcony was Lee Elder, the first African American to play in the Masters and one of Tiger's heroes. I glanced over and glimpsed a tear rolling down his cheek.

It did not begin well for Tiger—a missed fairway led to a bogey at the first and he added three more, including the eighth and ninth, to reach the turn in 40, 4 over par. Then, as if a switch flipped, he channeled the golf he'd played a week earlier in Florida with O'Meara and blistered the back nine with four birdies and an eagle to return in 30. His 2-under-par total staked him to a solo fourth place.

A 66 on Friday took him into the lead by three strokes over Colin Montgomerie, who in the pressroom that afternoon foolishly said, "The pressure is mounting and I have a lot more experience in majors than this kid does." The next day Tiger blew Montgomerie away, 65 to 74, and roared to a nine-stroke lead, whereupon Colin changed his tune, telling the media, "There's no chance humanly possible Tiger is going to lose this tournament. No way." When a reporter reminded Monty that only a year earlier Greg Norman had had a six-stroke lead on Nick Faldo going into the final round, Colin responded: "Faldo is not lying second, for a start. And Greg Norman is not Tiger Woods." When I read that in the *Augusta Chronicle* on Sunday morning, my already upbeat mood became even happier.

As was my habit, I watched the final round from a table in the club's grillroom, where various officials and members of the press gathered, occasionally joined by players who had completed their rounds and wanted to see the finish. On that Sunday afternoon there was no drama to watch—by the back nine Tiger's lead was in double digits—but there was one moment that caused me concern when he hit his second shot to the par-5 fifteenth a bit to the right, the ball coming to rest beside a woman's purse, necessitating a drop.

As he assessed his situation, I heard a pro at the table next to me say, "That's a tricky little drop there, I hope he does this right." A rules official appeared and seemed to inspect the scene, but I wondered, even after Tiger had played his shot to the green, whether something might have gone wrong. It was with that in mind that I stationed myself along with Earl and Tida behind the eighteenth green. I wanted to be sure that Tiger, before he signed his card, triple-checked with the scorer's tent that all had proceeded correctly at the fifteenth, so I conveyed that message to Earl. If you watch a videotape of the conclusion of that Masters, you'll see, after Tiger hugs Earl, that Earl engages him in a brief, serious conversation. That was the subject. I was probably being overly cautious, but I kept thinking, whereas a penalty stroke (or ten!) would be manageable, a DQ for signing for an incorrect score would be disastrous!

That evening I was fortunate to be among those included in the members dinner held in the Augusta National clubhouse honoring the champion. I'd never been to one of those, but I'm fairly certain this was the first one that began with a spontaneous ovation from the back of the room, where the clubhouse staff—chefs, servers, and bartenders—had assembled to applaud the first non-white winner of the Masters.

Later that evening at the home Tiger and his parents had rented for the week, a celebration was in full swing with friends, family, and a Masters champion cake that had been ordered the day before from a local bakery. Among those there were Kathy Repeta, Bev Norwood, John Merchant, Pete McDaniel, and two or three of Tiger's Stanford buddies, who had been there all week and had provided a valuable service—heading with Tiger after each round to a nearby Arby's, where they'd wolf down roast beef sandwiches before returning to the house to shoot baskets in the driveway and play ping-pong in the basement, thus keeping his mind off the tournament for a few hours.

When Tiger arrived, there was a huge cheer. We all toasted several times and the party went well into the evening, although an exhausted Tiger crashed early. I was about to head back to the IMG house, when Tida took my arm, put her fingers to her lips (*Shh . . .*), and wearing a big smile, walked me back to Tiger's bedroom. There he was, sound asleep on his bed, hugging the champion's green jacket with both arms, like a little kid with his blankie. Priceless.

Tiger had set or tied a total of twenty-seven Masters records, including the lowest seventy-two-hole total and widest margin of victory. Not surprisingly, a few days later he wanted to view the videotapes of his play. With some help from Jim Nantz I was able to get them quickly, and the next time Tiger and I were together we watched them.

I'd expected it to be a celebratory occasion, but it quickly became just the opposite: "Look at that swing, it's horrible . . . Ohmygod, I had no idea where that shot was going . . . I've got to change my swing."

"Tiger," I laughed, "it can't be that bad, you just won the Masters by twelve shots!" I then cautioned him that a couple of major champions (Hubert Green, Ian Baker-Finch) had lost their games dramatically after trying to change their swings. But Tiger was adamant.

"I don't like what I'm seeing," he said. "I need to get back to work with Butch."

It was a powerful statement and reminded me of something McCormack had once said about the top athletes he'd represented: "In the champion's mind he is never ahead. He distorts reality to serve his competitive purpose. He is always coming from behind, even when the score indicates he is destroying his opponent. He never believes he is performing as well as he actually is."

Tiger had exactly that mindset. His drive to improve would never end, his eyes would never leave the prize—and that message was not lost on me. As much as I had a duty to IMG to maximize income for my client, I had a higher obligation to Tiger, to give him the freedom to pursue his quest. If he succeeded, everything else off the course would take care of itself. In the meantime, I promised myself that any future deals I'd be presenting to him would require minimum commitments of his time.

That's not to say Tiger had life in general figured out. There would be a few more mistakes, a few learning moments along the way, notably the public embarrassment that resulted when he declined an invitation from President Clinton to join him at a Shea Stadium celebration commemorating the life of Jackie Robinson. John Feinstein ripped him, but so did a number of more prominent mainstream columnists, notably the *New York Times*'s Maureen Dowd in a column titled "Tiger's Double Bogey."

More bad press ensued when it became known that Tiger had rebuffed fellow Tour player Billy Andrade, refusing to sign a golf ball for a charity auction with which Andrade was involved, a violation of the code among Tour players.

And then there was the Fuzzy Zoeller incident. On the eve of Tiger's Masters victory, Zoeller, the 1979 Masters Champion and one of the Tour's jokesters, was on his way to the clubhouse, when he was buttonholed by a couple of golf writers. Asked what he thought of Tiger's three days of dominance, Zoeller made a racially insensitive comment, a remark he no doubt thought was clever at the time: "That little boy is driving well and he's putting well. He's doing everything it takes to win. So you pat him on the back, say congratulations and enjoy it, and tell him not to serve fried chicken next year [at the Masters Champions dinner the winner hosts] or collard greens or whatever the hell they serve."

Tiger knew Zoeller's reputation as a wisecracker and figured he meant no harm, but was nonetheless perplexed by the gratuitous dig. Initially he made no response, and he also did not respond when Fuzzy, after being skewered in the press, reached out to apologize. (And once again, my own PR efforts were ineffectual at best.) Earl seemed to almost enjoy watching Fuzzy twist in the wind for a few days as fitting punishment. Eventually Tiger did accept Zoeller's apology and everyone moved on.

Indeed, Tiger not only survived his missteps unscathed, but rose to the pinnacle of sport. A *Wall Street Journal*/NBC News poll published shortly after the Masters revealed that he had shot past Michael Jordan as the most popular athlete in America, with only 2 percent of the respondents giving him a negative rating. The poll, which extended beyond athletes, also showed Tiger was more popular than Generals Norman Schwarzkopf and Colin Powell, just weeks after the Gulf War.

Tiger would finish 1997 with four victories in the U.S. and one in Asia, with prize winnings of $2.3 million. On top of that, he earned $19.5 million in off-course income through the deals I'd made with Nike, Titleist, and the rest.

When at the end of the year Nike decided to produce a line of Tiger Woods golf shoes, I added a clause to the contract that guaranteed an annual royalty payment of $3,125,000. That instantly increased the total value of the five-year Nike deal from $40 million to more than $50 million. Think Nike overpaid? Before signing Tiger, Nike Golf was doing $30 million in annual revenue. Two years later, that number had increased to $300 million.

Tiger unquestionably benefited more than anyone from his success, but his tentacles were long and lucrative, and they spread to every corner of golf, beginning with the PGA Tour.

The timing could not have been better. Indeed it was somehow both ironic and fitting that Tiger's first step toward immortality, the 1994 U.S. Amateur, had come at TPC Sawgrass, headquarters of the PGA Tour. Equally poignant was the fact that, at the same moment Tiger was making his entrance, the man who'd built that grand arena, Deane Beman, was making his exit, retiring as Tour commissioner after twenty years in the job.

Beman had almost single-handedly transformed the game of professional golf from a floundering enterprise to a steamrolling juggernaut, leaving his successor, Tim Finchem, a relatively simple job. As Peter Jacobsen put it, "Deane built a Mercedes; all Tim has to do is keep his foot on the gas."

And once Tiger turned pro, all Finchem had to do was keep the car on the road. At the same moment that a record 20.3 million viewers were watching Tiger win the 1997 Masters, Finchem was in the middle of negotiating a renewal of the Tour's television rights. Over the next twenty-two years—the Tiger Woods era in professional golf—the value of those TV contracts would more than quadruple, from just under $100 million to more than $400 million a year. Those numbers bring to mind the words of journeyman Tour professional Frank Beard, who fifty years ago declared, "We owe eighty cents of every dollar we earn to Arnold Palmer." The same statement could be made today by any player who was a contemporary of Tiger Woods.

On the list of others benefiting directly from the Tiger tidal wave, IMG was surely at the top. Roughly 20 percent of every dollar we earned for him came straight back to Cleveland, which brought $4 million to IMG Golf in year one.

But IMG was continuing to expand and thrive even without Tiger. In the works was a $900 million deal with the New York Yankees that would involve the creation of a TV network to broadcast their games. That would lead in turn to the signing of Derek Jeter as a client and would bring him a ten-year Yankee contract worth $189 million.

In tennis, the two hottest young players were sisters, Venus and Serena Williams, and they became the newest additions to the galaxy of stars in IMG Tennis.

Meanwhile, during the 1990s we'd gotten into a decidedly non-sports arena, classical music, by hiring music agents from a number of other firms who brought with them close to one hundred artists and vocalists, making IMG the second-largest agency in the classical music world. In addition, and in keeping with the holistic IMG strategy, we hosted music productions, released live and archival recordings, and provided consulting services in arts management. We even launched a new trend—arena opera.

Other notable IMG developments had included the signing of the Rock & Roll Hall of Fame as a client in 1993; the addition of the Kennedy Space Center as a client in 1997; the establishment in 1996 of TWI Interactive, a media arm under Mark McCormack's son Todd that handled website development for Manchester United, FC Barcelona, and the British Open; and in 1998 the launch of a private equity fund, formed with Chase Capital Partners, to invest in the sports industry. As the end of the century approached, IMG had eighty-five offices in thirty-three countries and more than one thousand clients. Our annual revenue had risen to $1.5 billion.

IMG was larger, more powerful, and more broadly based than ever, and thanks to the relationship I'd built with Tiger Woods, I was once again on top of my own little world. When Mark, at the end of 1997, moved my salary to $750,000, with a large additional bonus, it felt great. But the best recognition came from Tiger one day when he said, "Hughesy, you and I make a great team—we're both number one in the world at what we do."

9

······

Fired

Year two of my tenure as Tiger's handler-in-chief began far less frenetically than had year one. For one thing, Tiger's game cooled down a bit. In the first four months of 1998 his only victory came in January at the Johnnie Walker Classic in Thailand, where he came from eight strokes back in the final round to beat Ernie Els in a playoff. He would not add a PGA Tour win until May at the BellSouth Classic. This comparatively fallow spell, on the heels of his meteoric start, had led some to speculate that Tiger had been overrated—oversold—and, not surprisingly, one of the lead critics was the perpetually insecure Greg Norman, smarting no doubt from the indignity of being toppled by Tiger, swiftly and permanently, from his perch as the game's dominant player. "Tiger is proving to be a lot like everybody else on the PGA Tour," said Norman. "He got off to a phenomenal fast start but he's come back to reality and he's just another golfer out there."

Most of the golf world, however, remained Tiger crazy, and I'd done my best to act as his buffer, allowing him to navigate within the eye of the hurricane swirling perpetually around him. He and Butch Harmon had worked hard on his swing change, and both of them were pleased with the progress made. At the same time Tiger had become a gym rat, adding a two-hour workout to his daily schedule of practice and play. The result was that he'd put on twenty pounds of muscle, suddenly had the physique of an NFL defensive back, and was hitting the ball longer than ever with little if any loss of accuracy. At age twenty-two he'd become the number-one-ranked player in the world, the youngest and fastest ever to ascend to that spot. Bottom line, life was good for Tiger, and by extension, good for me.

Then I made the worst strategic decision of my career—I agreed to co-operate with *Golf World* on a cover piece about me. The tacit policy at IMG had always been, the less publicity for agents the better. But the writer who'd approached me, Tim Rosaforte, was someone I considered a friend. He assured me the piece would be positive and also said *Golf World* was going to run it, whether I participated directly or not. I ran it by Mark, and in the end I reluctantly decided to oblige them, thinking I'd rather have a say in what the magazine wrote about me than not. I also figured a fully detailed account of Tiger's commercial success could only enhance IMG's future ability to attract superstar athletes.

What a mistake. The cover photo—a staged studio shot with me posing goofily between a smiling Tiger and Earl—was superimposed with the headline "The Father, the Son, and the Holy Ghost," the last three words in huge type. As I began reading the piece, I cringed.

Walk into the locker room of any PGA Tour event, the marketing department of any major golf company, or the boardroom of any sports business agency that isn't the International Management Group, and toss out the name of agent Hughes Norton. You'd get a more subdued reaction if you walked into the Oval Office and asked Bill Clinton what he thinks of Kenneth Starr.

"Hughes Norton? I wouldn't piss on him if he was on fire."

"He's the crookedest son-of-a-bitch I know."

"Turn off the tape recorder."

"[Bleep] Hughes Norton."

An awful lot of people in the golf community would like to "bleep" Hughes Norton: agents who say he stole clients from them; players he discarded like old lovers; executives who say he double-crossed them; and dozens of others who made the mistake of turning their backs on him a moment too soon. They'd all like to bleep him, but they can't. Norton, 50, manages Tiger Woods—negotiates his deals, sets his schedule, runs his life. When Woods walked off the 72nd green at Augusta last year, Norton was the third person to congratulate him, after Woods's parents. When Woods celebrated his 22nd birthday, Norton received an invitation to the private party. When Woods attended the ESPY awards, he sat next to Norton. Anyone who wants Tiger—and these days everyone wants Tiger—has to pay homage to Norton. Kowtow to him. Kiss his ring. Tell him he's having a good hair day. Bleeping him is pretty much out of the question.

It didn't get much better. Following those malevolent—and maddeningly unattributed—opening quotes came weigh-ins from rival agents, accounts of my rocky marriage/divorce and the tension and eventual breakup with Greg Norman, and a sneering rehash of my hiring Earl Woods as a talent scout. Maybe worst of all, an IMG senior executive, Alastair Johnston, in a textbook example of Freudian projection, had characterized me as "economical with the truth." Imagine saying that to the media about a colleague of twenty-five years—betrayal by my own teammate.

I suppose I should have expected as much. And to be fair, the piece also included strong words of support from Tiger, Mark McCormack, and others, as well as a reasonably accurate account of what I'd done to make both Greg and Tiger multimillionaires. But as a profile, it was anything but positive.

Surprisingly—blessedly—there was little reaction to it. Maybe I've sublimated whatever negative fallout there was, but I know there was no response from Tiger or Earl. If other clients didn't like it, I never heard from them or from any coworkers, and since *Golf World* was little more than a trade magazine, almost none of my friends saw the article. Nonetheless, agreeing to do that piece was a dumb mistake, a further example of my public relations naiveté—still stumbling, bumbling, fumbling after all those years.

What's more, I'm convinced the piece actually did have an impact—a delayed and devastating impact—as a few months later Tiger fired me.

His call came on September 26, 1998. I don't remember the exchange verbatim, but it went something like this:

Hughes: "Hey, Tiger, what's up?"
Tiger (voice emotionless): "I've decided to make a change. I no longer
   want you as my agent."
Hughes: "What . . . Why?"
Tiger: "I don't want to go into it."
Hughes: "Whoa, we can't do this over the phone; let's sit down and talk
   about it."
Tiger: "Nope, it's over."
Hughes: "Tiger, we've been through too much together. I can be on
   the next plane."
Tiger: "No, Hughes. That would be a waste of time; my mind's made up."

Finally, he reluctantly agreed to see me. After a sleepless night, I flew
the next morning to Orlando. Tiger had told me to meet him at the front
door of the Isleworth clubhouse. I figured he didn't want to sit down at his
house, so we'd go somewhere private in the clubhouse and talk it through.

When I arrived there he was standing literally at the front door of the
clubhouse. His eyes were zombie-like, his face expressionless.

"Can we go inside and talk?" I said.

"No," he said, "I told you it was over, not to come down here. My mind
is made up. We're through." And with that he turned and walked away.

In the twenty-five years since, I have not heard one word from Tiger Woods.

It didn't take long for the word to get out. One of the first reports, from
Thomas Bonk in the *Los Angeles Times*, began, "Only a couple of months
ago *Golf World* ran a cover story on Hughes Norton featuring a photo of

Tiger Woods, Earl Woods, and Norton with the headline 'The Father, Son and the Holy Ghost.' This week, Norton was downgraded from Holy Ghost to just plain ghost." Within twenty-four hours it was all over the internet, had appeared in every major newspaper, and on numerous radio and television broadcasts including a full discussion on Golf Channel.

As with the *Golf World* piece, the reaction was muted. I heard from very few people. I suspect some were respecting my privacy; others saw me as damaged goods, someone no longer worth cultivating. It was one of those moments in life when you find out who your true friends are.

Among those who did call was Peter Jacobsen. One of the good guys, he'd also reached out to me a few years earlier after Norman had bailed. Peter is much more than the glib TV analyst you now see occasionally on NBC. Following a great playing career—a dozen wins worldwide including the 2004 U.S. Senior Open—he achieved equal success as CEO of his own sports marketing and event management company, and a big key to that success was his ability to connect with people.

Just after the news broke I got a totally unexpected call from another IMG client, one I'd come to know only recently, Wayne Gretzky. "I see where Earl says, 'Hughes is all about the money,'" he said. "Well, duh, wasn't that your job? Surely Tiger didn't object when you were putting that first hundred and twenty million dollars in the bank!" On the same day, a call came from Jim Nantz, who was equally incredulous, and with typical warmth and sincerity did his best to console me. It meant the world to me in that moment to hear from those two. Wayne and Jim remain, in my book, in a class by themselves, the rare genuine superstars who are also first-class human beings.

The arguments against firing me were, in my mind at least, so numerous and compelling I couldn't process what had happened. I'd set Tiger up financially for life; I'd employed his dad so that father and son could travel the amateur circuit together for years, all expenses paid; I'd sensed his discomfort with the demands of fame and had shielded him as best I could; and at his request I'd limited the time required for photo sessions and commercial appearances to an absolute minimum compared to the time commitments other superstars, such as Arnold Palmer, devoted to endorsements paying them far less per year.

Why—and how—had Tiger reached the decision to do this? In the absence of any clarification from him, I could only speculate. I wondered briefly whether Earl might have been behind it. He liked to assert his paternal influence every now and then, and as Gretzky had mentioned, a CNN/ *SI* report had quoted Earl saying, "The business stuff is a tremendous weight on Tiger and has affected his performance on the golf course . . . Hughes overcommitted him and was only interested in the almighty dollar."

That didn't ring true with me for a couple of reasons. Only a few weeks earlier, during a lengthy conversation with Earl, I'd jotted down a note of something he'd said: "Tiger is so lucky to have you and the group of people you have put together around him to do what you have done for him . . . It's right for Tiger and it is only going to continue to get better."

Even if Earl had for some reason changed his mind about me, his comment about overcommitting Tiger was disingenuous, since Earl himself had been involved in every business agreement—and commitment—I made. He may not have signed the contracts, but he read them, and both he and Tiger knew exactly what Tiger was getting into.

Then I wondered, could Tida have been the instigator? Years later, a biography of Tiger by Jeff Benedict and Armen Keteyian included this exchange:

Earl: "Hughes has been good to us, let's give him another chance."
Tida: "No. Tiger don't like Hughes. He don't want to be with Hughes. I don't like Hughes. He gotta go."

Again, that didn't ring true. Not long after Tiger's Masters victory, Tida had presented me the gift of a unique ceramic multicolored globe, crafted in her home country of Thailand. Someone estimated it was worth $10,000. It's been on my desk ever since. Tida was not prone to such generous expressions of gratitude, and my sense was she had always liked me, and I her.

I eventually reached the conclusion that Earl and Tida had decided, whatever their feelings about me, that they needed to be supportive of the son they so loved. This was Tiger's decision—his first major decision since leaving the nest—and it was important for his parents to have his back.

No, the more I thought about what had happened, the more convinced I became that if anyone had influenced Tiger it was Mark O'Meara. I'm not sure what prompted him—I suspect he was swayed by the *Golf World* piece—but in the summer of 1998 Mark had decided to switch from me to another IMG agent. "Hughes was a hard-driven guy," he later said. "He would go for the jugular. I wanted an agent who was less confrontational and a little more professional." It was a curious statement coming from someone who, when he signed with IMG, insisted that he be represented by me.

O'Meara's characterization of me brought to mind something Jean-Claude Killy had observed years earlier about Mark McCormack. "The McCormack image is not very good in France," he said. "He is seen as too professional, too hard." What O'Meara had failed to add, as Killy did: "But we must have the best people—and IMG is the best."

I make no apologies for the way I did my job. I believed my duty was to be the strongest possible advocate for the people who entrusted me to manage their careers. If doing that meant some people didn't like me, so be it. I wasn't worried about whether those on the other side of the negotiating table would be my pals afterward; it was my job to get every possible dollar for my client, and by extension for IMG. In fact, as hurtful as it was to be disparaged as ruthless and unyielding, it was almost a badge of honor, confirmation that I was doing what I'd been hired to do.

Irving Azoff, the famed music agent with a reputation as a fierce negotiator, was someone who would do anything to get as much as he could for his clients, damn the consequences. Don Henley, one of the lead vocalists for the Eagles, whom Azoff represented, when asked why his band had put up with such a roundly reviled, tough son of a bitch for decades, said: "Irving might be the devil, but he's *our* devil." Henley got it. I'm not sure O'Meara ever did.

In any case, in the summer of 1998 Mark and Tiger were well into the bromance I'd fostered. I can just imagine Mark, flipping burgers in his Isleworth backyard one evening and saying to Tiger, "Did you see that *Golf World* article? Do you really want a guy with Hughes's reputation representing you? And by the way, shouldn't a cover story be about you, Tiger, not your agent?" As Tiger's best friend and someone who spent more time with him than anyone, O'Meara was basically saying to a still-impressionable twenty-two-year-old, "If Hughes isn't right for me, he isn't right for you."

Thinking back to the phone call I'd made to O'Meara eighteen months earlier, I was struck by the irony. "Mark," I'd said, "I'm too old to be Tiger's big brother, but I think you'd be perfect. This kid has never been on his own, and I realize it's a lot to ask, but I think Tiger could learn a lot from you and you could be a great help to him settling into his new world." And Mark's reaction had been just as I'd hoped: "Hughes, I'd be happy to; it would be an honor. I'm really flattered you've asked me to do this, I'd love to get to know the kid."

I'd brought Mark together with Tiger—then Mark had influenced Tiger to fire me. If that wasn't betrayal, I don't know what is.

I called O'Meara and he vehemently denied it, but not in a way that was credible to me. Ten years later, when I happened to see him again—and the subject came up again—he became extremely defensive in the way only a guilty man can. If there was any lingering doubt in my mind, it was settled years later by one line in the Benedict/Keteyian book: "Nobody on Tour had more influence over Tiger than O'Meara, and once he said goodbye to Norton, it was only a matter of time before Tiger did the same."

That fall of 1998 quickly became the most emotionally difficult period of my life. At the same moment that my career was tanking, I was dealing with a couple of serious family issues. My mother, who years earlier had moved to an assisted-living facility in Florida, was nearing the end of her

life, and my daughter Stephanie had just been diagnosed with schizophre-
nia. Virtually overnight, my first child had become a different person, a
stranger, and it was both heartbreaking and frightening.

Uncertainty reigned in my life, both personally and professionally. Back
in Cleveland, I still had a job, still had an office, but suddenly had nothing
to do. The atmosphere was eerie, as few of my coworkers dared come near
my office, and those who did asked questions about my status and my future that I couldn't answer. It was an embarrassing and unprofessional void
of information. People inside the company and the outside world deserved
to know what was happening.

Shortly after returning from my non-meeting at the front door of Isleworth, I'd suggested to Mark that he get ahead of the situation by issuing
a public statement. There was no need to defend me, but he could say that
Tiger's decision was not abnormal or cataclysmic, just part of the nature of
player-agent relationships. I even prepared a draft for Mark to release. But
for reasons never explained, and which I still don't understand, IMG never
made any announcement to its staff or the media. Silence. As if Mark was
embarrassed to publicly acknowledge he had terminated such a key contributor, or worried that reaction would be negative to IMG.

At first, I thought it was just another example of Mark's aversion to
public relations, a preference to ignore—or at least not confront—the uncomfortable. Then I realized Mark had a more pressing concern at that
moment—keeping Tiger as an IMG client. That "key man" clause I'd kept
in Tiger's contract, allowing Tiger to bail on IMG if for any reason Hughes
Norton was no longer his agent, was now a major threat. Within hours of
learning Tiger had fired me, Mark had gotten on the phone to Tiger, assuring him that IMG had a number of talented agents ready to step in.

It was a measure of Tiger and Earl's overall comfort and confidence in
IMG (if not me) that Tiger opted to stay on, eventually choosing thirty-
year-old Mark Steinberg, a basketball player at the University of Illinois
who'd earned a law degree and joined IMG six years earlier, focusing on
women's golf, where he'd managed Karrie Webb and Annika Sorenstam.

Tiger's continued loyalty came at a steep price to IMG, however, as he negotiated a significant reduction of his commission fee.

The only substantive assignment during my post-Tiger purgatory thus became the briefing of Steinberg on all things Tiger—an A-to-Z run-through of every contract and the people associated with it. ("These are the guys at Nike you'll enjoy working with; these are the ones to be wary of.") The two of us met in a conference room, where for four and a half hours I talked and he took notes. It was an uncomfortable session for both me and Steinberg, but we got through it and I think he may even have thanked me. But as with Tiger, I've never heard a word from Steinberg since.

Otherwise, in the days and weeks following the Tiger debacle, I had little to do besides contemplate my future. And I did come up with a plan. I'd never worked anywhere else in my career, but as a business school grad I had read enough about other companies to realize IMG was a bit weird. At Goldman Sachs or General Electric, the company culture is carefully instilled into new employees. Not at IMG. There was no orientation week, no corporate manual or written history of the company. The only training I ever had was reading McCormack's book *Arnie*—and I'd done that on my own the third week I was in Cleveland. "Make it up as you go along" is not the greatest way to develop young executives! Which is why I saw my next incarnation at IMG as a mentor, passing along to upcoming executives the art of agenting and the unique culture of IMG. Agenting 101: the things I've learned, the mistakes I've made, where the bodies are buried—the works.

Knowing Alastair Johnston had Mark's ear, I figured I'd pretest the idea. Over a drink at a nearby bar I laid it out in detail. The goal, I told him, was to give the next generation of IMG executives the sort of training and mentoring that he and I never got from Mark when we started out.

Alastair's reaction was positive. "I hear you, and I agree we could have had more guidance all those years ago," he said. "This might work." I was encouraged and figured he'd set the table for the full-blown pitch I was now going to make to Mark.

Mark, when he was in the office, had not reached out to me at all—part of his avoidance of confrontation. But, as I would learn later from Bob Kain, the boss had not been insensitive to my situation—he just wasn't sure what to do. So he'd called a meeting of the executive committee—Kain, Johnston, and Jay Lafave, along with corporate advisors Ben Bidwell, Ray Cave, and Chris Lewinton—with a simple agenda: What are we going to do with Hughes? According to Kain, the general tone of the discussion was: "This guy has been a tremendous asset to the company for two and a half decades; we can't just neuter him, stick him in an office on the eleventh floor with nothing to do."

Then one day in mid-December, a couple of days after my chat with Alastair, I finally heard from Mark, an invitation for breakfast at Cleveland's Ritz-Carlton hotel, a few blocks from the office. This was something he and I had done many times over the years. I figured he'd finally come up with a plan on how to deploy me, and if not I was ready with my mentoring proposal, buoyed by Alastair's words of support.

After we sat down, Mark simply handed me a two-page document.

"This is a termination agreement," I said incredulously.

"Yes, and a very generous one," he said.

"Mark, before we go there, let me tell you about an idea I have." I then explained it briefly. "I think you should consider giving this—and me—a try, even on a short-term basis."

It fell on deaf ears. Mark was such a self-starter, he probably thought a position like this was superfluous. Young IMG executives could pick it up as they went along, just as he had in the early days with Palmer. Or maybe he thought I'd never accept the significant cut in compensation such a new role would require. I might have. You never know unless you ask for it—you taught me that, Mark.

Sensing I was losing the battle, I reached for my ace in the hole. "Mark, I've run this idea past Alastair and he's supportive. Like me, he had little guidance in the early years and he agrees this is something worth trying."

"No he doesn't," said Mark.

"What do you mean? I talked to Alastair at length about this just two days ago and he agreed it had merit."

"That was just lip service. He has no interest in this."

"Mark, that's an outright lie."

"You're calling Alastair a liar?"

"You bet I am—why don't we call him right now?"

We got up from the table and went to a house phone in the lobby. It was just after 7 a.m., and knowing Alastair's slacker style, I figured he'd still be in bed, which he was.

"Alastair, I'm at the Ritz having breakfast with Mark," I said, holding the phone out so Mark could hear. "I just pitched him on my idea about mentoring that we talked about two nights ago. When I told him you really liked it, Mark said that's not true."

"Mark's right."

"What? What are you talking about? You were encouraging to me about it two nights ago!"

"No I wasn't—not then and not now."

In that second it dawned on me what had happened. Mark, a day earlier, had told Alastair, "I've made a decision on Hughes," and when Alastair heard that, backstabber that he was, he jumped in and said something like "Good move, boss. Just yesterday he came to me with this cockamamie idea of becoming the company mentor."

It was classic Alastair Johnston. Twenty years earlier, Ian Todd had thought about breaking away from IMG, taking his top client, Björn Borg, with him, until Mark got wind of the impending defection. Who betrayed Ian to McCormack? We were never one hundred percent sure, but all signs pointed to Alastair, someone who never seemed to work as hard as the rest of us except when it came to sucking up to Mark. At executive committee meetings he always positioned himself in a chair at the head of the table where we got to watch him make little asides to Mark throughout the course of the meeting. Alastair had become

Mark's Iago, informing him about what the rest of us were saying and thinking, posing as our friend while ever ready to sell us out. None of us ever trusted him thereafter. Now he'd done his thing once again.

Snapping the phone back, I screamed at him, "You fucking traitor!" and hung up.

Mark and I went back to the table, but it wasn't more than a few seconds before I said, "I can't deal with this right now," stood up, and went home.

So once again, faced with a bitter reality, what did I do? The same thing I'd always done in such moments—I ran. On that cold Cleveland morning, I went out and ran as far as my body would let me.

I guess the mix of emotions is pretty much the same for everyone who gets fired—disbelief, recrimination, self-pity, self-doubt, shame, fear, and ultimately some sort of acceptance. It was like a death. All of a sudden I'm standing there on the edge of a cliff and I no longer have a job—no longer have what I called my livelihood for the past two and a half decades. It felt like the end of the world. Anger, hurt, and bitterness toward IMG. A loss of my identity. I needed time to get over that—I felt it every day. I had to go through a period of grief and then try to recover.

I was far more fortunate than most. During that same executive committee meeting where my fate had been discussed, the corporate advisors had spoken up. Their message to Mark was: "If you're going to get rid of Hughes, you have to give him a helluva severance package. Everyone at IMG will be watching closely how we treat a guy who has been this valuable and loyal." The result was that Mark put together the largest severance package in IMG's history.

The total value was just under $9 million ($16.5 million in today's dollars), paid out over ten years. Roughly a third of that was income I would have been due anyway—deferred compensation, benefits—but the remainder came straight from Mark. We never had employment contracts at IMG, so he didn't owe me a cent, at least not in a legal sense. My boss could be ruthless, but he also had a soft spot—I guess this was his way of saying thanks or sorry or both.

In return, I had to agree to a non-compete clause and a gag order; I would not go to work for a rival agent or start my own agent business, nor would I share with the world any details of my IMG career or severance for the same ten-year period. It all struck me as a bit strange—Mark was not interested in paying me to continue to work for him, but was willing to pay multiple millions for me not to work against him.

I was appreciative of my package, but there was something I didn't get from Mark—a clear and cogent explanation for why he'd fired me. Like Tiger, he'd never had the courage to express to me in person what his thinking was. All of it deserved some sort of closure, but I never got it.

A few years later I was reading *USA Today* when I saw a syndicated column by Mark based on his book *What They Don't Teach You at Harvard Business School*. In the column was a line that caught my eye: "The real reason that anyone gets fired is that the people above you don't like you."

I clipped it out and sent it to Mark with a handwritten note: "Why didn't you just tell me the truth, when we sat down that December day?" His return note was a bit weird: "You know perfectly well the reason behind your leaving IMG . . . I hope someday we can sit down and talk about the past, present, and future."

That was the closest I got to an explanation. I never had the chance for that sit-down because not long after writing that note, Mark McCormack had a heart attack, fell into a four-month coma, and on May 16, 2003, died at the age of seventy-two.

The company had always been Mark McCormack's and his alone, and now he was gone. Through all the decades, Mark had never cared about profits, only growth. Under the able leadership of new president Bob Kain, IMG quickly became more disciplined and more profitable than ever before.

Betsy, Mark's widow, was suddenly the largest shareholder. She had no expertise or interest in running the company and her advisors convinced her to sell. In October 2004 the McCormack family accepted an offer of $750 million from private equity firm Forstmann Little. Ted

Forstmann was a difficult guy to work for, to say the least, but Kain agreed to stay on for two years, in order to make sure the right people remaining at IMG received equity. They did.

Client management, the original DNA of IMG, was not a priority to Chairman Forstmann. Event management and television grew enormously; top IMG client agents started to look elsewhere. That led to the defection of Mark Steinberg, who took Tiger with him.

Alastair Johnston, having lost the company's top client, along with several other golfers, was defiantly defensive. "Our representation of the R&A and British Open is far more valuable to us than our representation of Tiger," he said. "Exponentially so." Meanwhile, his golf division's recruiting and client management were crumbling.

Teddy Forstmann died of brain cancer in late 2011. Two years later Forstmann Little sold IMG to the entertainment talent agency William Morris for $2.3 billion. By this time, IMG's golf client management had dramatically eroded. And the IMG name itself had virtually disappeared. Not the legacy Mark McCormack ever envisioned.

Epilogue

....

As I now look back on the course of my life, I realize it has unfurled rather neatly in three distinct phases, each roughly twenty-five years in length—my youth, my career, and everything since—three periods of preparation, perspiration, and contemplation.

The third stage, the quarter century since my departure from IMG, has brought plenty of time to reflect—not just on my own rise and fall but on the arena I so fervently embraced, the world of big-money professional golf, which, over the same period, has expanded explosively—some would say grotesquely—to the point that it now faces a crisis. At the same time, I've tried to take a hard look at myself—at the role I played in that turbulent world, and the lasting effect it's had on me.

It took me a while to deal honestly with the shock and embarrassment of losing my job. Every morning, for several months, I'd reach impulsively for my yellow pad—my to-do list—except there was no pad, no list, nothing to do. My knee-jerk response was to console myself, tell myself I was fine, that I no longer needed that kind of engagement or validation.

I actually managed to convince myself that the thrill was gone, that my crowning achievement—signing and representing transcendent superstar Tiger Woods—had never delivered the level of joy and satisfaction I'd expected it would, but had instead left me wondering, *Is that all there is?* I decided I'd become an unknowing victim of career burnout—no mountains left to climb, and no energy left to climb them. Genuinely relieved to be out of the agent rat race: forever chasing the next superstar, working my butt off for unappreciative clients, living a never-ending roadtrip, perpetually having to defend the firm I was proud to work for. Getting fired, I told myself, was actually the best thing that could have happened to me.

But that was all a rationalization, a comforting self-delusion. Further reflection led me to see the truth, which was just the opposite. Up until the day I received that fateful phone call from Tiger, I absolutely loved my job. I was on top of the world, repping the hottest athlete on the planet, and reveling in my role as rainmaker. My job had defined me, had made me who I was. I hadn't burned out, I was on fire, making millions of dollars for my clients, for IMG, and for myself. The money-grab era of professional golf was roaring at full throttle and I was front and center, fueling it, loving it, fully energized.

In those days, there was a nickname for me within the golf business—Huge—which some of my competitors, and I suspect more than a few others, used derisively as a reference to my ego. The actual genesis for "Huge" was Seve Ballesteros; it was his Spanglish pronunciation of my name, and it caught on, first within IMG and then beyond. That said, there was, I see now, justification for the darker interpretation.

My workaholism had left me little time for introspection. I'd always thought of myself as humble, self-effacing, appreciative—the way I was raised. Intense, to be sure, confident, but also terrified of coming across as arrogant or egotistical. But the evidence to the contrary was hard to deny—the horrific quotes in the *Golf World* profile, the realization that I had casual acquaintances but few real friends, my inability to sustain a serious relationship, whether with prospective paramours or superstar clients. It certainly seemed as if Hughes Norton was someone nobody wanted to be with long-term. Did I unknowingly project a demeanor the opposite of my own true values? Maybe what I'd needed during my IMG glory years was someone to say to me what I made a point of saying to those superstar clients when they became too cocky: "You're full of shit."

On the day Tiger told me the exact opposite, "You and I are a great team because we're both the best in the world at what we do," I'd taken it—and myself—too seriously. I'd had the audacity to believe he and I were equals. Now, I may have shared Tiger's ambition and work ethic, and maybe even a bit of his creativity, but he was the number one golfer in the world, an athletic genius. I was just an agent. There were countless guys out there who, had they been lucky enough to get hired by Mark McCormack, might have produced just as emphatically as I had. I'd overvalued myself, overvalued the job I'd done—and then I'd made a fatal mistake: I'd *overdone* my job.

And that, I finally came to accept, is why Tiger fired me—for doing what I'd been so proud of—overdelivering. I'd given him more than he wanted or needed in terms of both income and contractual obligations, and he'd decided he'd had enough of that—and me.

Tiger had told me on more than one occasion that the time commitments to Nike, Titleist, and the rest were too much for him, but I'd chosen not to hear his protests, telling myself that he and Earl knew exactly what he'd gotten into. The reality was, Tiger was a twenty-one-year-old kid who didn't know much about anything except how to strike a golf ball better than anyone alive. It was my duty to know things for him. More to the point, it was my responsibility to do him no harm—to protect him—and I hadn't done that to the best of my ability. I could have pressed a couple of those corporate clients to relax their contract demands on Tiger's time, and they would have caved rather than risk losing him. It would have meant less income for Tiger, to be sure, but he wouldn't have cared. I was the one who cared, so instead of listening to him and making his life easier, in my zeal to produce for IMG I plowed forward. Until Tiger stopped me.

It came down once again to that old conundrum—balance—and the hard truth was that I'd lost mine. The same monomaniacal focus that had cost me my marriage had cost me my relationship with Tiger. Ultimately it would cost me my job at IMG, and therein lay an irony: overdelivering, something Tiger didn't want, was precisely what Mark McCormack insisted on. Once Tiger fired me, however, it became a simple equation for Mark—my days of overdelivering were clearly behind me, so the smart business move was to fire me.

That said, Mark was sufficiently paranoid to include a ten-year non-compete clause in my severance package. He needn't have worried. Once I'd come to grips with the reason for my fall, I had little desire to keep working as an agent—not for another firm, not for myself, not at all. Redemption? I didn't need it or obsess over it. I was bitter about betrayal by clients and colleagues, but proud of what I had accomplished and at peace with it. In the years since, I have never said to myself, "I wish I were back in the golf business." Not once.

People in the golf industry, journalists, former IMG colleagues, kept asking, "Has anyone heard from Hughes? . . . It's as if he's disappeared . . . What's he doing these days? Surely he's into something, some new chapter of his life." Nope. Start over in some new business? No thanks. Luckily, I didn't have to. Virtually overnight, I transformed from a type A to a near recluse—made a 180-degree lifestyle change—and have remained in that state of self-imposed exile for the past twenty-five years.

During the same two and a half decades that my life has become less complicated and more tranquil, the arena in which I worked, professional golf, has taken the opposite path, expanding explosively—and following the money—to the point that it today faces a moment of turmoil and an uncertain future.

Throughout the Tiger era and beyond, steady increases in corporate investment drove more and more advertising dollars to the PGA Tour, which boosted TV rights payments, increased tournament purses, and made multi-millionaires out of dozens of players. In 1996, the last year before Tiger turned pro, the total purse played for on the Tour was $101 million. Last year it was $563 million—shared by roughly 150 players. That works out to an average of roughly $3.75 million per player.

In addition, thanks to the emergence in 2007 of the FedEx Cup, a season-long competition ending in a series of playoff events, another huge pot of money became available. Last year the leading money winner was twenty-six-year-old Viktor Hovland, who finished third on the official money list, but then took home an additional $18 million bonus for winning the FedEx Cup, bringing his total earnings to just over $33 million. And as if that bonanza weren't enough, two recent initiatives—the Comcast Business Tour Top 10 and the Tour's own Player Impact Program—have pumped another $140 million into the jackpot, all of it going to the top twenty players. As a result, the divide between the elite players and all the others is wider than ever.

But far be it from me to pass judgment. When I started my career, pro golf was relatively poor and pure, and as proud as I was at the time that I earned Tiger an unprecedented $100 million in endorsement income, I see now that I was literally an agent of the wretched excess that pervades the game today. Money is all that counts, whether it's an agent's commission, the smorgasbord of corporate logos plastered across Tour players' apparel, or the legalized gambling that is spreading like a virus, part of every tournament telecast. Six betting websites, including FanDuel and DraftKings, are now official partners of the PGA Tour, with a potential for substantial harm if it's all allowed to go too far.

Of course, the most disruptive development has been the emergence of LIV Golf, backed by the Saudi government's $700 billion Public Investment Fund, which in 2022 paid several prominent players eight- and nine-figure bonuses to resign from the Tour and join an upstart circuit of fifty-four-hole events with shotgun starts, fields of just forty-eight players, and bigger purses than at PGA Tour events. Initially the Tour dismissed the upstart league, but as players began to defect, changes were made to slow the exodus. The Player Impact Program was one such inducement, as were tweaks to the FedEx Cup, a rejiggering of the Tour's schedule around eight lucrative "signature events" with limited fields, and a major jump in prize money and FedEx Cup bonuses. (In 2024, the FedEx Cup champion will be paid a bonus of $25 million.)

But all this did nothing to deter LIV, which not only proceeded with its schedule of events, but sued the Tour for restraint of trade. The Tour promptly countersued, and a bloody battle seemed to loom until June of last year, when the surprise announcement came that the PGA Tour and LIV Golf had formed an alliance. Almost no specifics were issued, except that each side had agreed to drop legal action against the other. Meanwhile, both tours completed their 2023 seasons—relatively unheralded American Talor Gooch led the LIV money list with total earnings in excess of $36 million—and both tours remain in place for 2024, with Jon Rahm the most recent and ominous defection to the Saudi side.

I've watched all this develop with particular interest because the two most prominent combatants have been my two former clients—Greg Norman and Tiger Woods. In a way it's fitting that they assumed the roles they did. Each of them was a major figure in the game's big-money explosion and each is suited perfectly to the role he's playing in the still-unfolding drama.

Norman, swaggering narcissist that he is, has always loved commanding the arena. Being the world's best player fueled his ego, but ultimately I believe golf was primarily a means to an end for him, a way to acquire luxury homes, Ferraris, airplanes, yachts, and fame by wheeling and dealing in business. He went at these extracurricular pursuits full bore, perhaps as an alternative scorecard to make up for his golf achievements falling short of expectations. Greg once told me his goal was to become identified with a brand that was completely independent of his golf fame. When Reebok started a Greg Norman line of apparel, I think he had dreams of it going on forever, well beyond his playing days, his name mentioned in the same breath as Giorgio Armani and Yves Saint Laurent. That never happened, but I suspect he still dreams of his Shark logo reaching a status like that of the Lacoste crocodile, which originated with French tennis star René Lacoste.

Certainly, no individual in the game of golf—no player past or present— has ever been aligned more perfectly with the motives of the Saudis: power, money, and image burnishing. And as the most polarizing superstar the game has produced, he's the perfect leader of the renegade LIV circuit. Greg has always been a disrupter, someone who perceived enemies, beginning with a father who disapproved of his becoming a golf pro and thereby became estranged from him, and continuing through a succession of business managers that included me, along with three or four caddies and three wives. His attitude has always been: "It's me against the world. I'll get back at you all, prove you wrong."

Interestingly, among the first to call for Greg's ouster as LIV CEO and commissioner was Tiger Woods. When Norman learned of that, he responded by calling Tiger "a mouthpiece for the PGA Tour." I suppose that was accurate enough, not because Tiger had been co-opted in any way, but because, just as Norman's persona fits with the disruptiveness of LIV, so does Tiger's align with the tradition (if not the current state) of the Tour. As I've said more than once in the course of this narrative, Tiger has never cared about the money. From the time he was a toddler, his sole joy was playing the game. Hours and hours practicing, grinding on the range, working out in the gym, competing—that was his fun. He could not have cared less about the trophies, or the massive financial payoff. Resented all that, actually. It was an *intrusion* into his everyday happiness. Like Arnold Palmer and Jack Nicklaus, Tiger played not for money, he played for the glory, the history, the legacy, a reminder that not every reward is monetary.

Honestly, I suspect a player tends to set his future priorities at least partly according to the nature of the success he's already had. Those who have won multiple major championships always ascribe more importance to those big events. If Greg had not frittered away his chances in so many majors he might have developed a slightly different posture, although in his case, I doubt that it would have altered things too much.

Where will the PGA Tour/LIV thing sort out? It's probably easier to sort Greg and Tiger. As part of the framework agreement that exists between LIV Golf and the Tour, Tour officials have insisted that any future LIV may have must not include Greg Norman, so if by the time you read this a more firm agreement has been reached, I'll be surprised if Greg is still around. He will likely have moved on, taken his $50 million or whatever of Saudi up-front money, and started prowling for the next way to feed his obsessive need to be in the spotlight.

As for Tiger's future, in the near term, as the newest and most prominent member of the PGA Tour Policy Board, he's been a lead dog in forming—or dissolving—the agreement with the Saudis. And as one of the founders, along with Rory McIlroy and former Golf Channel President Mike McCarley, of TGL, the new indoor golf league expected to launch in 2025, of which the Tour is part owner, he's literally invested in the future of professional golf, no matter what shape it may take.

But don't let that fool you into thinking his days of competitive golf are over. In a couple of years, assuming both he and the Champions Tour stay healthy, don't be surprised if he dominates senior golf. Even after his multiple surgeries, Tiger still hits the ball plenty long, still has all the shots. Walking is the only thing holding him back. Once he's allowed to use a cart, I suspect he'll take dead aim at adding to his legacy because competition is still what he lives for. Think Bernhard Langer's record forty-six victories on the senior circuit is safe? Try telling that to Tiger, one of the most ruthlessly competitive athletes in the history of sports. Five wins a year between ages fifty and sixty is perfectly feasible to me.

As for the future fabric of professional golf, who knows? One speculation is that in 2025 we'll see an elite global golf tour, featuring players from the PGA Tour, LIV Golf, and Europe's DP World Tour—eighteen events (not counting the four major championships), twelve of them to be played in the United States. Each of the three independent tours would continue in some form, and players from all three would be able to cross over and compete in events outside their home tour, a major change from what prevails now. It might be funded by Saudi billions, by corporate investment, or both. Or it might not happen at all.

To what extent this grand scheme may succeed remains to be seen. At the same time that purses have exploded to an unconscionable level, the star power of global golf has diminished. Tiger is all but gone, and no one player has stepped up to replace him—in fact, no two or three players have risen to dominate in any sustained or compelling way. The main revenue driver—television—has changed in both viewer demographics and the way it's delivered—and the ratings for golf telecasts, never particularly strong, today are unstable at best. There's a sense that golf's fan base is waning, perhaps becoming both bored and peeved by the decadence of the show-me-the-money era. Meanwhile, in the wake of all the machinations with the Saudis last summer, a bill was introduced in the U.S. Senate to strip the PGA Tour of its tax-exempt status.

Professional golf, if it isn't careful, may well become a victim of its own greed.

As for me, well, I'd like to think my unstable up-and-down career has been replaced by a life that's more centered, serene, and self-aware. A couple of years ago my friend John Hanley at J.P. Morgan Private Bank in Denver asked me to give a short presentation to its top executives about my years as a golf agent. I labeled one of my talking points that day "Things I've Learned." I guess you could say these have become my retroactive Ten Commandments:

1. Talk is cheap. Deeds, not words.
2. If you don't know where you're going, any road will take you there.
3. Nobody goes through life undefeated. And nobody said life is fair.
4. Lighten up a little. You can try too hard and care too much.
5. Regrets will kill you.
6. "I don't know." "I was wrong." "I need help." Hard things for anyone to say.
7. It's the journey, not the destination. The sooner you figure that out, the better.
8. Stay humble, appreciative, grateful. It's not easy.
9. Success? Finding a couple of people in life who really "get" you.
10. Exercise: the best RX any doctor ever writes.

These days, I occasionally find my mind wandering back to that Saturday in Maine so many years ago when I somehow outlasted Ray Lebel to win the Portland Country Club men's golf championship. On that golden summer afternoon, fresh out of college, I was ready to conquer the world. I had no idea what my future held, but I couldn't wait to get started.

Everything that lay ahead of me then is behind me now, and I sometimes wonder if the life I've led has measured up to the hopes and aspirations of that young man on the eighteenth green. If I could sit down on a bench with him now and say, "Kid, here's what we did," I'm not sure what his reaction would be. But I'd like to think he'd listen patiently to my whole saga—the ups and downs, the good and the bad—and when he'd heard it all he'd look me in the eye, shake my hand with a smile, and say, "Wow, it's going to be a great ride."

Acknowledgments

....

Big thanks to our editors at Atria Books: Amar Deol, who believed in my story and critically improved it; and Sean deLone, who stepped in toward the end to quarterback the narrative through to completion. Kudos to the rest of the team at Atria and Simon & Schuster: Hannah Frankel, Shida Carr, Dayna Johnson, Libby McGuire, Lindsay Sagnette, and Annette Pagliaro Sweeney.

If you found the book a good read, credit goes to George Peper. No other collaborator could have written so authentically in my voice or made it all flow together so seamlessly. George's call after listening to my No Laying Up podcast—"so are we finally going to do that book?"—is the reason the whole thing came together.

And sincere appreciation to this long-time agent's first-ever agent, Susan Canavan at Waxman Literary Agency—who made our original concept bigger and better and then worked tirelessly to make a terrific deal with a great publisher.

A Note on Sources

....

The anecdotes and stories contained in this book are based on personal recollections, contemporaneous notes, emails and text messages, public records, and other sources. Where notes or records did not exist for a particular conversation, we have reconstructed the exchange to the very best of my recollection and/or in consultation with subjects who were involved in or aware of those conversations. Where portions of books or articles are quoted verbatim, we have so acknowledged.

Index

....

Page numbers followed by *t* refer to tables.

Aaron, Tommy, 45, 65
ABC, 29, 31, 60, 71, 80–81, 145
ABC Sports, 29
Action Network, 197
Adams, Gary, 85
Adidas America, 172
Advantage International, 84
Affleck, Ben, 171
Agassi, Andre, 149, 171, 173, 174
Agnes Scott College, 7
Air (film), 171
Air Jordan shoe, 171
Air Rabbit commercial, 179
Albertville Olympic Committees, 147
Alcaraz, Carlos, 157
Ali, Muhammad, 94
All England Club, 109
American Brands, 179
American Express, 186–187, 190*t*
American Gladiators (TV show), 150
American Professional Golfers, Inc. (APG), 26
Andrade, Billy, 203
Anselmo, John, 167
Aoki, Isao, 76
Approved Tournament Player card, 20
Arizona State University, 150
Arledge, Roone, 31
Armani, Giorgio, 228
Armour, Ryan, 164
Arnie: The Evolution of a Legend (McCormack), 17, 18, 67, 78, 216
Arnold Palmer Enterprises, 34
Arnold Palmer Invitational, 164
Arter, Hadden, Wykoff & Van Duzer, 17

Asahi, 190*t*, 191
Asia Golf Circuit, 107
Associated Press, 59
Atlanta Athletic Club, 114
Atlanta Country Club, 52
AT&T Pebble Beach Pro-Am, 129, 154–155, 196
Augusta Chronicle, 201
Augusta National Golf Club, 17, 63, 79–80, 83, 109, 125, 192, 198–201, 209
Australian Amateur Championship, 138
Australian Masters, 106
Australian Open, 39, 77, 106
Azoff, Irving, 213

Bacon, Sir Francis, 93
Baffler 3-wood, 138
Baillie, Bill, 105
Baker-Finch, Ian, 90, 107, 202
Ball, C. Jordan, Jr., 62, 63, 88
Ballesteros, Manuel, 116
Ballesteros, Seve, 74, 104, 106, 107, 108, 109, 114, 117, 158–159, 171, 224
Baltimore Ravens, 120
Baltusrol, 24, 43
Barner, Ed, 46, 50, 54, 65–66
Barnett, Mike, 151
Baseball Hall of Fame, 81
Bateman, Jason, 171
Baugh, Laura, 52–56, 65, 84, 123
Bayer, George, 136
Bay Hill Classic, 99, 125
Bay Hill Club, 99, 164
Bean, Andy, 83, 100
Beard, Frank, 205

Beatles, 62
Beaver College, 57
Begay, Notah, 155, 164, 186, 194
Bel-Air Country Club, 80–81
Belfry, The, 108
Bell, Judy, 178
Bell Canadian Open, 185
Bellerive Country Club, 123
BellSouth Classic, 207
Belmont Country Club, 21
Beman, Deane, 68–72, 96–101, 111, 114, 145, 147, 205
Benedict, Jeff, 212, 214
Ben Hogan Tour, see Korn Ferry Tour
Berry, Chuck, 6
Betty Ford Clinic, 55
Bidwell, Ben, 46, 217
Bidwell, Candy, 56–57, 73, 91, 92, 103, 117–119
Bies, Don, 82
Big "I" Insurance Classic, 158, 184
Big Three, 21, 43, 54, 88, 103, 143
Bing Crosby Open, 135
Bob Hope Chrysler Classic, 98
Bob Hope Desert Classic, 24, 75, 98
Bo Knows commercial, 179
Bollettieri, Nick, 149
Bonk, Thomas, 210
Borg, Björn, 39, 218
Boston Red Sox, 120
Bowdoin College, 187
Brandweek, 150
Breyers ice cream, 191
Brigham Young University, 46, 88
British Amateur Championship, 61, 68
British Open, 25, 28, 77, 109, 126, 206, 221
Brown Deer Park course, 159, 184
Brunza, Jay, 194
Bugs Bunny, 179
Buick Open, 194
Burke, Daniel, 12, 14
Burns, George, 61
Bush, George H. W., 145
Business Week, 198
Butler National Golf Club, 50

Calcavecchia, Mark, 126
Caldwell, Allen, 198
Cameron, Scotty, 176
Canadian Amateur Championship, 48
Canadian Open, 28, 100, 185

Canon Greater Hartford Open, 98
Canterbury Country Club, 50
Canyon Country Club, 24
Capital (Cap) Cities, 12, 14, 54
Capriati, Stefano, 195
Captain Kangaroo, 5
Caracas GM Open, 46, 49
Caribbean Tour, 44, 46
Carmel, California, 88
Carnoustie Golf Links, 48, 65
Carpenter, Bill, 67
Cave, Ray, 217
Caves Valley Golf Club, 121
CBS, 1, 31, 70, 71
CBS Golf Classic, 71
CBS Sportsline, 190t
Ceballos, Jorge, 115
Centenary College, 112
Cerrudo, Ron, 45, 47
Cessna Aircraft, 198
Chamberlain, Wilt, 94
Champions Tour, 18, 230
Chase Capital Partners, 206
Chenault, Ken, 187
Clampett, Bobby, 87–90, 92, 103
Clay, Cassius, 94
Cleveland Browns, 120
Cleveland Open, 49
Clinton, Bill, 203
Cobb, Ty, 23, 81
Cobra Golf, 138–140, 176
Cole, Bobby, 55
Cole, Eric, 56
Colgate-Palmolive, 28, 54, 95
Collins, Bud, 95
Comcast Business Tour Top 10, 227
Complete Book of Running, The (Fixx), 91
Cook, John, 134
Corcoran, Fred, 21–23, 44
Cornerstone Sports, 170
Costas, Bob, 31
Couples, Fred, 82, 84, 86, 111, 131–132
Courier, James, 149, 173
Cowan, Mike "Fluff," 193
Crampton, Bruce, 49
Crenshaw, Ben, 75–77, 76, 77, 83, 87, 100
Crooked Stick Golf Club, 135
Crosby, Bing, 23
Crow, Tom, 138
Curtis, Tony, 37
Curtis Cup, 52, 58

Daikyo, 106
Daly, John, 135–136, 159
Damon, Matt, 171
Daniel Island Club, *47*
Dartmouth College, 27
Deane Beman: Golf's Driving Force (Schupak), 69
De Beers Diamond company, 75
Dell, Donald, 86
Demon Deacons team, 17
Dennis the Menace, 29
Derby, Lord, 108
De Vicenzo, Roberto, 45
Devlin, Bruce, 49, 104
deWindt, E. M. "Dell," 100
Dey, Joseph C., 27, 68–69
Diaz, Jaime, 200
Dickerman, George, 138
Dobyns, Stephen, 40
Dole Foods, 132
Doral Open, 85
Dowd, Maureen, 203
Dowling, Brian, 63
DP World Tour, 230
DraftKings website, 227
Duran, Rudy, 167
Duval, David, 154, 169, 196
Dye, Pete, 114

Eagles (rock group), 213
EA Sports, 188–189, 191
Eichelberger, Dave, 45
Elbin, Max, 24, 26
Elder, Lee, 200
Electronic Arts, 188–189
Eliot, T. S., 79
Els, Ernie, 107, 207
Epson computers, 105
Epstein, Brian, 62
Erskine, James, 105–106, 140
ESPN, 1, 188, 199
European Tour Order of Merit, 115, 137
Evert, Chris, 134, 147
Exxon, 117

Faldo, Nick, 107, 108, 136, 158, 201
Family Matters (TV show), 187
FanDuel website, 227
FC Barcelona, 206
FedEx Cup, 226–227
Feinstein, John, 195–196, 199–200, 203

Finchem, Tim, 205
Fireman, Paul, 139–140
Firestone Country Club, 71
Fischer, Bobby, 94
Fixx, Jim, 91
Fleisher, Bruce, 48
Floyd, Maria, 85–86
Floyd, Ray, 27, 44–55, 58, 65, 75, 85–6, 88, 89, 100, 112, 125
Foot-Joy, 80, 139
Forbes, 172, 198
Ford, Gerald, 145
Ford Maracaibo Open, 46
Ford Motor Company, 46
Forstmann, Ted, 220–221
Forstmann Little equity firm, 220
Fought, John, 82
Fox Broadcasting Company, 31
Fox Sports, 142
Francis, Connie, 6
Frank, Barry, 31, 110
Fred Corcoran: The Man Who Sold Golf to the World (Corcoran), 23
French Open, 49, 66
Frost, David, 125
Fyles, Alfie, 48

Gamez, Robert, 125
GB&I, 108
Geiberger, Al, 47
General Electric, 216
Gentleman's Quarterly, 194
Georgia Tech, 154
Giles, Marvin M. "Vinny," 61–63, 65, 75, 83, 114, 134–135, 171
Glasgow Rangers soccer team, 32
Golden Handshake, 18
Goldman Sachs, 216
Golf Channel, 99, 183, 211, 230
Golf Digest, 4, 52, 54, 99, 133, 154, 161, 190*t*, 191–192, 194, 199–200, 244
Golf magazine, 89, 106, 112, 199–200
Golf World, 141, 153, 169, 170, 208, 209, 210–211, 213–214, 224
Golf Writers Association of America, 23
Gooch, Talor, 228
Gordon, Joel, 19
Grady, Wayne, 107
Graham, David, 49, 75–76, 104, 106
Grammys, the, 92
Grand Slam, 39, 174

Greater Hartford Open, 98
Greater Milwaukee Open, 1, 178
Greatest Game of All, The (Nicklaus), 19
Green, Hubert, 90, 202
Greg Norman Golf Course Design, 106
Greg Norman Holden Classic, 140
Gretzky, Wayne, 151, 211–212

Hagen, Walter, 24
Hambric, Rocky, 170
Hamill, Dorothy, 95
Hamlet, The, 53
Haney, Hank, 169
Hanley, John, 231
Harmon, Butch, 167, 179, 180, 194, 207
Harmon, Claude, 167
Harrison, Bob, 106
Harvard Business School (HBS), 11–12, 13, 15, 28, 29, 56–57, 118
Harvard University, 11, 12, 14–15
Haskins Award, 194, 196
Hassan II Trophy, *47*
Havlicek, John, 40
Hawaiian Open, 135
Hayes, Woody, 63
HBS, *see* Harvard Business School
Heard, Jerry, 46, 51–52
Helene Curtis cosmetics, 191
Hemisphere Cup, 145, 147
Henley, Don, 213
Herron, Tim "Lumpy," 168
Hertz, 28, 92, 147, 171
Hillman, Dennis, 164
Hills, Arthur, 44
Hogan, Ben, 49, 167
Holly, Buddy, 6
Honors Course, The 168
Hope, Bob, 23, 160
Houston Baptist University, 136
Hovland, Viktor, 227
Hubman, Chris, 193

Iger, Robert, 16
Ihrie, Bob, 56
IMG Broadcasting, 29
IMG Golf, 45, 49, 85, 153, 158, 205
IMG Literary Management, 29
IMG Motor Sports, 39
IMG Skiing, 39
IMG Team Sports Division, 59
IMG Tennis, 30, 39, 149, 171, 174, 205

Inglis, David, 131
Inkster, Juli, 84–85
International Management Group (IMG), 2, 13, 15, 16, 20, 21, 27–31, 32, 34, 35–36, 39–40, 43–49, 52–54, 57, 59, 60–64, 65–68, 72, 73–80, 82––88, 92–96, 99, 100, 103–107, 110, 112–120, 123, 128–129, 129*t*, 131, 133, 134–137, 139–142, 145, 146–154, 147, 157–158, 162, 165–166, 168, 171, 174, 175, 181, 184, 189, 190, 192, 193, 196, 199, 202–203, 205–206, 208, 209, 211, 213, 215–216, 217, 218, 219–221, 223–226
Inverness Country Club, 125, 127
Irwin, Hale, 65, 76, 100, 109
Isaacson, Rick, 27–28, 30, 45

Jacklin, Tony, 9, 39, 44, 47, 65, 87, 151
Jack Nicklaus Western Hemisphere Trading Co., 21
Jackson, Bo, 179
Jacobsen, Peter, 73–74, 115, 154, 171, 172, 175, 205, 211
Jacobus, George, 21
Jaeckel, Barry, 45
Jake Trout and the Flounders, 74
Jantzen, 48
Japan Senior Amateur Championship, 155
Jenkins, Dan, 32, 87, 120, 126
Jenkins, Sally, 119–120
Jeopardy!, 47
Jerry Maguire (film), 166
Jeter, Derek, 205
Johnnie Walker Golf Classic, 91, 207
John Paul II, Pope, 92
John Player Classic, 66
Johnson, Peter, 59, 119
Johnston, Alastair, 32, 66, 99, 119, 153, 209, 216–218, 221
Jones, Bobby, 24, 46, 125, 168
Jones, Clarke, 193, 199
Jones, Fletcher, 88
Jones, Grier, 46
Jordan, Michael, 171, 173–174, 179, 194, 204
J.P. Morgan Private Bank, 231

Kain, Bob, 30–31, 34, 119, 149, 171, 217, 220
Kaiser International Tournament, 44
Kansas State University, 160, 173
Kemper Open, 123
Kennedy, Ray, 21, 53, 96
Kennedy Space Center, 206

Ketcham, Hank, 29
Keteyian, Armen, 212, 214
Key Man clause, 181
Killy, Jean-Claude, 39, 189, 213
King, Billie Jean, 30–31
King Cobra irons, 138
Kite, Tom, 61, 100
Knight, Phil, 171–173, 175–176, 178–179, 198
Koch, Gary, 61
Korn Ferry Tour, 27, 135
Kramer, Hans, 97
Kuehne, Hank, 168
Kutner, Kirsten, 133–134

La Costa resort, 187
Ladies Professional Golf Association (LPGA), 23, 53–54, 56, 58–59, 65, 85
Lafave, Jay, 67, 217
La Grange Country Club, 58
LaManga Golf Club, 115
Lancôme Trophy, 35, 50, 66
Langer, Bernhard, 107, 108, 112, 158
Latrobe Country Club, 25, 26
Laurence M. Crosbie Fall Golf Championship, 9
Laver, Rod, 39, 189
Leadbetter, David, 167
Lebel, Ray, 3, 11, 231
Lehman, Tom, 187
Leonard, Justin, 154, 159, 184
Levy, Lawrence, 130
Lewinton, Chris, 217
Lietzke, Bruce, 76
Liggett & Myers, 45
LIV Golf, 25, 67, 100, 132, 141, 144, 163, 227–230
Lochinvar Golf Club, 167
Long Beach State College, 134
Lopez, Domingo, 58–59, 88
Lopez, Nancy, 57–59, 65, 80, 84
Los Angeles Open, 23
Los Angeles Times, 200, 210
Love, Davis III, 185
Loy, Steve, 152
LPGA, *see* Ladies Professional Golf Association
LPGA Skins Game, 110
Lye, Mark, 74
Lyle, Sandy, 76, 107, 136, 158
Lyle & Scott, 106

Mackenzie, Keith, 109
Madden, John, 31, 147
Mahaffey, John, 48
Maine Sports Hall of Fame, 3
Manchester United, 206
Mangijo Country Club, 155
Mantle, Mickey, 94
Marr, Dave, 9, 34, 45, 50, 72, 74
Marshall, James, 104–105
Marucci, George "Buddy," 168
Masters Tournament, 1, 9, 20, 25, 45, 62–63, 65, 79, 83, 86, 88, 104, 107, 109, 115–116, 123, 125, 127, 161, 167, 179, 197, 198, 200, 201, 202, 203, 204, 205, 212
Maxfli, 154
Mays, Willie, 94
Mazda, 157
McCarley, Mike, 230
McCormack, Betsy, 220
McCormack, Grace, 16
McCormack, Mark, 12, 13, 14, 15, 16–21, 25, 27–41, 43–45, 48, 49, 50, 52, 53, 56, 61–63, 65–68, 73, 78, 79, 80, 82, 84, 86–87, 90, 92, 93–94, 95–96, 99, 100, 103, 104, 109, 111–113, 115, 118, 123–124, 133, 136, 140–143, 145, 147, 148–153, 158, 184, 194, 198, 203, 206, 208, 209, 213–221, 225–226
McCormack, Ned, 16
McCormack, Todd, 206
McDaniel, Pete, 194, 200, 202
McDonald's, 132, 185
McDonnell Douglas, 165
McIlroy, Rory, 230
Melnyk, Steve, 48
Memorial Tournament, 50, 99
Merchant, John, 181, 194, 202
Merv Griffin Show, The, 160
Meyer, Russ, 198
Michaels, Al, 31
Michaels, Jay, 38–39
Mickelson, Phil, 150–152, 169, 189
Mikita, Stan, 40
Mill, Andy, 134
Miller, Allen, 48
Miller, Johnny, 43–44, 46, 89, 100, 109, 114, 127–128
Miller, Steve, 172–173
Miller Brewing, 28
Milwaukee Open, *see* Greater Milwaukee Open

Missouri State Amateur, 48
Mize, Larry, 126–127
Mizuno irons, 176
Modell, Art, 120
Modell, David, 120
Monahan, Jay, 100
Money magazine, 150
Montgomerie, Colin, 136, 137, 200
Morgan, Brian, 89
Morrow, Larry, 79
Motor Marketing International (MMI), 29
"Mr. Skins," 11
Muirfield Village Golf Club, 87, 108, 126, 168
Murdoch, Rupert, 93
Murdock, David, 132
Murdock, Dustin "Dusty," 84, 114, 119
Murphy, Tom, 12, 16

Nagelsen, Betsy, 56, 184
Nagle, Kel, 123
Nantz, Jim, 31, 146–147, 202, 211
National Sports Management, 17, 19
NBC, 71, 110, 148, 204, 211
NCAA, 48, 61, 62, 75, 83, 150, 163, 168–169
Nelford, Jim, 82
Nelson, Byron, 60–61, 124
Nelson, Ricky, 6
Nestlés, 148
NetJets, 198
Nevada Bob's, 85
Newberg, Esther, 196
New Orleans Open, 78, 125
Newport Country Club, 168
New South Wales Open, 78
New York Times, 22, 64, 143, 203
New York Yankees, 205
Nichols, Bobby, 51–52
Nick Bollettieri Tennis Academy, 149
Nicklaus, Barbara, 79
Nicklaus, Jack, 3–4, 9, 13, 19–21, 24, 25, 40, 61, 72, 81, 99, 108–109, 110, 116, 125, 126, 132, 140–141, 161, 173, 176, 193, 229
Nike, 1, 2, 106, 115–116, 135, 177–180, 183, 186, 189–91, 190*t*, 198, 204, 216, 225
Nike Golf, 173
Nike Tour, *see* Korn Ferry Tour
Nissan, 106
Nissan Open, 1, 179
Nobel Foundation, 92
Norman, Greg, 103–107, 112, 115, 117, 123–135, 137–145, 147, 152–153, 158, 161,

163, 167, 170, 171, 174, 177, 180–181, 201, 204, 207, 209, 211, 228–229, 244
Norman, Gregory, 129
Norman, Laura, 104–105, 129–130, 133–134
Norman, Morgan-Leigh, 129
Northern Telecom Open, 150
Norton, Hughes, 5, 79, 151, 175, 181, 208, 210, 215, 224
Norton, Virginia "Gini," 6, 7
Norwood, Bev, 31–32, 192–193, 199, 202

Official World Golf Ranking (OWGR), 111, 154, 175
Ohio State University, 63
Ohlmeyer, Don, 110
Olazábal, José María, 107
Old Course at St. Andrews, 3, 89, 120
Old Marsh Golf Club, 163
Olympic Club San Francisco, 43, 81
Olympic Games, 32, 148
O'Meara, Alicia, 184
O'Meara, Mark, 134–135, 184, 196–197, 200, 213–214
Oney, John, 193
Oosterhuis, Peter, 65
Open Championship, 3, 31, 45, 48, 65, 76, 89, 90, 107, 108, 114, 120, 125, 154
Optimist Junior World, 158
Oregon Open, 73
Out of the Rough (Baugh), 55
OWGR (Official World Golf Ranking), 111
Oxford University, 150

Packer, Kerry, 133
Page, Paul, 168
Palm Beach, 126
Palm Beach Gardens, 163
Palmer, Arnold, 13, 17–19, 20, 21, 24–26, 29, 31–32, 34, 37, 40, 43, 44, 50, 62, 65, 72, 74, 79, 89, 97, 99, 100–101, 109, 110, 115, 124, 125, 141–143, 153, 170, 174, 184, 189, 194, 205, 212, 217, 229
Palmer, Winnie, 79
Panama Open, 49
Parker, Colonel Tom, 38
Pate, Jerry, 61, 114, 117
Pebble Beach, 89, 154–155
Pelé, 40
Penick, Harvey, 75
Peper, George, 89, 192, 199
Peper, Libby, 192–193

Perlman, Itzhak, 92
Peters, Greg, 115
PGA Championship, 18, 21, 24, 25, 26, 45,
    50, 81, 86, 88, 108–109, 112, 125, 126, 135
PGA of America, 20, 21, 22, 23, 25–27, 50,
    69–71, 85, 100, 108, 142, 145
PGA Tour, 21, 23–27, 26, 44, 46, 47, 49, 52,
    56, 67–70, 73–75, 82, 84, 86, 88, 89, 97,
    99, 100–101, 103–107, 110, 111, 112, 115, 123,
    132, 143–146, 150, 154, 159, 169, 170–171,
    177, 184, 187, 192, 194, 230–231
PGA Tournament Players Division, 69, 71
PGA Tour of Australia, 107
PGA Tour Policy Board, 68, 230
PGA Tour Productions, 97
Phillips Exeter Academy, 7–9, 118
Phoenix Open, 50
Pierce, Andy, 120
Pierce, Charles, 185
Pierce, Chris, 9, 28, 57
Pilic, Nikki, 94
Pinehurst, 21, 64
Player, Gary, 9, 13, 19, 20, 21, 24, 25, 27, 37,
    44, 48, 65, 67, 79, 106, 110, 111, 123–124
Player, Vivienne, 79
Player Impact Program, 227
Players Championship, 97, 114, 154
Polo Ralph Lauren, 154
Portland Country Club, 3, 4, 8, 11, 232
Portland Press Herald, 135
Portuguese Open, 137
Powell, Colin, 204
Presidents Cup, 31–32, 145–147
Presley, Elvis, 6, 183
Price, Nick, 107, 145, 152
Princess Hotels, 28
Pro Serv, 86
Pros Inc., 61, 135
Psychology Today, 126
Public Investment Fund, 227
Pumpkin Ridge Golf Club, 168–169, 177, 178
Purkey, Mike, 199

Qantas Airways, 105, 132
Quad Cities, 185
Qualifying School (Q-Schools), 59, 64, 174

RadarOnline, 134
Ram Golf, 48, 154
Rand, Ayn, 154
RBC Canadian Open, 100

Reebok, 106, 139, 171, 228
Rees, David, 29
Reilly, Rick, 126, 130
Repeta, Kathy, 192–193, 202
Revere Knitting Mills, 19–20
Rice, Jerry, 173
Ridley, Betsy, 83
Ridley, Fred, 83–84, 112
Riswold, Jim, 179
Roach, Lynn, 84
Robert Trent Jones Golf Club, 145
Robinson, Brooks, 40
Robinson, Jackie, 203
Rock & Roll Hall of Fame, 206
Rogers, Beth, 77
Rogers, Bill, 75–79, 83
Rolex, 28, 54, 95, 147, 189–191, 190t
Ronald McDonald Children's Charities, 132
Rosaforte, Tim, 208
Rosburg, Bob "Rossie," 80–81
Royal and Ancient Golf Club of St. Andrews,
    3, 32, 89, 109, 120
Royal Birkdale Golf Club, 28, 89, 109, 114
Royal Golf Dar Es Salam course, 47
Royal Lytham, 154
Royal St. George's Golf Club, 76
Royal Troon Golf Club, 90, 92, 136
Rubin, Chuck, 48, 100
Russo, Lou, 155
Ruth, Babe, 23
Ryder Cup, 23, 26, 31, 107–108, 137, 145

Saint Ignatius High School, 63
Saint Laurent, Yves, 228
Sampras, Pete, 149
Sandburg, Carl, 16
Sander, Bill, 81–82
Sanders, Doug, 3, 4, 45
San José State University, 47
Santulli, Rich, 198
Sarazen, Gene, 22
"Saturday Slam," 125
Saudis, 100, 144, 227–230
Schenkel, Chris, 29, 60
Schupak, Adam, 69–70, 97, 100
Schwarzkopf, Norman, 204
Scott, Steve, 168, 178
Seagram's, 28
Sea Pines Heritage Classic, 76
Second Tour project, 67, 142
Senior Tour, 52, 74, 97, 110

Shakespeare, William, 93
Shark Shootout, 132, 143, 146
Shark (St. John), 143
Sherwood Country Club, 132
Shinnecock Hills Golf Club, 125
Shipnuck, Alan, 195
Shrimpton, Jean, 29
Simons, Jim, 46
Simpson, John, 158
Sinatra, Frank, 24
Singer Sewing Machine, 94
Singh, Vijay, 145
Skins Game, 110–111
Sky TV, 145
Smokey Barwood (fictional character), 32
Snead, Sam, 22, 24, 44
Snyder, Bill, 173
Sony, 111–112
Sorenstam, Annika, 215
Southern Hills Country Club, 16
Spalding, 21, 105, 127–128, 137–138
Spalding Tour Edition golf ball, 127–128, 138, 177
Spitz, Mark, 94
SportsCenter, 188
Sports Illustrated (SI), 17, 21, 53, 59, 66, 94, 96, 126, 130, 147, 185, 195, 212
Sports Reporters, The (TV show), 199
St. Andrews Golf Club, 3, 32, 89, 109, 120
St. John, Lauren, 143
Stadler, Craig, 74, 100, 109, 127–128
Stanford University, 47, 52, 81, 154, 164, 169, 172, 177–178, 187, 202
Stanner, Bud, 33
Starr, Kenneth, 208
Stars on Ice, 35
Star Television, 145
Steinberg, Leigh, 166
Steinberg, Mark, 215–216, 221
Stetson University Law School, 83
Stewart, Jackie, 39, 189
Stewart, Jimmy, 160
Stewart, Payne, 74, 131
Strange, Allan, 62
Strange, Curtis, 32, 61–65, 73–75, 83, 85, 88, 103, 115, 118, 158, 169, 171, 175
Strange, Tom, 62
Strasser, Rob, 171, 172
Suntory Open, 77
Superstars, The (TV show), 150
Survival of the Fittest (TV show), 150

Sutton, Hal, 112, 113, 117
Suzuki, 54
Swan beer, 106
Swift, E. M., 147

Tarde, Jerry, 200
Tarkenton, Fran, 40
Tatum, Frank "Sandy," 165
Taylor Made, 85
Team Europe, 108
Texas Open, 78, 185
Thatcher, Margaret, 150
30 Days of Lee Trevino, The (IMG documentary), 28
Tigermania, 183, 198
"Tiger's Double Bogey" (Dowd), 203
Tiger Woods 99 PGA Tour Golf game, 188–189
Tiger Woods Foundation, 190
Tiger Woods Signature Tudor watch, 190
Tin Cup (film), 74
Tirico, Mike, 31
Titleist, 2, 80, 127–128, 139, 146, 147, 154, 169–171, 176–177, 180, 183, 186, 190, 191, 204, 225
Titleist Tour Edition ball, 125–128, 138
Todd, Ian, 30, 119, 136, 218
Tommy Hilfiger, 154
Top-Flite ball, 127
Torrey Pines Golf Course, 187
Tournament of Champions, 187
Tournament Players Club (TPC), 97
Tournament Players Division (TPD), 26, 69, 70, 71, 108
TPC Sawgrass, 97, 168, 205
Trans World International (TWI), 29, 31, 39, 150
Trevino, Lee, 28, 43–44, 51–52, 74, 87, 89, 100, 140
Troon Open Championship 1982, 92
Tufts, Richard, 21
Turnberry, 125, 129–130, 137
Tway, Bob, 125–127
TW Foundation, 191, 200
TWI Interactive, 206

Uihlein, Wally, 80, 146–147, 176
Ultra-Brite toothpaste, 54
Unilever, 191
University of Connecticut, 10
University of Illinois, 215
University of Oregon, 171

University of Texas, 75
U.S. Amateur Championship, 1, 16, 43, 47,
    48, 61–62, 68, 80–81, 83, 134, 150, 168, 169,
    177–178, 179, 194, 204
U.S. Girls' Junior Championship, 58
U.S. Lawn Tennis Association, 95
U.S. Open, 9, 16, 24–26, 28, 31, 39, 43, 46,
    50, 58, 64, 65, 74, 76, 86, 88, 109, 114, 123,
    125, 126, 158, 187
U.S. Senior Open, 74, 211
U.S. Women's Amateur, 52, 84
U.S. Women's Open, 58
USA Today, 220
USGA, 26, 83, 147, 154, 164–166, 176–178
USGA Championship, 23
USGA Junior Championship, 154, 164, 167,
    168, 176

Vaseline, 191
Vassar College, 7
Vaughan, Bruce, 155
Vokey, Bob, 176
Volkswagen, 94
Volpe, Ray, 59

Wadkins, Lanny, 43–44, 46, 48, 50, 83, 85,
    86–87, 88, 100, 112
Wake Forest, 16, 31, 43, 46, 61–62, 169
Walker Cup, 61, 62, 68, 75, 83
Wall Street Journal, 1, 186, 198, 204
Walt Disney Classic, 185
Walt Disney Company, 16
Washington Post, 120, 195
Washington State Open, 83
Wasserman, Lew, 37–38
Watson, Tom, 47–49, 54, 61, 65, 80, 88, 89,
    99–100, 103, 109, 110, 141, 154
Waverley Country Club, 164
Way of the Shark, The (Norman), 141, 144
Weatherhead, Olwen, 120–121
Weaver, DeWitt, 45
Webb, Karrie, 215
Weiskopf, Tom, 100, 108
Western Open, 50
West Lakes Classic, 104
WGAN, 11
What They Don't Teach You at Harvard
    Business School (McCormack), 36, 38, 148,
    220
Wheaties, 190
Wieden & Kennedy agency, 179

Wilkinson, 107
William & Mary, the College of, 16
William Morris Agency, 166, 221
Williams, Frank, 140
Williams, Serena, 205
Williams, Ted, 23
Williams, Venus, 205
Wilson, Mark, 154, 164
Wilson Golf, 54
Wilson Sporting Goods, 17, 77
Wimbledon, 39, 94–95, 109, 147, 149
Winged Foot, 65, 89, 123–124, 167
Winston-Salem Journal, 31
Winter Olympics, 39
WKBW, 6, 12
WNHC, 12
Wollaston Golf Club, 164
Woodlands Club, The, 135
Woods, Earl, 159–167, 169, 175, 177–178, 180,
    181, 185–186, 190, 194, 195, 200–201, 204,
    208, 209, 211–213, 215, 225
Woods, Kultida "Tida," 159–162, 188, 194,
    201, 202, 212–213
Woods, Tiger, 1–2, 157–181, 183–206,
    207–221, 223–230
Woosnam, Ian, 107, 136, 158
World Amateur Team Championship, 178
World Championship Tennis tour, 95
World Cup, 49, 52, 58
World Golf Hall of Fame, 23, 60, 76, 109,
    126, 134, 173
World Golf Tour, 142, 145
World Match Play Championship, 35, 66, 76
World of Professional Golf, The (McCormack),
    31, 111
World Series of Golf, 70, 77
World's Strongest Man (TV show), 150
Woy, Bucky, 28
WPEA, 8
WWWE, 79
WYBC, 10

Yale University, 9–10, 17, 63, 118
Yamada, Masashi, 155
Yonex, 75
Young Thunderbirds, 46
Yugoslav Tennis Federation, 95

Zaharias, Babe Didrikson, 23
Zoeller, Fuzzy, 76, 123, 203–204
Zwetschke, Brad, 164

About the Authors

....

Hughes Norton is best known as golf's superagent for his work representing giants of the sport such as Tiger Woods and Greg Norman. Twice named one of the "Most Powerful 36 People in Golf" by *Golf Digest*, he lives in Chagrin Falls, Ohio.

George Peper, currently the editor of *Links* magazine, was editor in chief of *Golf* magazine for twenty-five years and is the bestselling author of nineteen previous books. He lives in Charleston, South Carolina.